*Harold Bloom*

To Audrey Sullivan
without whom this book would not have been written.

# Harold Bloom
## A Poetics of Conflict

Graham Allen

*Department of English Literature, University of Dundee*

New York   London   Toronto   Sydney   Tokyo   Singapore

First published 1994 by
Harvester Wheatsheaf
Campus 400, Maylands Avenue
Hemel Hempstead
Hertfordshire, HP2 7EZ
A division of
Simon & Schuster International Group

© Graham Allen, 1994

All rights reserved. No part of this publication may be reproduced, stored in a retrieval system, or transmitted, in any form, or by any means, electronic, mechanical, photocopying, recording or otherwise, without the prior permission, in writing, from the publisher.

Typeset in Ehrhardt 10.5pt
by Inforum, Rowlands Castle, Hampshire

Printed and bound in Great Britain by
Biddles Ltd, Guildford and King's Lynn

British Library Cataloguing in Publication Data

A catalogue record for this book is available from the British Library

ISBN 0–7450–0943–3 (hbk)
ISBN 0–7450–0944–1 (pbk)

1 2 3 4 5   98 97 96 95 94

The following titles are available in the Modern Cultural Theorists Series:

*Roland Barthes* by Rick Rylance

*Harold Bloom* by Graham Allen

*Hélène Cixous* by Verena Andermatt Conley

*Jacques Lacan* by Madan Sarup

*F. R. Leavis* by Anne Samson

Imagine that you enter a parlour. You come late. When you arrive, others have long preceded you, and they are engaged in a heated discussion, a discussion too heated for them to pause and tell you exactly what it is about. In fact, the discussion has already begun long before any of them got there, so that no one present is qualified to retrace for you all the steps that had gone before. You listen for a while, until you decide you have caught the tenor of the argument; then you put in your oar. Someone answers; you answer him; another comes to your defense; another aligns himself against you, to either the embarrassment or gratification of your opponent, depending upon the quality of your ally's assistance. However, the discussion is interminable. The hour grows late. You must depart. And you do depart, with the discussion still vigorously in progress.
Kenneth Burke, 'The Philosophy of Literary Form'.

What makes us free is the knowledge who we were, what we have become; where we were, wherein we have been thrown; whereto we speed, wherefrom we are redeemed; what is birth and what rebirth.
Valentinus, second-century Gnostic.

How is it that they don't bore themselves to death? I can walk into the Yale Library periodical room any afternoon I want to, and I swear that I can read fifteen to twenty fresh attacks upon me for forgetting that the social world exists. They thus proclaim their critical originality and genius, by simply discovering what I say all the time anyway. Which is: forget it; it is not your function; you deal with a solitary pleasure which it is immensely difficult to impart usefully to others.

The only critical wisdom I know is that there is no method except yourself. Everything else is an imposture. There is only yourself.
Harold Bloom, interview with Imre Salusinszky.

# Contents

| | |
|---|---|
| Acknowledgements | ix |
| Preface | xi |
| Chronology | xv |
| Historical and cultural context: movements beyond formalism | xvii |
| 1  Bloom and the re-evaluation of Romanticism | 1 |
| 2  Anxieties of influence: deidealisation, reduction and Bloom's poetics of conflict | 12 |
|     *Yeats, Bloom and the composite god* | 12 |
|     *Influence revised: critical reduction, deidealisation and the repetition of Romanticism* | 16 |
| 3  Maps of misreading | 41 |
|     *Ant-agon-ism and the question of misreading* | 41 |
|     *Forms of totality* | 43 |
|     *Critical persuasion* | 56 |
|     *Counter-reading: Bloom and the Comedian* | 61 |
| 4  Scenes of instruction: the limits of Bloom's psychopoetics | 69 |
|     *The anxiety of choice* | 69 |
|     *Bloom, Derrida, Freud and the question of origins* | 73 |
|     *Counter-reading: Milton, Wordsworth, Bloom* | 87 |
| 5  Lies against time: transumptive allusion, diachronic rhetoric and the question of history | 105 |
|     *Poetic echo: substance and effect* | 105 |
|     *Transumption, Gnosticism, history* | 110 |
|     *Counter-reading: Transumption and/in history: the figure of the poet and the figure of the future in Shelley* | 116 |
|     *Transumption, Emerson and the American difference* | 128 |
| 6  Literary cultures: facticity and the return of originality | 134 |
|     *Bloom and current critical trends* | 134 |

| | |
|---|---|
| *Difference and power* | 143 |
| *Counter-reading: canny fathers and uncanny daughters:* | |
| *Bloom, Freud and the question of authority* | 150 |
| Notes | 163 |
| Glossary of terms | 178 |
| Bibliography | 189 |
| Index | 197 |

# Acknowledgements

My thanks go to all who have read or commented on the various drafts of this book or who have offered advice and encouragement along the way. There are too many, particularly in the last category, to name here, but my special thanks go to: Stephen Bygrave, Mark Currie, Alex Davies, Lily Forrester, Philip Grover, James Knowles, Sandy Lyle, Pam Morris, Ken Newton and Stan Smith. They each know what part they have had to play in the development and production of this book; it goes without saying that none of them is responsible for any errors or misjudgements contained herein. I would also like to thank Peter de Bolla and Roy Sellars for their willingness to discuss aspects of Bloom's work with me.

This book started as a PhD thesis (Sheffield), a project it took me much too long a time to complete. Over that period I have been encouraged and assisted by many non-academic friends, among whom I must name the following: Mike and June Hitchen, Richard Howells and Tony Bond, Alan and Ann Travers (the Zebra Pub, Cambridge) and Priscilla Gillum-Webb. This book is dedicated to the person to whom I have owed the most over this period. I would also like to thank my editor at Harvester, Jackie Jones, for her encouragement and patience.

The author acknowledges with thanks permission granted to reproduce in this volume the following material previously published elsewhere.

From Harold Bloom, *The Anxiety of Influence* and *A Map of Misreading*, reprinted with the permission of Oxford University Press; from *Wallace Stevens: The Poems of Our Climate*, Copyright 1976, 1977, by Cornell University, used by permission of the publisher Cornell

University Press; from *The Ringers in the Tower*, Copyright 1971, 1973, with the permission of the University of Chicago Press; reprinted by permission of the publishers from *Ruin the Sacred Truths: Poetry and Belief from the Bible to the Present*, Cambridge, Mass.: Harvard University Press, Copyright 1987, 1989 by Harold Bloom. Quotations from Wallace Stevens, from *Collected Poems* by Wallace Stevens, Copyright 1923 and renewed 1951, are reprinted with permission of Alfred A. Knopf, Inc. and by Faber and Faber Ltd.

# *Preface*

This study seeks to perform three functions which may not be compatible. Taking the complete oeuvre of the American critic and theorist Harold Bloom, it seeks to be an introduction, a critique and a revision.

Bloom's theoretical works are less widely read today than they were in the 1960s and the 1970s. During that period his seminal role in the re-evaluation of Romanticism and in the attempt to find alternatives to a temporarily dominant deconstructive movement guaranteed him a large audience. Students now get their Bloom through the numerous introductions he has contributed to the various Chelsea House series. At this juncture, it seems to me that an introduction to the theorist behind those often gnomic editorial pronouncements is not only justifiable but essential. What seems equally essential is to develop a fundamental critique of Bloom; that his 'poetic' version of literary history, his defiant repetition of the Romantic ideology and his psychopoetic theory of intratextual modes of misreading leave out of an account of poetic meaning its social and historical dimensions.

Literary theory and criticism is currently being revitalised by a concerted effort, in both America and Britain, to return the text to history. The most important methodological decision I have had to take has been whether to read Bloom from a non-Bloomian perspective or in his own terms. To be extrinsic or intrinsic: that seemed to be the question.

For a good while I thought that I had chosen the latter of the two options, this seeming the only manner in which I could resolve the tension between my three discursive functions: introduction, critique, revision. For a long while I contented myself that there was indeed a choice to be made. But of course, it is not possible simply to leave one's own presuppositions and theoretical allegiances (however xii *Preface*

inchoate, however precise) at the door which leads 'inside' the work of an author, only to pick them up once again, like an umbrella, as one leaves the premises. These figurations, 'inside' and 'outside', are just that, figurative. Acknowledging their tenaciousness, it is clear that we enter 'into' a reading of an author with our own relation to an 'outside' already assimilated into the very fabric of our outlook. With friendly or aggressive intentions one enters, as it were, bringing an internalised exteriority, into a textual interior space and immediately looks around for confirmations of its presumed autonomy, its interior design. But the bookcases are crammed with texts which do not bear the occupier's name. The bookcases themselves were clearly made elsewhere; as were the chairs, tables and all the other objects which furnish the room. At last, perhaps in desperation, one turns to the bricks which constitute the very limit of that assumed division between the room and the world 'outside'. Inscribed in bold figures into the surface of these bricks are names which advertise their place of production: Chicago, New York, the London Brick Company. 'But this is supposed to be New Haven!' you exclaim. As you leave this interior, somehow at once disarranged and yet untouched by your stay, you realise that you take with you a slightly disarranged interiority, which now includes not only what you first brought with you but, equally, the trace of that space you have briefly (dis)honoured with your presence.

A major subject of this study is Bloom's vestigial adherence to such an untenable rhetoric of interiority, of immanence with regard to the poetic tradition. 'Inside' and 'outside', as these terms apply to our reading of individual texts and what traditionally is styled text and context, or literature and history, are finally resistant to separation, perpetually exhibiting themselves as the 'host' of the other. The methodological implications of this should be clear as the reader makes his or her way through this study. I have attempted to resist a quick translation of the Bloomian vocabulary into other vocabularies. I have attempted to read Bloom clearly in his own terms, feeling that not only does his work deserve such treatment, but that too few accounts of that work have followed such a path. The effect is thus to create the impression that reading 'through' Bloom I have slowly found a way of passing 'beyond' him, carrying whatever I have managed to establish as useful and promising out into a new domain, which is, inevitably, not submitted to a definitive cartography within the pages that follow. The reality, however, is that my own presuppositions and affiliations are at work throughout, slowly translating and transforming Bloom into an object which I can finally appropriate in ways which have been prepared from the very beginning. The largest methodological decision, in other words, has concerned the issue of pace, of the quickness of translation. This lesson, of the slowness of reading, despite frequent appearances and polemics, is, or at least should be, the principal lesson of literary theory.

# *Chronology: Harold Bloom*

Born in New York, 11 July 1930, son of William Bloom and Paula Lev.

| | |
|---|---|
| 1951 | BA from Cornell University, Ithaca, New York. |
| 1954–5 | Fulbright Fellowship at Cambridge University. |
| 1955 | PhD awarded from Yale University. |
| 1955–60 | Instructor in English at Yale. |
| 1956 | Awarded John Addison Porter Prize. |
| 1958 | Married Jeanne Gould. |
| 1959 | *Shelley's Mythmaking* published. |
| 1959 | Visiting Professor at Hebrew University, Jerusalem. |
| 1960–3 | Associate Professor at Yale. |
| 1961 | *The Visionary Company* published. |
| 1962 | Awarded Guggenheim Fellowship. |
| 1963 | *Blake's Apocalypse* published. |
| 1965–74 | Professor of English at Yale. |
| 1965 | Commentary to *The Complete Poems of William Blake*, edited by David V. Erdman, published. Editor, with Fredrick W. Hilles, *From Sensibility to Romanticism*. Visiting Professor at Breadloaf Summer School at Vermont (and 1966). |
| 1967 | Received Newton Arvin Award. |
| 1968–9 | Visiting Fellow at the Society for the Humanities at Cornell University. |
| 1970 | *Yeats* published; also editor of *Romanticism and Consciousness*. Received Melville Cane Award from the Poetry Society of America. |
| 1971 | *The Ringers in the Tower* published. |
| 1973 | *The Anxiety of Influence* published; also two volumes of The Oxford Anthology of English Literature, |

|  | *Romantic Poetry and Prose* and *Victorian Poetry and Prose*, edited with Lionel Trilling. |
| --- | --- |
| 1974–7 | De Vane Professor of Humanities at Yale. |
| 1975 | *A Map of Misreading* and *Kabbalah and Criticism* published. |
| 1976 | *Poetry and Repression* and *Figures of Capable Imagination* published. |
| 1977 | *Wallace Stevens* published. |
| 1979 | *The Flight to Lucifer: A Gnostic Fantasy* and *Deconstruction and Criticism*, edited by Bloom, published. |
| 1981 | *Agon* and *The Breaking of the Vessels* published. |
| 1982 | Awarded Zabel Prize by the American Institute of Arts and Letters. |
| 1982–4 | Visiting Professor at New School of Social Research, New York. |
| 1983– | Stirling Professor of Humanities at Yale. |
| 1984 | Begins General Editorship for Chelsea House series. |
| 1985 | Awarded MacArthur Prize Fellowship. |
| 1987–8 | Charles Eliot Norton Professor of Poetry at Harvard University. |
| 1988 | *Poetics of Influence* published. |
| 1988– | Berg Visiting Professor of English at New York University. |
| 1989 | *Ruin the Sacred Truths* published. |
| 1990 | Interpretation of *The Book of J* published. |
| 1992 | *The American Religion* published. |

# Historical and cultural context: movements beyond formalism

Given Harold Bloom's[1] antagonism to rival or alternative movements in contemporary literary theory, and given the complex nature of the history of that field since the early 1970s, it is a difficult task to locate Bloom's place within the Anglo-American critical scene. Bloom's fiercely individual stance, his constant effort to distance himself from all movements, from what he sees as the weak rhetoric of consensus, militates against the drawing of neat lines of association between his 'antithetical criticism' and other more popularly understood and inclusive approaches.

One solution to the problem is to begin by focusing on the various critics and theorists who have utilised aspects of the Bloomian project. Most of these critics, however, have not so much followed the Bloomian way as plundered various theoretical terms and often reduced versions of his theoretical principles, ensuring that their own work is properly distanced from Bloom's own practice. Such a situation is encouraged by Bloom's own theories concerning critical misreading.

A better way to understand Bloom's relationship to contemporary theory is to begin with those rare moments in which he associates his own work with other contemporary movements. In *The Anxiety of Influence* he asserts:

> in the contemporary criticism that clarifies for me my own evasions, in books like *Allegory* by Angus Fletcher, *Beyond Formalism* by Geoffrey Hartman, and *Blindness and Insight* by Paul de Man, I am made aware of the mind's effort to overcome the impasse of Formalist criticism, the barren moralizing that Archetypal criticism has come to be, and the anti-humanistic plain dreariness of all those developments in European criticism that have yet to demonstrate that they can aid in reading any one poem by any poet whatsoever. (AI, pp.12–13)

This is, with hindsight, an interesting assessment of theoretical affiliation. The ascription to Paul de Man of an attempt to provide a defence against the anti-humanism of an insurgent, Continental, philosophical movement says far more about Bloom's own resistance to post-structuralism than it does about de Man. The more precise assessment concerns the description of these books as constituting a generally discernible movement within American criticism in the late 1960s and early 1970s to go 'beyond formalism'. Both Hartman's and de Man's texts contain a number of essays which call for and/or exhibit such a movement. It is clear also that in its stated promise of a 'more antithetical practical criticism than any we now have' (AI, p.13), its rejection of the concept of the literary text as an aesthetic monad in favour of a conception of each text as a 'dyad', its emphasis on the revisionary nature of both poetry and criticism, and other issues I intend to discuss in what follows, the theory of the anxiety of influence was consciously created by Bloom as his own version of such a movement.

That such a desire to go 'beyond formalism' does not cover the whole history of literary theory in Anglo-American criticism should be noted: many feminist, Marxist and psychoanalytical approaches would be greatly distorted if reduced to such a perspective. Indeed, it is by no means clear that the New Criticism ever achieved the uniformity or academic hegemony ascribed to it by various, more recent critics. However, as a motif bearing on those critical issues and traditions most directly influencing the work of Bloom, it remains more productive than most and, as I have already indicated, close to Bloom's conception of his own enterprise.

The general drive to pass 'beyond formalism', which can be said to have greatly assisted in the acceptance of post-structuralist theory into the Anglo-American critical scene around the beginning of the 1970s, led in a number of distinct, if frequently interrelated, directions. Of course, each different 'post-formalist' movement has defined what it takes to be the principal limitations of New Criticism/formalism in terms that open a space into which it can position itself. The rise of what is commonly styled as a 'new historicism' exhibits one route. Edward Said exemplifies this movement:

> My position is that texts are worldly, to some degree they are events, and, even when they appear to deny it, they are nevertheless a part of the social world, human life, and of course the historical moments in which they are located and interpreted.[2]

A different set of criteria can be said to have fed into the deconstructive approach to the going 'beyond formalism' question. A concern with the unbridgeable gulf between signified and signifier, the consequent problematisation of epistemology and interpretative accuracy, the emphasis on textuality over standard, 'humanistic' value-terms such as 'history', the writing and reading 'subject', the 'literal'/'figural', 'form'/'content', 'presence'/'absence', 'speech'/'writing' oppositions: all these concerns combined in the emergence of a deconstructive movement in certain key institutions within the American academy in the mid-1970s.

In such critics as J. Hillis Miller and Geoffrey Hartman the deconstructive view of textuality promoted assertions of the 'literariness' of criticism itself and generated virtuoso displays of critical freedom. On the other hand, as Hillis Miller points out, the work of Paul de Man, with its 'painstaking', 'Apollonian' rigour, based itself on a 'prodigious effort in the disarticulation of the major texts of Western metaphysics, philosophical and literary . . .'[3] Generally speaking, deconstruction represented a textualised unravelling of most of the concepts on which not only the New Criticism but equally any positive form of historiography up to that point had been based. To those concerned with history, deconstruction in America seemed to be a kind of nightmare extension of the New Critical project.

In contrast to this, the deconstructors were at pains to illustrate the unsupportable metaphysical assumptions on which historicism generally founds itself: Hillis Miller's review of M. H. Abrams's *Natural Supernaturalism* being a famous example.[4] It would be wrong, of course, to portray the recent history of criticism in the Anglo-American world as a simple fight between historicist and deconstructive or post-structuralist movements. Much post-structuralism is deeply engaged with history and the question of literary historiography; deconstruction, if it has been used to deny history, is not in itself necessarily anti-historical. In outlining the history of movements 'beyond formalism' in the early to mid-1970s, however, I am less concerned with developing an adequate account of the twists and turns of theory in that period than in establishing the best context within which to read Bloom's particular intervention into that discursive realm.

Commentators on Bloom's work have characterised it as a movement 'beyond formalism' towards a new form of historicism. Said writes that, along with the work of Raymond Schwab, Michel Foucault and Walter Jackson Bate, Bloom's approach should be read as 'exemplifying a possible trend for criticism to be taken seriously only if literature is going to be studied in a more situated, circumstantial, but no less theoretically self-conscious way'.[5] On the other hand, many commentators have highlighted similarities between Bloom's approach and certain anti-historical tendencies in deconstructive practice. Other critics have read Bloom's anti-New Critical theorising as being as much a rhetorical ploy as a substantial move away from formalism.[6]

Bloom's move 'beyond formalism' can be said to contain vestiges of both the directions I have outlined: it subjects every poetic text to an historicised brand of interpretation, reading each text as having its meaning only in terms of its position within a tradition of textual utterances; yet it reduces the notion of poetry's historicity to a textualised framework. This combination is engineered to save the Romantic 'subject'. It promotes a vision of poetry as a personal, 'experiential' mode of desire or will-to-power, which ultimately resists explanatory contexts on both linguistic and historical levels, and can only properly be accounted for by an equally 'experiential' brand of criticism, founded on a similar will-to-(interpretative)-power.

Bloom can be said to have appropriated whatever among the dominant theoretical approaches could be utilised in order to safeguard this vision of the poetic 'subject' and his belief in the essential autonomy of the poetic tradition; what Northrop Frye called 'the literary universe'. In this sense, Bloom's approach can be understood as one outcome of the formalists' attempts to produce a satisfactory form of literary history.

If formalism is defined as the attempt to describe the 'literariness' of literary texts, then formalist literary history is an attempt to produce a form of historiography which properly represents the 'intrinsic' modes of development and transformation presumed to be the foundations of that history. Formalist literary history, in other words, requires some intrinsic dynamic, some properly 'literary' principle of transformation, if it is to be a viable proposition. Whether or not New Criticism rejected historiography is a question beyond the scope of this introduction. What can be asserted with reasonable confidence, however, is that for critics of Bloom's temperament and generation the quest for a truly formalist theory of literary history appeared to have only properly been established when Frye, developing the suggestions of T. S. Eliot in his 'Tradition and the individual talent', published *Anatomy of Criticism*, with its first chapter on 'Historical criticism'.

If Frye can be said to have reintegrated the formalist project with its Romantic antecedents, then Bloom's work can be read as continuing that movement towards a Romantic formalism by dragging the Fryean–Eliotic emphasis on the dynamic function of interpoetic relations into a post-structuralist context. While the defining terms in Frye's criticism remain 'identity', 'progression', 'liberation' and 'similarity', the key terms in Bloom's version of the 'literary universe' are the characteristically post-structuralist ones of difference, discontinuity and rupture.

The important point is that Bloom's historicism is tied to and determined by his version of Romanticism and the formalistic presuppositions it helped to foster, while his post-structuralist tendencies are similarly oriented towards a defence of those primary positions. We can see this more clearly if we compare Bloom's 'antithetical practical criticism' with Paul de Man's important essay 'Literary history and literary modernity'.[7]

In this essay de Man draws a distinction between modernity, conceived as an event or act, and the discursive (reflective) concepts of literature and history. This distinction looks forward to de Man's subsequent theories concerning the nature of rhetoric, theories we will observe playing an important part in Bloom's own development of a theory of poetic rhetoric. In de Man's argument, modernity, conceived as a drive towards an act of utterance freed from historical contexts and constraints, pits itself firmly against the very categories of continuity and tradition which make literature and history possible. This situation leads de Man to an understanding of the literary text as constituting a radical contradiction in its intentions and directions. Literature, viewed as expressive of a drive towards modernity and thus as a drive towards discontinuity with the very tradition upon which it relies for its status *as literature*, comes to be seen as a form of discourse which 'both betrays and obeys its own mode of being', which 'exists at the same time in the modes of error and truth'.[8] Such an insight, the characteristic de Manian location of a textual aporia beyond interpretative resolution, produces a radical questioning of the very possibility for literary history. A history of literature depends, according to de Man, not only on the possibility of treating literary texts as 'a collection of empirical data',[9] but traditionally also on the interpretative construction of a genetic narrative, providing the appearance of an historical shape and significance to such a collection of texts. Such a geneticism is, however, deconstructed within the text's own aporetic status.

xxii  *Historical and cultural context*

No 'positivistic history of literature', relying on the assumption that we can 'know' what a text means and is, can escape the abysmal fate of becoming 'a history of what literature is not'. 'At best', de Man affirms, such histories 'would be a preliminary classification opening the way for actual literary study, and at worst, an obstacle in the way of literary understanding'.[10] However, as he continues, 'the intrinsic interpretation of literature claims to be anti- or a-historical, but often presupposes a notion of history of which the critic is not himself aware'.[11] De Man's essay thus moves towards a characteristic irony, in which a concept such as historiography is at one and the same time deconstructed and yet shown to be most powerfully and subversively present where, from an orthodox perspective, it is considered not to be present at all (i.e. in formal or formalistic close reading). A potential solution to the problem de Man has established with regard to 'doing' literary history begins to emerge here. Having discovered that the contradictory drives of modernity and history exist simultaneously within the literary text, the opportunity arises to envisage a form of literary history as the reading of a text's own aporetic demonstration of these antagonistic forces. Literary history, on this model, begins to become synonymous with a deconstructive critical interpretation, since texts are seen as containing their own struggle with the 'history' within which they take their appearance of meaning. Such a form of historiography, if we can still call it that, represents a rejection of the traditional positive projection of genetic patterns and paradigms and becomes implicated within the 'history' it reads in the single literary text.

De Man's approach continually forces him back on a form of close reading in which the literary text's own deconstruction of historical assumptions is thoroughly explored *in preparation* for a form of historiography. This will be constructed on the kind of 'proper' understanding of such texts, which his own theories concerning rhetoric and interpretation do not appear to sanction as a viable possibility.

De Man's resistance to literary history stems from his focus on the epistemological status of literary texts and their interpretation, his emphasis on the fact that genetic narratives 'can only be metaphorical, and history is not a fiction'.[12] Bloom, however, can actually develop the kind of historiography which 'Literary history and literary modernity' postulates only eventually to disallow, because for him the focus of critical interpretation is not epistemology but power. This 'power' is remarkably close to the kinds of conflict highlighted by de Man in his meditation on the relationship between literature's drive towards modernity and its concomitant defence against tradition (history and literature). As de Man writes, paraphrasing his source-text, Nietzsche's 'On the uses and disadvantages of history for life': 'The parricidal imagery of . . . the weaker son condemning and killing the stronger father, reaches the inherent paradox of the denial of history implied in modernity'.[13] Bloom's theory of the poetic anxiety of influence takes this 'parricidal [Oedipal] imagery' and, in centring his account of the basis of poetic articulation and meaning on it, fulfils de Man's notion of an historiographical method centred in the practice of literary interpretation. At the same time, it swerves dramatically away from the de Manian concern with evacuating all metaphors (particularly the genetic fallacy) from the post-formalist, deconstructive project of reading.

Bloom's approach, *contra* de Man, seeks to present the genetic patterns of progress, decline and the authoring power of individual poetic 'subjects' as actually defining the nature of poetic meaning and tradition itself. This allows Bloom to absorb the sophisticated attention on figural schemes of representation developed by deconstruction into a practice which in some senses fulfils the formalists' desire for an appropriately intrinsic literary history-writing. It does this at the same time as it insists on its own position 'inside' the history it seeks to uncover. This post-formalist approach can be characterised as a modern extension of what Jerome J. McGann has called the 'Romantic ideology' and has defined as the 'idea that poetry, or even consciousness, can set one free from the ruins of history and culture'.[14]

The formalist project for an intrinsic literary history and the Romantic ideology of literature's essential autonomy from political and social realities come defiantly together in Bloom's 'antithetical criticism'. What I am particularly concerned to establish is why and how Bloom has chosen such a route 'beyond formalism'.

What I will argue throughout this study is that Bloom retains a significant relation to that aspect of Romantic historicism we can call, following Nietzsche, monumentalism. Nietzsche, in his essay on history, compares monumentalism to two other modes of historical consciousness – antiquarianism and critical historicism – and asserts that its *use* is that it provides us with models of greatness and a sense of the possible greatness within our own selves and our own age, while its *disadvantages* are that it tends both to foster a resentment and hatred of the past by the present and also to dwarf the present by the past. However, perhaps the most important problem in monumentalism is its severe reductiveness: 'whole segments' of the past, Nietzsche writes, 'are forgotten, despised and flow away in an uninterrupted colourless flood, and only individual embellished facts rise out of it like islands: the few personalities who are visible at all have something strange and unnatural about them . . .'[15]

This tension between a positive focus on past instances of greatness and the repressive illusions concerning history which such a focus entails is the kind of ambiguity which de Man has brought out so well in his reading of Nietzsche's essay. As this study will endeavour to point out, it is not simply the case that monumentalism – defined as the focusing on or even the hypostasisation of single authorial figures from the literary past – is a wholly misguided or even avoidable tendency in literary discourse, be it poetic or critical. My point in citing the question of monumentalism here is to introduce the assertion that Bloom's theory of inter-poetic relations, and more generally his account of influence as it pertains to literary texts, tends to read these complex issues through a too rigid theory of psychopoetic relations between 'latecomer poet[s] and precursor[s]'.

Bloom's various theorisations of poetic influence neither take full cognisance of the plethora of influences which affect the modern poet nor recognise that the 'story' of influence changes radically through time. This resistance to the 'full story' of influence is not to be read as a simple oversight; rather, it represents a crucial element in Bloom's defence of those post-formalist and Romantic presuppositions to which I have referred.

The purpose of this study is to think through Bloom's account of the poetic anxiety of influence in an attempt to locate precisely where a revision of that account is needed. Is a revised conception of influence available, a conception of influence which can form the basis of a theory and method capable of recreating the ideological, social and aesthetic 'wars and revolutions' which the managing of the intertextual medium of literary language discloses and elides?

# Chapter One | Bloom and the re-evaluation of Romanticism

Unlike older scholars of literary Romanticism such as Northrop Frye and M. H. Abrams, Harold Bloom belongs to a generation of critics whose careers appear to fall into a developmental narrative of the 'before' and 'after' variety. In contrast to his former Yale contemporaries, Geoffrey Hartman, Paul de Man and J. Hillis Miller, however, all of whom registered the arrival of Continental theory on the Anglo-American critical scene by affecting profound transformations in their own interpretative styles and practices, the reasons for the shift in Bloom's critical vision are somewhat harder to explain.

Beginning as a scholar of Romantic poetry, Bloom, between 1959 and 1973, produced a number of scrupulously argued readings of that tradition, which mixed an admirable attention to the detail of individual texts with a lively tendency to defend his version of the Romantic tradition against the Modernist, New Critical tenets, which appeared to dominate the academic study of poetry, at least at the onset of this phase of his career. These texts helped establish Bloom at the vanguard of the 're-evaluation of Romanticism', which characterised much of the most important work produced in the American critical scene in the 1960s and early 1970s.

To read these texts as a succession of studies arguing for a stable, fully coherent account of Romanticism is, however, to erase the dramatic twists and transformations which occur within them. By the time of his study *Yeats* and the later essays collected in *The Ringers in the Tower*, Bloom's view of the nature of the Romantic tradition, its successes and limitations, had changed considerably. Not only do these later texts exhibit a similar tendency towards theory to the work of many of his American contemporaries in the late 1960s and early 1970s, they bring to an intense focus problems and doubts concerning the effectiveness of his version of Romantic humanism, which now, with hindsight, can be seen always to have been an important feature of his work.

It has frequently been remarked that, from the very beginning of his career, Bloom's critical stance was profoundly antagonistic to predominant critical assumptions. At least one element of his critical approach appears to have altered little, therefore. The theme of critical revisionism, allied to the question of poetic and critical canon-formation, forms a great part of Bloom's subject from first to last. His first publication, a review of Northrop Frye's *Anatomy of Criticism*, while declaring his debt to and respect for Frye's reading of Romanticism, immediately turns from Frye's desire to create a systematic form of criticism which could incorporate all previous approaches. Bloom insists, *contra* Frye, that there are positions to be taken in criticism as in poetry.[1]

From the beginning of his career, Bloom has striven to be not a 'reconciler' but a 'quarreller', as he puts it in his review. The justification for such a tendentious impulse is that only such a stress on conflict can properly reflect the nature of poetry's own polemical relationship to its subject-matter, to 'extra'-poetic contexts, and to the forms of the past. In a complete reversal of the tenets of Frye's inclusive system, Bloom has persistently declared that for the critic to do justice to the Romantic line of visionary or revisionary poetry he must join those poets in the practice of a rhetorical or 'poetic', rather than a logical or philosophical or scientific discourse. The terms in which Bloom has expressed this consciousness of the necessity of position-taking may have changed, yet the principal emphasis on conflict has remained constant.

There has been a sufficiently adept enough series of examinations of Bloom's antagonistic relationship with the New Criticism to allow me to pass quickly through this issue. The dominant critical ideas in the New Critical approach, the 'impersonality thesis', the notion of the poem as aesthetic monad, the heresy of paraphrase and the injunction against evaluative assessments, the emphasis on irony, paradox and the self-conscious detachment of artist from work, all fostering a general downgrading of the Romantic tradition in favour of what Bloom, in derisory fashion, styles the 'Line of Wit', are all critical commonplaces this far into the general reassertion of Romanticism. We need only refer to Bloom's short enumeration of the central themes of Shelley's poetry, in *Shelley's Mythmaking*, to register the differences between Bloom's Romanticism and the New Critical–Eliotic adherence to Catholic, classical and socially moderate principles:

> The remoteness of Divinity; the eternal gap between aspiration after the desired object and the means of attainment, between good and the means of good, poetry and the medium of poetry; the ultimate conflict between romantic humanism and the human condition; the inevitable collapse of a Thou into an It again, after the relational event has run its course . . . (SM, pp.33–4)

If Shelley's poetry had suffered more than most in the New Critical–Modernist devaluation of the Romantic poetry of imagination and vision, then Bloom's fiercely argued thesis sought to rectify the anti-Romantic tendencies in contemporary critical thought by presenting a poet in whom subject and mode of presentation are magnificently wedded. Combining Frye's influential theories concerning mythopoeic poetry with the terminology of Martin Buber's study of religious vision in *I and Thou*, Bloom presented a thesis on Romantic poetry in which the visionary, humanistic and apocalyptic desire of the poet was represented as being pitted against all natural contexts, including, importantly, the very language within which the poet's ascension to visionary relation with the experiential world is expressed: 'In Shelley's myth, a poem is a relational event which has run its course by being set down; once on the page a poem is an It. Shelley's poems generally begin in relationship, are defeated, and end as artifice' (SM, p.200).

Much of the commentary on Bloom's work at the time and subsequently has focused on his apparent adherence to a Blakean conception of the apocalyptic human imagination. Bloom's intense involvement with the far more ambivalent Shelleyan imagination is, however, equally important and, with hindsight, perhaps even more enlightening. Both Blake and Shelley in Bloom's readings share a radically visionary rhetoric, antithetical to all external contexts, including the chief context of *nature*. This was, for the time, a major reassessment of the dialectic between mind and nature in

Romanticism, and Bloom's principal precursor in this reading of Romantic vision was Northrop Frye. David Fite's judicious examination of this relationship can help us at this point. Both Frye and Bloom, he writes:

> seeing the world through a Blakean lens, glorify the power of the mythmaking visionary imagination; both insist, against established critical authority, that visionary poetry requires a reading in terms of *itself*, in terms of the types of visionary moments that it tries to present. And both critics go on, then, analogizing in Blakean fashion from these types, to construct an autonomy of the imagination out of the similitudes of imaginative quest.[2]

The concentration on Blakean 'similitudes' might be slightly exaggerated here, yet the emphasis on mythopoeia, on an intrinsic, critical approach and on the ultimate autonomy of poetic vision, is the correct one. Indeed, Fite usefully denominates four principal elements in Bloom's early reading of English Romanticism, all pertaining to the character of the 'mythmaking visionary imagination': (1) it is antinatural, pitted against all 'external' contexts; (2) it is, characteristically, presented in terms of the quest-romance; (3) the achievement of visionary imagination, the mythopoeic fusion of 'I' and 'Thou', is 'evanescent'; and, finally, (4) the achieved, if temporary, vision 'by virtue of its passage beyond all context . . . in some sense has no referent and is always focused on the problematics of pure visionary desire'.[3]

Bloom's definition of Romantic poetry in his early triad of books is, therefore, of an exercise of the human will seeking to transform the natural world into an apocalyptic realm of pure vision. Romantic poetry, Bloom asserts, following Frye, moves from the allegorical to the anagogic stage in which, to employ the explanatory passage Bloom takes from Dante, 'a scripture is spiritually expounded which even in the literal sense, by the very things it signifies, signifies again some portion of the supernal things of eternal glory' (quoted in SM, p.166). This anagogic level of Romantic poetry means that the mythopoeic poem must not be treated as an allegory, that is, translated into other, non-'mythopoeic' terms, but must be read in its own terms. Although the manner in which the reader can respect the poem's own mode of articulation and vision has modulated in Bloom, this general stricture remains constant.

The Romantic poet reimagines nature and then seeks to marry what has been created. Romantic poetry, for Bloom, is a refusal of dualism, particularly the dualism established by the Cartesian separation of intensive mind and extensive nature. For Bloom, Romanticism is a radical protest against the Enlightenment. This view differs significantly from the more orthodox conception of the Romantic co-operation or interrelationship of intransigently distinct entities represented, for example, in the work of M. H. Abrams.

The project of Romantic poetry, which Bloom wishes to extend back through Milton and Spenser to the Old Testament prophets and forwards in time to the most authentic poetic achievements of the modern century, is described in terms of the twin drive to humanise nature and to naturalise the imagination (see VC, p.8). The crucial aspect of this kind of poetry lies in the fact that it has an ultimately extra- or supraliterary objective: no less than the imaginative renewal of man himself. As Bloom writes in his experimental essay 'The internalization of quest romance':

> The deepest satisfactions of reading Blake or Wordsworth come from the realization of new ranges of tensions in the mind, but Blake and Wordsworth both believed, in different ways, that the pleasures of poetry were only forepleasures, in the sense that poems, finally, were scaffoldings for a more imaginative vision, and not ends in themselves. (RT, p.13)

Such a passage immediately leads us into a consideration of the principal ambiguity, even paradox, in Bloom's early work on Romanticism: a subject which has been analysed by Frank Lentricchia. If the objectives of Romantic poetry are finally extrapoetic, for what reason and on what grounds does Bloom so earnestly insist on an intrinsic critical account of that poetry? Lentricchia describes Bloom as having gradually turned away from an engagement with the social and political motivations of Romantic poetry towards a purely formalistic, aestheticised critical vision: 'In his refusal to recognize any longer the constitutive role of extraliterary forces ("differences in religion and politics") upon identity, Bloom turns himself into a remarkably odd scholarly creature: the historian as aesthete.'[4] This assessment, it seems to me, is rather simplistic, even consciously reductive, as it is clear that Bloom, even in his earliest works, did not advocate an extraliterary mode of interpretation and, as a consequence, found difficulty from the very outset in dealing with the direct social and political objectives which form part of the Romantic version of radical humanism.

As Kelvin Everest has pointed out, it is a characteristic of much criticism in America to reproduce a history of Romanticism which stresses an internalisation of radical humanism after the 'crisis' of the French Revolution. Everest's point is that such critics 'may be reading something of their own experience and background into their formulations of the Romantic ethos' and that it is 'equally possible to argue that there was a newly charged political dimension in the Romantic representation of private consciousness'.[5]

What both Lentricchia and Everest emphasise is the importance of internalisation as a cardinal theme in post-formalist approaches to Romanticism; a theme which plays an important role in Bloom's gradual resolution of the paradox I am focusing on here. Caught between a belief in intrinsic criticism and a view of poetry which stresses its basis in an apocalyptic human desire, Bloom increasingly moves to the theme of internalisation. In this way he protects his vision of Romanticism from the destructive, internal logic of its ultimately *extrapoetic* implications. We can see such a process occurring if we turn our attention to two essays, the first written by Bloom in 1966, ' "To reason with a higher reason": Romanticism and the rational' (RT, pp.323–37), the second, the already cited essay on the theme of the internalised quest-romance.

In the first essay, Bloom questions what he describes as the traditional view of Romanticism as an essentially anti-rational mode of consciousness, a celebration or exploration of those drives and desires repressed by and in European Enlightenment philosophy. He argues that such a view of Romanticism stems from 'Continental', particularly German, traditions of thought, and does not properly account for the specificity of English versions of Romanticism. This latter mode of Romanticism, he argues, has its basis in a more developed and sustaining prehistory; and it is not reason but 'premature modes of conceptualization that masquerade as final accounts of reason' (RT, p.323) which characterise the 'great Enemy' of Romanticism. On this view, a line of 'compass-wield[ing]' rationalists – Descartes, Bacon, Newton, Locke, Hegel, Marx, Freud – stand in opposition to Romantic poetry, ready to reduce it to their rival, non-poetic systems.

Romanticism is defined here as the 'doomed', 'yet perpetually self-renewing' attempt to demonstrate 'that the garments of ideology or of supposed thought that we wear must be thrown aside if we are to explore our human imaginative heights and depths' (RT, p.324).

Bloom, in this essay, promotes a reading of Romanticism in terms of an attempt to 'cure' self-consciousness through an intensified and properly humanised form of imaginative 'consciousness', a reading which was also being articulated at the same time by M. H. Abrams and Geoffrey Hartman.[6] The argument encapsulates many of the themes I have been stressing so far. It promotes the view that poetry is essentially anti-social, pitted against all dualisms and limitations, indeed against all forms of 'context' (philosophical, historical or ideological) save for its own basis in a brand of unfulfillable and yet indestructible human desire. Yet what is most interesting in the definition, apart from the emergence of Freud as at once the last in the line of Enlightenment 'compass-wielders' and yet a theorist who comes disturbingly close to reworking the Romantic conception of human desire, is the emphasis on failure. Moving the spotlight away from all social and ideological contexts, Bloom's version of radical (Romantic) desire has no *extrinsic* space towards which it can direct itself. What is left is the desire to attain an apocalypse of individual vision and the obvious inability of every Romantic quester, even the strongest, to achieve such an objective. The essay illustrates Bloom's movement towards a full articulation of the paradox inherent within his own account of Romanticism. In his preface to the Cornell paperback edition of *Shelley's Mythmaking*, Bloom states: 'It is evident to me only now, on re-reading, that the subject of this book is Shelley's internalized quest to reach the limits of desire' (SM, p.vii). Such a statement reflects the paradox inherent in Bloom's version of the Romantic project: it has an impossible goal, and because of this is at one and the same time perpetually defeated and yet fully immune to total extinction. It cannot be halted through success or through inertia. The essay also illustrates how Bloom's interests have shifted from the objectives of Romantic visionary poetics to the reasons why consciousness is its own impasse.

Bloom's desire to assert the autonomy of poetic vision, to defend the Romantic tradition from mind/nature, poet/society dualisms, leads him steadily to an emphasis on poetic psychology, on the consciousness of the Romantic visionary. More particularly, it leads him to centre the very dualisms against which Romantic desire is said to struggle within the individual consciousness of each aspiring poet. This movement reaches its initial and decisive climax in 'The Internalization of quest romance', in which Bloom can be said significantly to alter the balance between his early adherence to Frye's version of Romantic humanism and the insurgent influence of Freudian psychology, with its conceptualisation of the essentially dualistic nature of individual human consciousness. Criticising Frye's acquiescence to a vision of Romanticism as the attempted integration of mind and nature, Bloom substitutes a modified Freudianism to reassert the autonomy of visionary poetics:

> If the goal of Romantic internalization of the quest was a wider consciousness that would be free of the excesses of self-consciousness, a consideration of the rigors of experiential psychology will show, quite rapidly, why nature could not provide adequate context. (RT, p.21)

Employing terms taken from Shelley and Blake, Bloom asserts that the Romantic project cited above passes through two stages. In the first, 'nature is an ally, though always a wounded and sometimes a withdrawn one'. This stage is entitled 'Prometheus' and is likened 'to the libido's struggle against repressiveness' (RT, p.22). The second stage, in which nature becomes 'the immediate though not the ultimate antagonist', is entitled 'the Real Man, the Imagination' and represents the ascension to a 'widened consciousness' in which the 'final enemy to be overcome is a recalcitrance in the self' (SM, p.vii). The first stage gives us 'the poet-as-hero ... marked by a deep involvement in political, social, and literary revolution, and a direct, even satirical attack on institutionally orientated Christianity, and the neo-classical literary and intellectual tradition': the second presents us with 'a standing-aside from polemic and satire, so as to re-center the arena of search within the self and its ambiguities' (SM, p.vii).

From this description we can see how Bloom's alliance of Romantic terminology with terms taken from 'experiential psychology' allows him to construct a more rigorous and systematised theory of Romanticism; an account which can contain the social radicalism of poets such as Blake and Shelley within an overall pattern inexorably moving towards an internalised, autonomous, decontextualised mode of vision. The engagement with revolutionary politics in Shelley, for example, becomes a manifestation of a necessary stage in poetic psychology, where a general attempt to unleash all repressed drives and forces occurs as a necessary first step in a fundamentally psychological movement towards autonomy, originality and freedom from all internal and external constraints. Social objectives and desires are significant only in terms of their place within a system of psychopoetic motives; they are to be interpreted up into the realm of *poetry* and do not possess relevance in their own right.

The use of Freud in the essay is extremely tentative. Bloom is at great pains to explain how Freud himself, with his insistence on the 'reality principle, working through the great disenchanter, reason, the scientific attitude' (RT, p.23), ultimately succumbs to an anti-Romantic acceptance of dualism, a theme which, as this study will illustrate, continues throughout Bloom's career, motivating the various revisions Bloom makes of Freudian psychology as applied to poetry. However, the attempt to utilise the language of psychoanalysis as a means of ensuring Romantic poetry against extra-literary explanations remains obvious enough. With this more systematic account of Romantic desire, Bloom is able to assert:

> There are thus two main elements in the major phase of Romantic quest, the first being the inward overcoming of the Selfhood's temptation, and the second the outward turning of the triumphant Imagination, free of further internalizations, though 'outward' and 'inward' become cloven fictions or false conceptual distinctions in this triumph, which must complete a dialectic of love by uniting the Imagination with its bride, a transformed, ongoing creation of the Imagination rather than a redeemed nature. (RT, p.28)

This could be said to represent Bloom's correction of Frye's account of Romantic humanism.[7] The great breakthrough it exemplifies within the context of Bloom's career centres on the eradication of the inside/outside dichotomy. If the ultimate antagonist in the internalised quest-romance becomes a wholly internal 'blocking-agent', rather than nature or social injustice and repression, then poetry becomes a wholly autonomous realm of desire. Bloom, by focusing on the movement from self-consciousness to the triumph over self-consciousness, and by emphasising the Romantic inability to make such a movement fully, is able to reassert the Romantic ideology of tradition's essential autonomy and begin to develop a mode of criticism which can represent itself as fundamentally faithful to such a tradition. 'The internalization of quest romance' shows Bloom adding the final piece to his intrinsic critical system: that piece being the 'Covering Cherub' (the internalised blocking-agent which obstructs the passage from the Prometheus to the Imagination stage). As Bloom puts it:

> The hero of internalized quest is the poet himself, the antagonists of quest are everything in the self that blocks imaginative work, and the fulfilment is never the poem itself but the poem beyond that is made possible by the apocalypse of imagination. (RT, p.19)

This 'apocalypse of imagination' is, we must reflect, a severely limited concept, reducible to an evanescent moment of original vision, a 'privileged moment' or 'secularized epiphany' (RT, p.xi). Bloom's clarification and intensification of his vision of Romantic poetry can be said to have led him, in 'The internalization of quest romance', to a point where that tradition is conceived in terms of a constant struggle to attain an impossible autonomy of vision and thus a continual struggle against a perpetual 'recalcitrance in the self' (RT, p.22) blocking that movement to full autonomy and/or originality of vision. Bloom relinquishes the idea of the autonomy of Romantic visionary poetry only to secure it more firmly by locating the forces which disrupt it fully within the poetic 'psyche' itself. Reading the development of Bloom's early work on Romanticism in this way allows us to observe how and why the theory of the poetic anxiety of influence enters into his account of that tradition. Bloom concludes his essay with the following remark:

> The man prophesied by the Romantics is a central man who is always in the process of becoming his own begetter, and though his major poems perhaps have been written, he as yet has not fleshed out his prophecy, nor proved the final form of his love. (RT, p.35)

The 'central man' is a figure representing the ideal of self-origination; an ideal which every Romantic strives towards and yet is unable to reach due to a stubborn alienation with regard to their own selves as 'subjects'. Although the essay in itself does not fully explain what this alienation or 'recalcitrance in the self' is, Bloom's meditations on the relation between Freud's 'experiential psychology' and the Romantic dialectics of love can be said to have laid the foundations for the answer that was to come. At the beginning of his essay, examining the Freudian reading of romance as probably commencing with an 'experience whose "strong impression on the writer had stirred up a memory of an earlier experience, generally belonging to childhood, which then arouses a wish that finds a fulfilment in the work in question . . ." ' (RT, p.13), Bloom goes on to negotiate his attraction to this definition and his repulsion at Freud's insistence on measuring poetry in terms of actual psychological experience outside the realm of poetry. Freud's 'embryonic theory of romance', he explains, offers up a potentially useful account of Romanticism: 'particularly if we interpret his "memory of an earlier experience" to mean also the recall of an earlier insight, or yearning, that may not have been experiential' (RT, p.14).

Of course, the step that the essay as a whole appears to demand, and the step that Bloom was indeed already making in other related essays, such as 'Keats and the embarrassments of poetry' (RT, pp.131–42), was to define this 'source' or 'earlier insight' as the 'memory' of an earlier poetic text. The theory of the anxiety of influence allows Bloom to reiterate his belief in the autonomy of poetic vision and to establish a purely internalised account of both the objectives and the limitations of such a mode of consciousness. It also allows him to intensify his quarrel with all extrinsic accounts of the authentic Romantic tradition. Bloom turns the very force which now makes Romanticism such a diseased form of poetic utterance into a force which retains Romanticism's influence and priority over the supposedly post-Romantic poetic and critical tradition which follows in its wake.

CHAPTER
TWO

*Anxieties of influence: deidealisation, reduction, and Bloom's poetics of conflict*

### Yeats, Bloom and the composite god

*Yeats*, published in 1970, is a pivotal work in Bloom's critical canon, marking the conclusion of the early work on Romanticism and inaugurating the influence-based theoretical phase. It seems evident, in fact, as David Fite has suggested, that the paradoxes of Yeats's place within the Romantic tradition, his obvious affinities to the work of Blake and Shelley, tempered by his self-styled denunciation of Romantic origins from 1914 onwards, and the use made of this anti-Romantic trend by the New Critical–Modernist tradition of twentieth-century criticism, come as close as we are likely to get to a 'cause' for Bloom's alteration of critical approach. Bloom himself states: 'It is perhaps inevitable that Yeats, the conscious heir of the Romantics, compels us to a new kind of critical study of Romantic influences' (*Yeats*, p.7).

In a recent discussion of the work of Thomas Weiskel, Bloom has presented a fascinating insight into his own assessment of his work on influence. 'Throughout *The Romantic Sublime*', he writes, 'Weiskel works towards a difficult kind of literary criticism, at once moral or primary and de-idealizing or antithetical. This may not be possible; certainly I, for one, have failed to achieve it.'[1] *Yeats*, of all Bloom's critical works, comes closest to being a properly 'moral' or 'primary' work. As many commentators at the time perceived, it is precisely this tension between the 'primary' and the 'antithetical' which makes the book so unstable. One reviewer stated that the book's thesis 'impels the critic increasingly to shift his argument from critical to moral grounds as his demonstration unfolds and forces him to nervous feats of legerdemain, misemphasis, and falsely inspired indignation'.[2] Another commentator declared that Bloom's shifts between positions left the work a 'morally bifurcated response to poetry'.[3] Sandra Seigal summarises this general reception when she writes: '*Yeats* appears exceedingly ideological. The moral tone dominates; judgements abound. What accounts for this paradox is Bloom's belief that he is reading Yeats from the point of view of other poets who are themselves the measure of greatness.'[4]

*Yeats* represents Bloom's first book-length engagement with the issue of poetic influence. Concentrating on the complex relationship between Yeats and his two precursors, Blake and Shelley, Bloom analyses the poetry, plays and the system elaborated in *A Vision*, as creative misinterpretations of the work of these two High Romantics. The theory sketched in the book's first chapter views such misinterpretations as inevitable. Bloom asserts that each poet must create, in the sense of revise, his or her own literary 'father' (*Yeats*, pp.3–5). Bloom abstracts the complicated revisions of Blake and Shelley performed by Yeats into a rather symmetrical scheme when he writes: 'Yeats has read Shelley with great accuracy and insight, but will not abide in that reading . . . Yeats has read Blake with great inaccuracy and deliberately befuddled insight, so as to produce an antithetical poetic father to take Shelley's place' (*Yeats*, p.59).

Yeats, on this reading, can be said to arrange the work of his two poetic 'fathers' in such a way as to allow for the emergence of his unique stance and voice. Such an organisation of sources clearly makes the originality of that stance or voice rather more ambiguous and diluted than his precursors' work. Theoretically, however, such a contamination or decline in 'strength' is unavoidable and cannot constitute the basis for an evaluative judgement (see *Yeats*, p.219).

At the beginning of the text Bloom writes that 'the revisionary readings of precursors that are involved in Yeats's poems and essays are not being condemned by me, in anything that follows' (*Yeats*, p.7). Yet the judgement contained in Bloom's reading, in which the modern canonisation of the later phase of Yeats's career is rejected in favour of the Romantic faith expressed in the earlier phases, appears to do just that. The book's opening paragraph begins: 'Yeats was a poet very much in the line of vision; his ancestors in English poetic tradition were primarily Blake and Shelley, and his achievement will at last be judged against theirs' (*Yeats*, p.v).

Taking up an argument already presented in an earlier essay, and bearing similarities to a critique presented five years earlier by Frye,[5] Bloom endeavours to demonstrate the manner in which Yeats's later poetry relinquishes the 'faithless faith' of his Romantic inheritance. Yeats, according to Bloom, replaces this 'faith' with a theory of supernatural destiny and fate, what Martin Buber called the 'contemporary "composite God" of "possession by process, that is by unlimited causality" ' (*Yeats*, p.470). Yeats is condemned by Bloom for succumbing to a belief in historical determinism and, an even greater heresy, for projecting a form of such an anti-Romantic belief into the poetry of Blake and Shelley (see *Yeats*, p.471).

We begin here to be able to define more precisely the paradox that commentators have discovered in this text. Criticising Yeats for submitting to a version of historical determinism repugnant to the High Romantic ethos of Imagination, Bloom's book appears to inaugurate a theory of poetic influence equally grounded within a version of historical determinism. Daniel T. O'Hara writes that by the end of the 1970s, 'Bloom himself became an academic version of what he had beheld in Yeats: a "professor" of humane letters exposing what according to Bloom in *Yeats* is the modern form of Gnosticism: historical determinism'.[6] O'Hara makes much of the fact that by the time of his essay 'Yeats, gnosticism, and the sacred void' (PR, pp.205–34) Bloom feels it possible to present Yeats's Gnosticism not only as constructive but as an essential part of his Romanticism. Indeed, by the time of *Agon*, Bloom can describe himself as 'a Jewish Gnostic, trying to explore and develop a personal Gnosis and a possible Gnosticism, perhaps even one available to others' (*Agon*, p.4). Even if we object that Bloom's definition of Gnosticism has altered greatly in the decade between *Yeats* and *Agon*, it remains evident that his valorisation of Blakean humanism and apocalyptic Imagination in the former text stands in an uneasy alliance with the burgeoning theory of influence which frames it.

Criticising Yeats for misreading Blake and Shelley, Bloom inaugurates a theory of poetic influence which makes such a misreading inevitable. Censuring Yeats's acquiescence to a form of Gnosticism and a belief in historical determinism, Bloom establishes a theory of poetic influence which will, within a few years, assert a variety of both these 'errors'.

In coming to an analysis of Bloom's arguments concerning the nature of poetic influence we confront an attempt to produce a 'theory of poetry' and a form of 'antithetical practical criticism' which can read the phenomenon of inter-poetic relations in its own terms and which finds itself, in order to avoid a reduction and distortion of the full power and significance of such relations, incorporating into itself the very processes it is attempting faithfully to represent. If the shuttle between a more orthodox notion of critical judgement and a developing sense of the implication of criticism within the dialectics of poetic tradition helps to make *Yeats* such an discomforting and discomforted text, then the still relatively implicit 'crisis of vision' such a tone signifies becomes overtly bodied forth in the theoretical work which follows.

*Yeats* can be said to have left Bloom with an important decision: to develop the 'ethical' dimension of that work, judging modern poetry against a valorised standard of Romantic humanism, or to effect a radical transformation in the reading of Romantic tradition itself. I have begun to describe the reasons why Bloom chose the latter of these options. This choice was greatly determined by Bloom's resistance to critical reduction and his belief that criticism should ground itself on and teach 'not a language of criticism (a formalist view still held in common by archetypalists, structuralists, and phenomenologists) but a language in which poetry already is written'; a motive which becomes synonymous with a teaching of 'the language of influence, of the dialectic that governs the relations between poets *as poets*' (AI, p.25).

Bloom's presentation of his thesis in *The Anxiety of Influence* is bound up with a consideration of the possibility for a mode of criticism which might be able to respect the power of poetic utterance in its own terms. One might say that the undisclosed subject of that text is a defence against reduction, a desire, as Wordsworth puts it, to gain 'knowledge not purchased by the loss of power!'

It is necessary, then, to establish how Bloom presents his theory of poetic influence as a solution to such critical concerns: the desire to produce a properly *poetic* 'theory of poetry' and the desire to avoid reduction or the *non-poetic* rationalisation of poetic phenomena. In *The Anxiety of Influence*, Bloom begins to draw an association between the avoidance of such a reduction and the attempt to deidealise the orthodox conceptions of poetic influence. If such a project appears to leave behind the 'ethical' or 'primary' dimensions of *Yeats* in favour of a rigorously deidealising and 'antithetical' 'theory of poetry', then it does so merely to reinstitute a more fundamental tension between a critical repetition of Romantic tenets and a drive towards a deidealisation of our conception of that tradition. The separation between 'primary' and 'antithetical' modes of criticism, between a 'moral' and a 'deidealising' mode of reading, where deidealisation is conceived as an avoidance both of a repetition of poetry's own idealising self-representations and of an extrapoetic or ideological brand of interpretation, is not finally a project Bloom's theory of influence can achieve.

## *Influence revised: critical reduction, deidealisation and the repetition of Romanticism*

I

That *The Anxiety of Influence* is a work deeply concerned with the issue of critical reduction need hardly be in question, particularly if we look at the opening statements in the 'Interchapter: A manifesto for antithetical criticism'. Beginning with a reiteration of the revision of the poetic 'imagination' he is articulating in his new 'theory of poetry', Bloom sketches the basic processes involved in an 'antithetical' reading of literary influence. The interpretative practice he proposes involves a comparative reading of poets in terms both of their misreading of precursors and of the critic's own revisionary reading of that relationship. This approach requires Bloom to defend his method against the charge of reduction. He asserts, 'We reduce – if at all – to another poem. The meaning of a poem can only be another poem' (AI, p.94).

Reading through the mass of commentary which has accrued around Bloom's work of the mid-1970s is certainly instructive. Much of that commentary focuses on the issue of reduction, yet also highlights how easy it is to reduce what Bloom himself means by his key concept of the anxiety of influence. In this study I will draw on the most influential critiques of Bloom's work, illustrating how he absorbs and revises his critics through the production of ever more sophisticated versions of his original insights and positions.

A definable set of objections emerges as we read through the mass of reviews Bloom's tetralogy on influence inspired. There are objections, for instance, to Bloom's misreading of Freud, his apparent imposition of theoretical principles and paradigms on the delicate and defenceless realm of literature, for apparently raising criticism to the level of poetry itself, for filling his texts with esoteric and arcane baggage, and for ultimately, despite his theoretical pyrotechnics, reasserting a naive and 'mythical' historical narrative in which a fall into an age of anxiety and belatedness occurs after a golden or 'giant age before the flood' (see AI, p.11).

By far the most common complaint, however, was directed at Bloom's basic definition of poetic influence, its characteristics and its essential functions and implications. The principal charge against him revolves around his reduction of the concept of influence to a quasi-Oedipal, poeticised version of the Freudian 'family romance': a reduction which many commentators assert does not account for the multiplicity of influences – poetic and extrapoetic – which affect every poet ('weak' or 'strong').

Much of the commentary on Bloom recognises the challenge inherent within his work to go beyond its own methods of interpretation. The only way to meet this challenge properly, however, is to base such a revision on as thorough an understanding of the theories being transcended as is interpretatively possible.

Having established the importance of the theme of reduction in Bloom's account of influence, we should note the importance of not allowing our own reading of that account to collapse into what are now almost canonical reductions of Bloom's enterprise. That any reading of Bloom's theory of influence will not be able to avoid a certain form of reduction is, of course, part of the lesson Bloom should have taught his readers, a lesson which will play an important role in the later chapters of this study. Yet, given the tendentious nature of every interpretation, it is still possible to produce a description of Bloom's theory of influence which rectifies most of the standard misconceptions.

What are the major misconceptions concerning Bloom's account of the poetic anxiety of influence? I would suggest, following Peter de Bolla, that there are three basic misunderstandings which have accumulated around Bloom's definition of influence: the belief that it rests on the recognition of similarities in style, imagery and overt poetic articulations of affiliation – those aspects of poetic language commonly understood under the general term of influence; that it presents an Oedipal account of the influence process and thus constitutes a significant defence of the orthodox notion of the author;

and, lastly, that it offers up and supports a form of literary history, and is in itself part of a general reassertion of the historical or contextual understanding of literary texts.

Needing, at this stage, to begin to unravel the complexities of Bloom's 'theory of poetry', it will be useful to employ these major misconceptions as starting-points for a positive representation of the Bloomian project.

II

In chapter 1 of *The Anxiety of Influence*, Bloom asks: 'And what *is* Poetic Influence anyway? Can the study of it really be anything more than the wearisome industry of source-hunting, of allusion-counting, an industry that will soon touch apocalypse anyway when it passes from scholars to computers?' (AI, p.31).

As Robin Jarvis and Peter de Bolla point out, the orthodox practice of 'source-study', based on a 'positivistic' conception of literary influence, has a long history in literary criticism.[8] R. D. Havens' work on Milton, *The Influence of Milton on English Poetry* (1922), with its 'compendious' list of Miltonic echoes in a wide range of subsequent poets, is, as Jarvis points out, characteristic of this common critical procedure.[9] Yet, as de Bolla illustrates, and as the passage above already indicates, Bloom has continually emphasised the distance between his conception of poetic influence and this traditional sense of stylistic borrowing (see AI, p.8).

The tendency to interpret Bloom's conception of influence in terms which would pull it into the traditional practice of source-study stems from a fundamental mistake with regard to Bloom's representation of the poetic text. For Bloom, a proper study of influence means that we can no longer retain the belief that individual texts exist. If traditional source-study represents a certain wandering of images, allusions and phrases from one text to another, then the 'antithetical' understanding of influence destroys the very objects between which that 'wandering' is supposed to occur. This is an essential point which needs labouring, not only because it constitutes the foundation for all Bloom's other theoretical insights, but equally because it highlights the manner in which influence, for Bloom, destroys the formalistic approach in criticism.

If the New Criticism depended on the conception of the literary text as a monad – a 'verbal icon' or 'well wrought urn' – then an 'antithetical' reading of influence exposes the illusionary nature of such a perspective. Bloom's point is that when we begin to understand poems as misreadings of prior poems then our conception of what a poem *is* changes radically. In the *Anxiety*, Bloom styles poetic texts as 'dyads'; in *Kabbalah and Criticism* they become 'triads'. Poems are 'relational events', 'inter-texts' which can only be understood 'antithetically', that is, in terms of their relationship with other poems. It is only when we register this essential fact about Bloom's theory of poetry and the 'antithetical practical criticism' it inspires that we begin to recognise how far from orthodox conceptions it takes the notion of influence. Bloom spells out the difference:

> All criticisms that call themselves primary vacillate between tautology – in which the poem is and means itself – and reduction – in which the poem means something that is not itself a poem. Antithetical criticism must begin by denying both tautology and reduction, a denial best delivered by the assertion that the meaning of a poem can only be a poem, but *another poem – a poem not itself*. And not a poem chosen with total arbitrariness, but any central poem by an indubitable precursor, even if the ephebe *never read that poem*. Source study is wholly irrelevant here; we are dealing with primal words, but antithetical meanings, and an ephebe's best misinterpretations may well be of poems he has never read. (AI, p.70)

This last assertion has become a rather (in)famous example of what many take to be the essential eccentricity of Bloom's approach. Having moved the Bloomian project away from the conventional notion of the conscious employment of stylistic features from previous poetry, however, we begin to understand its proper significance. The defence against tradition, which is the act of misreading, does not need in any way to be – and indeed is usually most effective when it is not – a conscious defence. When we add to this the fact that misreading does not simply occur between two texts, but spans and in fact constitutes the *history* of the poetic tradition, then such a statement begins to prove both highly suggestive and rather devastating to conventional source-study.

We have not fully understood the importance of juxtaposing Bloom's version of influence with the more traditional varieties, however, until we have begun to address the manner in which Bloom suggests such intertextual relations of misreading are to be interpretatively recaptured. Bloom presents the method of his interpretative practice quite clearly in his 'interchapter':

The first swerve is to learn to read a great precursor poet as his greater descendants compelled themselves to read him.

The second is to read the descendants as if we were their disciples, and so compel ourselves to learn where we must revise them if we are to be found by our own work, and claimed by the living of our own lives.

Neither of these quests is yet Antithetical Criticism.

That begins when we measure the first *clinamen* against the second. Finding just what the accent of deviation is, we proceed to apply it as corrective to the reading of the first but not the second poet or group of poets. To practice Antithetical Criticism on the more recent poet or poets becomes possible only when they have found disciples not ourselves. But these can be critics, and not poets. (AI, pp.93–4)

It can be seen from this methodological statement that Bloom places the act of interpretation that a critic makes of the 'story' of influence squarely within the 'poetic history' produced by the various levels or stages of misreading. We also begin to see how a poet (or critic) can be said to be misreading a 'great precursor' via a misreading of a more recent poet. This explanation does not yet fully exhaust the strange, dialectical quality of the misreading event. For this we must jump a little ahead of our immediate focus to a passage from *Kabbalah and Criticism*:

A poem is a deep misprision of a previous poem when we recognize the later poem as being absent rather than present on the surface of the earlier poem, and yet still being *in* the earlier poem, implicit or hidden *in* it, not yet manifest, and yet *there*. (KC, pp.66–7)

Bloom illustrates what he means here by pointing to the influence of Shelley on Victorian and modern poets. Browning, Swinburne, Hardy and Yeats all exhibit fundamental relations to Shelley's poetry. Bloom argues that 'All four of these strong poets have styles almost totally antithetical to Shelley's style, yet he is the crucial precursor for all of them' (KC, p.67). The point is not just that Shelley influences these poets, but rather that their poetry can be said already to be implicitly hidden 'within' Shelley. We might say that for orthodox theorists of poetic influence Shelley's part in the production and meaning of a text such as 'Childe Roland to the dark tower came' is important but still ultimately peripheral. For Bloom, despite the absence of any truly striking verbal resemblances, Browning's poem is a misreading of certain key Shelley poems: the patterns of image, trope and defence which structure Shelley's 'strongest' work are reworked once again in Browning's text. In this way, it is possible to argue that 'Childe Roland to the dark tower came' already implicitly or potentially exists 'within' Shelley's key poetic texts; texts which are themselves, we should none the less note, intertextual acts of relation.

This strain within Bloom's approach to influence will eventually lead us to a consideration of his establishment of a complex, multiform map of misreading, meant to represent the overall manner in which poets within the post-Enlightenment or modern tradition can misread their precursors. At this stage it is necessary to move on to Bloom's explanation of how and why certain past poets can be said to become precursors for later poets. This area moves us on to a consideration of the second level of misconception to which I alluded earlier: the understanding of the Bloomian project as offering an Oedipal vision of poetic history and the concomitant error concerning Bloom's approach to the poet as an authorial 'subject'.

With regard to the question of psychoanalytic literary criticism, Bloom has frequently turned to comic irony, comparing it to the Holy Roman Empire: not Holy, not Roman, not an Empire; not psychoanalytic, not literary and not criticism (see BV, p.62 and PI, p.426).

To read Bloom's 'theory of poetry' as a simple translation of Freudian psychoanalysis into the realm of poetry is as great a mistake as to read him in the context of traditional views concerning influence. Just as Bloom dismisses the notion that there exist individual texts which can be interpreted and understood in their own right, so a similar relational characteristic is asserted for the poet him- or herself. As Bloom argues: 'We need to stop thinking of any poet as an autonomous ego . . . Every poet is a being caught up in a dialectical relationship (transference, repetition, error, communication) with another poet or poets' (AI, p.91).

I have already begun to discuss Bloom's ambivalent relation to Freud. According to Bloom, Freud's greatest contribution to the theory of poetry lies in his treatment of the motivations behind romance and thus by implication, given Bloom's reading of poetic influence in terms of a 'family romance', to the study of influence.

Despite Bloom's utilisation of the language of psychoanalysis we go astray if we interpret his work as arguing for a psychological or biographical reading of poetry. That such misconceptions are often encouraged by Bloom's own critical polemic (against the Eliotic/New Critical impersonality-thesis and the deconstructive critique of traditional humanist assumptions in particular) is a fact that should perhaps be acknowledged here. Such a polemic only goes to make more difficult a proper reading of Bloom's 'antithetical' approach to poetry, centred as it is in his sense of poetry as constituting primarily an act or utterance or discursive event. This vision of poetry, despite the appearance of many of Bloom's defences of the poetic 'subject', means that neither the text nor the psyche is to be given ultimate precedence. Throughout his theoretical work Bloom resists a purely linguistic or textual and a purely psychological context for the interpretation of poetry and its experientially felt pathos. This is a theme to which I will be returning in this study. We need, however, to gain a sense of how Bloom's utilisation of the language (or rhetoric) of Freudian psychoanalysis helps develop his theories concerning poetic influence.

For Freud, as Bloom continually reminds his readers, the function of art is to assist in the processes of sublimation (see AI, p.8). In this reading of poetry's basic motivations, Bloom locates Freud's greatest misreading of the literary tradition. To understand why, for Bloom, poetry is opposed to the logic of sublimation is to understand how great an error it is to ascribe to Bloom either an Oedipal theory of poetic influence or a traditional defence of the authorial 'self'. What is at stake in Bloom's rejection of the logic of Freudian sublimation is his vision of the essentially conflictual or agonistic nature of poetry itself: his sense of poetry as a drive against all constraining contexts.

Bloom's engagement with the language of psychoanalysis forces him into a re-evaluation and eventual transformation of his earlier figurations for poetry: blinded Oedipus comes to replace Prometheus, and the 'Real Man, the Imagination' of the essay on quest-romance disappears entirely (see AI, p.10). The vision of poetry we are left with is still clearly dependent on major Romantic themes and presuppositions, however. And the manner in which these themes and romantic tropes are retained is by maintaining the Freudian separation of art from life, while at the same moment incorporating into the realm of art the very principles of self-conflict, instinctual aggression and ambivalence Freud reserved for the experiential realm. Understanding this move is crucial if we are to go beyond the erroneous understanding of Bloom's use of the Oedipus complex and his version of the authorial 'self'.

As Bloom's 'poetic' reading of Freud grew in both confidence and depth during the 1970s and early 1980s, a central theme emerged, one which I will be returning to in chapter 6 of this study. Following suggestions made by Lionel Trilling in his seminal essay, 'Freud and literature', Bloom has developed a reading of Freud which presents him as a fundamentally 'literary' figure, basing his 'science' of psychoanalysis on prior 'poetic' insights, images and stances. The basic motivation for Bloom's assertion that what he himself has taken from Freud is precisely what Freud himself 'took from the poets' (MM, p.89) is clear enough. It allows Bloom to utilise the images, tropes and rhetorical figures which make up the text of psychoanalysis without collapsing the fundamental distinction between the realm of poetry and the realm of the extrapoetic, a separation which no form of psychoanalytic literary criticism worthy of the name could countenance.

What Bloom begins to develop in *The Anxiety of Influence* is a psychopoetic theory, a wholly 'poetic' rather than 'experiential' psychology of creation, which his earlier essay on quest-romance and his study of Yeats's system of antithetical masks had promised. The centre of this psychopoetics lies in Bloom's figuration of the 'poet-in-a-poet' or 'poet-as-poet', a figure which immediately illustrates the error of interpreting Bloom's representations as referring to the autobiographies of *real* historical men and women.

In my earlier discussion of 'The internalization of quest romance', I focused on Bloom's revision of Freud's 'theory of romance'. Bloom, it will be remembered, translates Freud's determining 'memory of an earlier experience' into 'the recall of an earlier insight, or yearning, that may not have been experiential' (RT, p.14). In *The Anxiety of Influence*, Bloom is in a position to explain properly the nature of this determining, even originating 'insight', 'yearning' or non-experiential 'experience'. It need not be surprising to assert that he does so by positing an initial act of influence which, quite simply, makes possible any person's transformation into a 'poet-as-poet'. Bloom quite defiantly employs religious terms for this originating moment, speaking of 'poetic incarnation' and the 'rebirth' any poet must pass through before becoming a 'poet-as-poet'. As if to resist the connotations of secondariness contained within such theological tropes, Bloom equally insists on a 'radical analogue between human and poetic birth, between biological and creative anxiety' (AI, p.58).

What his speculations on poetic origination ultimately produce, however, is a radical alteration in the application of Freudian terminology: for the poetic precursor, the apparent 'father-figure' for each new poet, comes to occupy not the poetic equivalent of the superego – as any psychoanalytic reading of the vicissitudes of poetic influence would presume – but rather comes to be absorbed as part of the poetic equivalent of the id-component. This point needs consideration, as it contains Bloom's most radical challenge to the logic of sublimation and thus stands at the very centre of the development of his poetics of conflict.

Bloom, in *Anxiety*, begins to argue a point he has reasserted consistently in his subsequent texts: the precursor, he informs us, 'is never absorbed as part of the superego (the Other who commands us), but as part of the id' (AI, p.71). This apparently eccentric notion begins to be clarified as soon as we remind ourselves of the equivalence Bloom wishes to draw between writing and (mis)reading, between the production of a poetic text and the defensive misinterpretation of previous, precursor texts. In perhaps his most profound essay on the relation between poetry and Freudian psychoanalysis, 'Freud's concepts of defense and the poetic will' (*Agon*, pp.119–44), Bloom reflects that 'to discuss Freud's concepts of defense is to discuss also what in Romantic or belated poetry is the poetic will itself, the ego of the poet not as man, but of the poet as poet' (*Agon*, p.120). The poetic 'will' is essentially defensive because it is the product of an original act of misreading, which is equally an original event of influence. To say this is equally to state that the poetic *will* is constituted by the influence of a precursor poet or poets. To put this more simply, when a poet is incarnated *as a poet* s/he first learns to desire his or her own power or *potentia*; yet this desire is learnt by recognising, however unconsciously, the power of an earlier poet. A poet's will-to-power or desire for poetic originality is from the very start the product of the influence of a precursor. On the level of rhetoric, this is equivalent to the recognition that the only *language* a poet has by which to prove his or her own originality and 'strength' is a *language* already possessed by past poets. The poetic 'will' *is*, essentially, that already possessed *language*; the images, tropes and defences of the precursor poet (see AI, p.71). Poets, in Bloom's account, do not defend against other anterior poets so much as against the presence of other poets within themselves, which becomes equivalent to the assertion that the poetic will to originality is concomitant with a defence against the 'self'.

These last points not only clarify the distance between Bloom's psychopoetics and anything classifiable as psychoanalytic literary criticism, they also begin to draw together our analysis of Bloom's account of influence and poetic psychology, establishing the remarkable shuttle observable in Bloom's work between text and psyche, between the explanatory languages of rhetoric and psychology.

This adaptation of Freud allows Bloom to develop a tragic reading of poetry, a reading based on an increasingly sophisticated version of quest-romance (see AI, pp.64–5).

If the desire for originality comes from a poet's recognition of such an originality in a previous poet, then, if the poet is not to relinquish that desire, s/he must necessarily become defensive about the very drives which constitute him or her as a poet. That defence is the anxiety of influence, an anxiety which requires poets to defend not against other poets but against the existence of other poetry within their own poetic 'psyches'. If s/he is to be 'strong', the poet must repress the recognition that his or her unconscious is largely made up of the language of prior poets – a motive which becomes equivalent to repressing the fact of belatedness, of having come late in the story of poetic history. The way in which poets do this is, again, analogous to the way in which Freud suggested people repressed their most authentic drives. These defence mechanisms, codified by Freud's daughter Anna into a sixfold taxonomy, become, in Bloom's analogous account of poetry, six ways in which poets defend against the recognition of their own belatedness, their own possession by the precursor poet. Bloom labels these defence mechanisms *revisionary ratios*, and invites us to read them as six interrelated ways in which influence operates between and within poetic texts.

As Bloom writes in his 'Freud and the sublime': 'Freud's rhetoric of the psyche, as codified by Anna Freud in *The Ego and the Mechanisms of Defense* (1946), is as comprehensive a system of tropes as Western theory has devised' (*Agon*, p.98). The way in which Bloom applies this comprehensive system to the interpretation of poetic texts can be seen in the following passage from 'The breaking of form':

> As I apply Anna Freud, in a poem the ego is the poetic self and the id is the precursor, idealized and frequently composite, hence fantasized, but still traceable to a historical author or authors. The defensive measures of the poetic self against the fantasized precursor can be witnessed in operation only by the study of a difference between ratios, but this difference depends upon our awareness not so much of presences as of absences, of *what is missing in the poem because it had to be excluded* . . . The authentic poem now achieves its dearth of meaning by strategies of exclusion, or what can be called litanies of evasion. (BF, pp.14–15)

By the time he wrote this essay, Bloom had developed the sixfold scheme of revisionary ratios first presented in the *Anxiety* into a complex map of misreading, which I do not intend to discuss in this chapter. Their presentation in *Anxiety* is speculative, helping Bloom to channel his material while representing his sense of the determinate shape potentially observable within the history of influence: 'The six revisionary movements that I will trace in the strong poet's life-cycle could as well be more, and could take quite different names than those I have employed. I have kept them to six, because these seem to be minimal and essential to my understanding of how one poet deviates from another' (AI, pp.10–11). The pattern that the ratios display, therefore, refers not merely to movements within an individual poetic text, but equally to the 'life-cycle' of a 'strong' poet and also, implicitly, to a potential narrative of post-Enlightenment poetry in general.

*Clinamen*, the basic form of revisionary swerve, corresponds to a form of irony in which a precursor's language is re-employed in a slightly different way. Bloom's illustration of this 'central working concept of the theory of Poetic Influence' (AI, p.42) is Milton's Satan and his relationship to Milton's God. The fundamental ratio of poetic influence, according to Bloom, establishes the modern poet within a version of the 'state of Satan', which Bloom defines as 'a constant consciousness of dualism, of being trapped in the finite, not just in space (in the body) but in clock-time as well' (AI, p.32). Milton's Satan becomes the 'archetype of the modern poet at his strongest' (AI, p.19), battling fiercely against a dualistic environment with the aid of the principal mode of defence Freud classified as 'reaction formation'. James Arrt Aune has usefully defined reaction formation as 'the fixation of an idea or affect that is opposite to a feared impulse in consciousness (e.g., homophobia as a reaction against strong internal homosexual drives)'.[10] *Clinamen*, in this way, sets up the fundamental irony of the story of influence: the poet's desire to be different from the precursor constantly being compromised by and exposing a desire to be the same as the precursor, or even simply to *be* the precursor.

The next ratio, *tessera*, takes Bloom into what appears to be a more fundamentally American mode of revisionism; a defensive turning against the self or reversal, in which the poet more overtly attempts to complete the precursor's language by employing it in a different way. Because of its closer relation to essential American modes of revisionism, Bloom's major example is Wallace Stevens's attempted completion of Walt Whitman (see AI, pp.67–9). With the next move, *kenosis*, we enter a stage in which the poet strategically humbles him- or herself, performing such a self-emptying in a manner similar to the defence mechanisms of undoing, isolation and regression – all mechanisms pitted against repetition-compulsion – and, by such a strategy, humbling the precursor more profoundly than the poetic 'self'. Such a strange sounding ratio is made somewhat more comprehensible as Bloom moves on to its major Romantic exemplars (see AI, pp.90–1). Bloom asks: 'Is the *kenosis* of Shelley in his "Ode to the West Wind" an undoing, an isolating of Wordsworth or of Shelley? Who is emptied more fearfully in Whitman's "As I Ebb'd with the Ocean of Life", Emerson or Whitman?' (AI, p.90). Bloom provides the following answer: '*Kenosis*, in this poetic and revisionary sense, appears to be an act of self-abnegation, yet tends to make the fathers pay for their own sins, and perhaps for those of the son also' (AI, p.91).

With the next two ratios Bloom enters into what is perhaps a more recognisable terrain, as the ratios of *daemonisation* and *askesis* appear to be central to that poetry we call Romantic. The former ratio corresponds to a poet's attainment of the sublime which, given Bloom's 'theory of poetry', must necessarily be a counter-sublime, a mode of *ecstasis* achieved at the expense of or in contradistinction to a previous sublimity. For Bloom, *daemonisation* is achieved through a form of repression, in which the power of the precursor's sublimity is contained, domesticated or absorbed 'more thoroughly into tradition than his own courageous individuation should allow him to be absorbed' (AI, p.109). Such a ratio is dominant in the 'Bards of Sensibility' and, as their legacy to the Romantics, leads Bloom to ponder the possibility that 'the *ekstasis*, the final step beyond, of Romantic vision' might be 'only an intensity of repression previously unmatched in the history of the imagination' (AI, pp.111–12).

*Askesis*, the next ratio, is the major Romantic response to such a problematic legacy of repression and involves an estrangement (internalisation, isolation, purgation) of the poetic 'self' from all contexts, from everything classifiable under the heading of the 'non-self'. Such a strategy is the major contribution of Wordsworth to the development of poetic tradition: 'An enormous curtailment made Wordsworth the inventor of modern poetry, which at last we can recognize as the diminished thing it is . . .' (AI, p.125).

The last of the revisionary ratios, *apophrades*, certainly provoked the most extreme responses in Bloom's commentators, for as a revisionary move which 'depends upon a successful manifestation of the dead in the garments of the living, as though the dead poets were given a suppler freedom than they had found for themselves' (AI, p.143) it produces the uncanny impression that temporal priority has been reversed – 'as though the later poet himself had written the precursor's characteristic work' (AI, p.16). This ratio corresponds to the defence mechanisms of introjection and projection and, whilst rather sketchily developed in *Anxiety*, will form the basis of Bloom's later theory of transumption.

Bloom's chosen examples in his discussion of *apophrades* are wide-ranging but can be said to centre on John Ashbery's relationship with his central precursor, Wallace Stevens. Bloom reflects that 'the achievement of John Ashbery in his powerful poem "Fragment" . . . is to return us to Stevens, somewhat uneasily to discover that at moments Stevens sounds rather too much like Ashbery, an accomplishment I might not have thought possible' (AI, p.142). *The Anxiety of Influence* thus concludes with an example of the 'survival of strong poetry' in the present moment and, as my brief survey of the revisionary ratios should have suggested, there remains an implicit historical narrative within the book's presentation, moving us from the Miltonic establishment of the post-Enlightenment tradition with its central dynamic (the anxiety of influence) through the inevitable diminishments such a dynamic entails to a qualified conclusion. Bloom's account of poetic tradition, in other words, emphasises an inevitably increasing distance between the priority of origins and the revisionary compromised nature of contemporary poetry. Yet this theory holds out the hope for continued 'strength' if the lessons of revisionism are correctly understood.

Elizabeth Bruss has described *Anxiety* as founded on 'the familiar pattern of glory, fall, and qualified recovery in the form of affiliation, denial, and renewed affiliation'.[11] Bloom's own description of his 'theory of poetry' as constituting 'a severe poem, reliant upon aphorism, apothegm, and a quite personal (though thoroughly traditional) mythic pattern' (AI, p.13), along with this description by Bruss, seems to be corroborated in the development of the revisionary ratios. Their presentation in *Anxiety* seems to contain Bloom's sense not so much of the actual as the still possible historical narrative of modern poetry, from the post-Miltonic 'fall' into anxiety to the potential 'restoration' in a heightened sense of the demarcations of such a belated state.

The fact that Bloom has recently regretted his attempt to 'rationalize and historicize' the final draft of *Anxiety*, indicates his own awareness that the implicit historical narrative ('mythic pattern') contained within it has led many of his commentators to emphasise this aspect at the expense of the 'theory of poetry' it was designed to present.[12] Despite this aspect of *Anxiety*, the theory of poetic influence presented within it is anything but historical.

The last of the three misconceptions I referred to earlier is surprisingly common, considering Bloom's continued denial of the relevance of history to the study of poetry. This misconception can be discovered within some of Bloom's most sophisticated commentators. Frank Lentricchia states that 'Few have succeeded, as Harold Bloom has succeeded, in returning poetry to history' (Foreword to BV, p.x). I have already referred to Edward Said's similarly confusing assertion. It is not simply that Bloom rejects the analysis of poetic meaning in terms of its supposed reflection of or context within social, ideological and political environments. More importantly, the account of poetic texts I have been outlining so far makes any attempt to produce an historicised reading of poetry inconceivable.

If Bloom's approach is to be described in terms of a return to some form of historicism, then that form must be recognised as an interpretation of modes of defensive misreading within *and* between texts. This becomes synonymous with the reading of poetic tradition itself as the wandering of poetic meaning in-between 'strong' poetic texts. Poetic history, on this model, becomes 'a vast visionary tragedy' describable on the model of the 'family romance'. Poetic history is understood in terms of a process in which a prior, original meaning is reimagined, revised; a process which makes each 'strong' text a new layer in a palimpsest. For Bloom, 'poetic history' *is* that palimpsest, and the task of an 'antithetical practical criticism' is, if I may slightly alter the metaphorical freight of John Hollander's description, to rectify the two-dimensional formalist approach, which treats merely its surface 'face', by moving to a three-dimensional conceptualisation of its depth (Hollander, 'Introduction' to PI, pp.xx–xxi).

*The Anxiety of Influence* represents not a return to history but the establishment of a method for the understanding of poetic texts as defensive turnings of a temporalised form of ('poetic') meaning. Poems, for Bloom, are neither linguistic, nor historical, nor psychological products, but rather, varieties of 'utterance, within a tradition of uttering' (BV, p.4). To develop further our understanding of the vision of poetry at the heart of such a theory we need now to turn our attention to the conception of poetic meaning presented in *Anxiety*; an issue which will return us to the theme of reduction.

### III

If a reader were asked to compile a list of the most controversial elements within Bloom's 'theory of poetry', the association between poetic *meaning* and *property* would surely emerge near the top. Bloom's poetics of conflict are predicated on a vision of poetic discourse as competition, an unremitting agon between warring forces. In 'The necessity of misreading', Bloom reflects on the fact that 'In psychic life, as in international affairs, "defense" is frequently murderous.' Undaunted by this insight, he goes on: 'Reading is defensive warfare, however generously or joyously we read, and with whatever degree of love, for in such love or such pleasure there is more-than-usual acute ambivalence' (KC, p.104). A little later in the same essay, Bloom condenses this vision of poetry into perhaps the most memorable of its representations: 'A new poem is not unlike a small child placed with a lot of other small children in a small playroom, with a limited number of toys, and no adult supervision whatever' (KC, p.121).

For Bloom 'priority in the natural order and authority in the spiritual order' are one and the same; which means that poetic meaning is equivalent to having *named something first*. If to possess 'strength' in poetry is to possess meaning, then 'strength' becomes not merely the inevitable but the natural characteristic of those texts which come early in a culture's tradition. For the texts which come late, which are *belated*, the only 'strength' on offer becomes what Bloom comes to call the text's defensive *lying against time*, a rhetorical assertion of 'strength' *qua* meaning which, sadly, is more figurative defence than fact. Bloom's entire 'theory of poetry' can be said to be built on this association of meaning and authority with priority, and on his parallel assertion that 'strong' poetry is always and inevitably produced by a refusal, in belated poets, to accept such a fact. This set of assumptions brings Bloom directly into conflict with a number of critical theorists, most significantly at this point with his Yale colleague, Geoffrey Hartman (see AI, pp.9–10).

Hartman's objections to Bloom's theory were not published until his review of *Anxiety*, 'War in heaven'. This is an attempt to outline and judge the 'many assumptions' within Bloom's 'brief epic',[13] and the critique such an analysis generates can help us greatly at this point.

Hartman's first and major critique is directed towards the slippage observable within Bloom's theory between natural and aesthetic (or 'spiritual') dimensions: Bloom's overly 'condensed' analogue between two modes of psychology, *natural* and *poetic*. This critique is encapsulated in the following paraphrase of Bloom's utilisation of the the 'family romance':

The blood-parent (Nature) is eventually denied in favour of an imaginative adoption. The ephebe-quester does the same. He myth-takes his parents or 'creates his own precursors', as Borges would say. For, in the realm of art, where no natural fathers are, greatness begins by choosing a worthy obstacle. If there were no precursor he would have to be invented. The imagination needs a blocking-agent to raise itself, or not to fall into solipsism. We become great, Kierkegaard said, in proportion to striven-with greatness.[14]

While this may sound like a simple description or paraphrase of Bloom's theory of poetry, Hartman's witty ventriloquism actually effects an important revision of Bloom's overcondensed account of the influence process. Hartman stresses the need for a blocking-agent, its necessary creation *by* the 'strong' poet. Bloom's emphasis is not so much on the need as on the inevitability of such a process. Hartman's account separates natural and aesthetic dimensions, while admitting that there appears to be a poetic need, if only temporarily, to fictionalise or fantasise their commensurability. Hartman's critique is founded, in other words, on Bloom's refusal of the 'second chance' in art. For Bloom there is only ever a 'history . . . of "one story and one story only" '.[15]

Hartman accuses Bloom of reducing poetry by restricting both poetic meaning and the motivations for the production of poetry to a single drive or process. Bloom's collapsing of the categories of the natural and the aesthetic tends towards an essentialistic account of poetic production and meaning. By essentialism I mean precisely that process in which cultural and social phenomena, which necessarily must be (*as* cultural and social phenomena) subject to the vagaries of history, which must inevitably change and mutate as they are subjected to the pressures of changing sociohistorical contexts, are presented as unchanging entities, or as entities which are dependent on unchanging, *natural* motives and/or laws. I am taking Hartman's critique of Bloom here into an area which he does not himself enter. Throughout this study I will argue that such a direction is a necessary next step after having gained the kind of insight Hartman presents in his review. The issue clearly revolves around the manner in which we interpret the terms *poetry, literature, tradition* and *culture*, and how the manner in which we come to interpret them affects our sense of the proper, critical response to those categories. Approaches which depend on a recognition of the historical forces impinging on these terms will resist the attempt to discover within them any single, universal and unchanging dimension. The attempt to avoid critical reduction will, in an approach of this kind, manifest itself through an effort to resist critical totalisation. Emphasising the constructedness of the very concepts in question, the kind of historicising approach to reading I am referring to here must locate the problematics of reading in the difficulty, even the impossibility, of fixing a stable relationship between those *entities* and their critical reception and interpretation. Such a problematics clearly involves us in the question of intrinsic and extrinsic representations of the reading process. If not merely the meaning of literary texts but the very concept of literature is determined by sociohistorical pressures and contexts, then we can neither locate literary meaning *inside* literary texts or literary tradition nor can we describe our relation to those texts as intrinsic, as an *inside* relationship.

I have already begun to outline the radical engagement with these figurations in Bloom's work and I will be returning to it throughout this study. What I am attempting to establish at this point is the reliance within Bloom's approach, despite its theoretical problematisation of the terms, on the inside/outside opposition: a reliance which manifests an a- or anti-historical definition of poetry's *essence*.

Bloom, throughout *Anxiety*, characterises his theory of poetry as a fundamentally deidealising one. This principle of deidealisation depends on Bloom's continued effort to read poetry in its own terms, without imposing extrapoetic criteria and contexts on it. As we have already observed, this attempted 'poetic' reading of poetry represents Bloom's cardinal defence against the reductiveness he criticises in other, rival forms of interpretation.

Seen from the perspective of traditional approaches to literary influence and meaning, Bloom's form of deidealisation does indeed appear highly persuasive. Even Hartman's reassertion of artistic freedom from natural and literal determinism is threatened with the appearance of naivety until it accounts for the ways in which individual, social and ideological determinates affect the poet's choice of particular 'blocking agents'. However, as Bloom himself has subsequently recognised, it is not as easy to avoid critical reductiveness as the bold, polemical assertions within *Anxiety* make it appear. The alliance between deidealisation and an intrinsic theory and reading of poetry remains under the sign of a circular pattern between interpretative fidelity and theoretical presupposition.

Bloom defines his approach to critical interpretation as a defiantly 'experiential' one. This experiential approach is meant to protect Bloom's work from reductiveness and from idealisation through its very subjectivity, making every reading of a text a recognition scene between text and reader: a scene in which the power of the text over the reader and the reader's desire for power over the text is rigorously played out. Such an approach, which makes reading 'a relational event, a concept of happening and not a concept of being' (BV, p.32), forms the basis for Bloom's description of his critical method as a 'poetic' brand of criticism, a reading with the poets. Such an apparently 'poetic' form of reading, however, immediately reinstitutes the threat of reductionism and idealism even as it appears to protect the antithetical practical critic from philosophical and ideological reductions and obfuscations of the 'poetic'. In *Poetry and Repression*, considering the nature of his own Kabbalistic paradigm (the map of misprision), Bloom states: 'The proper use of any critical paradigm ought to lessen the dangers of reduction, yet clearly most paradigms are, in themselves, dangerously reductive' (PR, p.14). By the time of *Agon* and *The Breaking of the Vessels*, Bloom's description of the relationship between criticism and poetry has become dominated by the former's desire to usurp the place and strength of the latter.

Although it may seem as if Bloom's insistence that 'All criticism that matters is experiential criticism' (BV, p.29) has led him to relinquish his desire to avoid reduction and has problematised the fideistic rhetoric of *reading with the poets*, Bloom's sense of the 'poetic' nature of his own approach has been quite tenacious. Recognising the difficulty of retaining a positive mode of critical interpretation *and* the rhetoric of deidealisation, Bloom has endeavoured to sidestep this situation by demonstrating how the very processes which make his own readings reductive, defensive and imaginary are precisely the same processes which mark every 'strong' example of poetry as a form of reductive, defensive and imaginary misinterpretation. Bloom represents his own falling away from critical accuracy and intrinsicality as the proof of his theory of influence in poetry and criticism. Bloom's swerve from deidealisation into the imaginary and the defensive is to be understood, in Bloomian terms, as the greatest demonstration of the success of his own mode of deidealisation and fidelity to the dialectics of poetic creation. To write 'poetically', for Bloom, is ultimately to perform a defensive act or to take part in an agonistic, relational event. This point explains why Bloom can describe his own criticism as 'poetic' even while cramming it with various discursive and terminological registers traditionally conceived as *extra*poetic. It also explains why his examples of 'strong' poetry can contain such figures as Freud and Nietzsche, and the prose writings of Pater and Emerson.

This complex and frequently persuasive account of the 'poetic' nature of 'antithetical criticism' does not, however, resolve the basic problem of how Bloom initially comes by his sense of the 'poetic' itself. As he is well aware, no amount of exemplification of the agonistic strain in his own (mis)interpretations of poetic texts, and no amount of interpretative representations of the apparent agonistic basis of poetic meaning, can escape the fact that poetry, as a concept, is never in itself a *given*, never precedes a theoretical definition and delimitation of an area of discourse designated as such. Even if we accept Bloom's account of poetry as a relational event which remains resistant to all philosophical and mimetic criteria of judgement and definition, it is still clear that such a view of the poetic remains just as compromised by the shuttle between presupposition and interpretative practice as any other mode of reading.

Many commentators on Bloom's work have addressed the issue of reduction by citing works which Bloom either ignores or which appear to offer the possibility of radically alternative readings to the ones performed by Bloom. Bloom has noted that the three major theoretical models which most positively rival his own are the Freudian, the deconstructive and those ideologically oriented approaches which are commonly grouped under the aegis of Marxist literary criticism (BV, p.40). Given this study's concern to establish a more historical understanding of the processes of poetic influence, the last of these three approaches is most significant at this stage.

I have already referred to various critiques of Bloom which focus on his repetition of a Romantic ideology concerning art's essential autonomy from the sociohistorical realm. From this point of view, Bloom's constant assertions that poetry is a nonideological mode of discourse repeat in a supposedly deidealised but in reality a tragic, belated and/or ironic fashion what McGann has characterised as the Romantic ideology.

Much of the language Bloom employs to describe the processes involved in poetry and criticism seems remarkably similar to the combination of psychoanalytical and Marxist terminology utilised by some of the most influential of recent theorists who have examined the ideological characteristics of literature. Fredric Jameson describes history as an 'absent cause' perceivable in the text only in terms of the discontinuities and contradictions within its aesthetic or formal element. The aesthetic form of a text is thus described in terms of an attempt to invent 'imaginary or "formal" solutions to unresolvable contradictions', a point emphasised also by Pierre Macherey.[16] In this manner, a text's 'unconscious' can be said to be the repressed social context which must be defended against if the text is to attain for itself the impression of aesthetic totality and/or autonomy. Bloom's postulation of the absent yet determining precursor, and this alternative kind of recovery of the absent yet determining social situatedness of the text, both rely on the language of the unconscious, of repression, defence and forms of antithetical (mis)interpretation. Both modes rely on a language if not originated, then at least brought to a modern culmination in the work of Freud. They also rely on distinct versions of that fundamental poststructuralist concept, intertextuality.

One of the elements which produces the essentialist trend in Bloom's theory of poetry depends on and is produced by his translation of the concept of intertextuality into what he styles intratextuality. Bloom explains that 'since "inside" and "outside" are wholly figurative notions in relation to poems', his preference is for the term intratextuality rather than intertextuality. He asserts: 'What matters is the sense or senses in which poems are internal to one another, say as the *Ode on a Grecian Urn* of Keats internalizes itself as "porcelain" in Stevens's poems . . .' (*Agon*, p.46).

We see here how Bloom's intratextuality problematises the figures of *inside* and *outside* in terms of the interpretation of poetic texts, only, eventually, to reinstate the sense of an inside – the internalised poetic history we call tradition – in opposition to an outside – the sense of history, or *extra*-poetic contexts, which for Bloom are an irrelevance. The absent cause in poetic texts is always and only an intratextual affair. Such an approach evades historical considerations of textual meaning in favour of an 'historicism which reduces to the inter-play of personalities' (MM, p.71). Yet such an approach is not so much the cause as the product of Bloom's fundamental presuppositions concerning the nature of poetry, presuppositions which are fundamentally Romantic and ideological in their implications. It is precisely in this issue of the relationship between intertextuality and intratextuality that an historicising revision of Bloom's approach must be located.

Intertextuality is a notoriously difficult concept to define and just as notoriously easy to (mis)use. Jay Clayton and Eric Rothstein, for example, focus on three distinct applications of the term in literary theory and practice. They point to the manner in which deconstruction has employed the term in order to highlight the uncertainty of any reading of a text. This stands in contrast to the manner in which a theorist such as Riffaterre has employed the term, taking it as the means by which interpretative certainty can be achieved. Finally, they point to the Foucauldian emphasis on the social and political applications of the concept.[17] Susan Stanford Freidman has produced a useful account not only of the development of the concept of intertextuality but of the manner in which it has been defined against the older concept of influence. Freidman adds that even in the work of Kristeva and Barthes, who first coined it, there is a certain contamination of the newer by the older term.[18] This fact could be said to generate even greater difficulties for a study such as this one, which needs to posit a distinction between intertextuality and influence without collapsing one of the terms into a valorised representation of the other. Much of this study will be involved in thinking through the relationship between influence and intertextuality. This still does not answer the question of what I mean by that latter term, however.

Because intertextuality is a concept always in the process of becoming, it has seemed best to let my own conceptualisation of it emerge largely through critical use rather than through programmatic statements. Freidman writes of the critic's need to retain a 'flexible concept of intertextuality that examines the clashing and blending of texts from the biographical, literary, and cultural records'.[19] However, it should be noted that my use of the term represents a belief in its importance for historical understanding, my sense of it as a phenomenon which positions the authoring subject in history. This is an important point because intertextuality in certain of its forms has been a major contribution to a de-authoring of texts. Intertextuality does not need to be a means of folding the subject into language; it can be a means of reaffirming the subject's position in history.

It is important to establish that intertextuality does not merely have to do with the relations between specific texts or textual units but is, more importantly, a way of discussing the inclusion of a text within the large signifying systems, codes and practices which make up particular sociocultural fields. A recent commentator writes that 'Bloom's genetic chain, in which the tensions of intertextual production are resolved by strong personal "misreadings" of particular precursors and origins inevitably reduces the "dialogic struggle" to the armwrestling of strong poets.'[20] Such a statement points to the difference between Bloom's account of intratextuality as a diachronic or what we might call a vertical doubling of specific precursor texts within a particular object-text with the understanding of intertextuality developed by Julia Kristeva. Following the work of Bakhtin, Kristeva argues that the 'literary word' is 'an *intersection of textual surfaces* rather than a point (a fixed meaning), as a dialogue among several writings: that of the writer, the addressee (or the character) and the contemporary or earlier cultural context'.[21] Reducing this complex view of intertextuality for our present purposes, we can say that it stresses a synchronic or *horizontal* understanding of the term, to the extent that it emphasises the text's positioning of itself within the larger 'signifying practices' which make up the socio-cultural realm. The fact that there are always at least two synchronic fields in the reading event – that of the author and that of the reader – does not, I think, invalidate but adds to the benefit of this pragmatic opposition here. The practices or formations on the synchronic plane will include the current assimilation within them of past texts, and this fact becomes important in our assessment of the relationship between intratextuality and intertextuality. However, given that I wish ultimately to question the separation of its two constituent parts, the fundamental opposition I wish to employ here is that between a vertical (diachronic) and a horizontal (synchronic) account of intertextuality.

If we take the position that there are at least two directions or dimensions of intertextuality, then we might be led to argue that there is a repression of the horizontal form within Bloom's theory of poetry; a repression which amounts to an evasion of the sociohistorical determinates of poetic meaning. Bloom argues that the proper poetic and critical understanding of the anxiety of influence can protect the poet or critic from what I am styling the synchronic dimension of intertextuality. In his essay 'First and last Romantics', Bloom refers to a speech made by E. R. Dodds at Berkeley University in 1949 in which he 'prophesied the troubles to come some fifteen years later when he quoted T. H. Huxley as epigraph to his lecture: "A man's worst difficulties begin when he is able to do as he likes" '. Bloom continues: 'Romantic poetry, in its long history, has been saved from those worst difficulties by its sense of its own tradition, by the liberating burden of poetic influence' (RT, pp.9–10).

Bloom, in this essay, characterises the anxiety of influence as a saving, determining form of influence-anxiety and compares it to an alternative, devastating freedom of choice offered to the modern author. For Bloom, the modern world offers such a complete freedom and range of choice, is so overdetermined an environment, that there is simultaneously too much and too little influence to choose from. Bloom's position relies on an alternative anxiety of choice to his own theory of the anxiety of influence; an alternative between two modes of influence. In contrast to the potentially positive features of an anxiety of influence, Bloom contrasts a contemporary brand, marked by the wholly negative characteristics of excess, accumulation and an anti-apocalyptic dispersal of meaning.

This alternative form of influence-anxiety emerges sporadically throughout Bloom's work.[22] At the beginning of his chapter on 'Emerson and influence' in *A Map of Misreading*, Bloom juxtaposes the authentic anxiety of influence still observable in American poetry, and which constitutes the foundation for any 'authentic' poetry American culture still has to offer, to 'the immediate sorrows of poetic over-production and the erosion of a literate audience' (MM, p.161). He goes on to cite Pope's *The Dunciad* by way of describing modern culture as an 'Age of Sirius' in which, as Pope puts it, 'The dog-star rages! nay 'tis past a doubt,/All Bedlam, or Parnassus, is let out', going on to discover a bathetic, *Dunciad*-like parody of the anxiety of influence in a reference to 'an educational hour [spent] watching an array of revolutionary bards, black and white, chanting on television' (MM, p.161).

In a recent interview Bloom asks:

> What are we to do? Why, after all, do we have one friend rather than another? You must choose. It isn't chosen for you. Why do we read one book rather than another? Why, for that matter, do we read one critic rather than another? Time is very limited. You can read all your life, for twenty-four hours a day, and you can read only a portion of what is worth reading. You can know only so many people. You can look at only so many sunsets. A fresh poem written now, a fresh critical essay written now, a fresh story or novel, competes against a vast overpopulation. That, I think, is what criticism must address itself to. But that is not the class-struggle: it is a question of how we individuate.[23]

This sense of contemporary culture exhibiting an 'over-population' of forms and meanings, indeed simply of texts, is not of course synonymous with the concept of intertextuality. It is, however, I would suggest, Bloom's way of representing the intertextual dimension of meaning. Such a representation provides a basis for Bloom's rejection of an historical understanding of poetry. Establishing an opposition between the 'liberating burden' of the anxiety of influence and a bathetic contemporaneous world of excess and 'overpopulation', Bloom locates meaning within and only within the former. An intra-textual understanding of poetic production and meaning is privileged at the expense of an understanding of the position of poetic texts within a contemporary realm of socio-culturally specific meanings. Poetic history is valorised at the expense of an historical understanding of poetry.

As Bloom has been at great pains to point out, this whole issue exhibits the fundamental relationship between critical interpretation and canon-formation. Arguments concerning the canon have swept through the British and the American academies in recent years. It does not take a particularly perceptive onlooker to recognise that this situation has come about largely because arguments about the canon reflect and frequently rehearse fundamental issues concerning the nature of modern society, of national, class and gender identities, and of the inclusion or exclusion of particular groups in a society's dominant modes of representation. As Frank Kermode rightly observes in his 'Institutional control of interpretation', the issue of canon-formation has, since its origins in the establishment of the Old and New Testaments, revolved around an axis of inclusion and exclusion.[24] As previously excluded groups within society gain entrance to university education and to the debate over the nature of culture and tradition, the pressures on the kind of liberal belief expressed by Kermode in the ultimately inclusive ('pluralistic') tendencies of the canon-forming process intensify.[25] The very idea of the canon, in fact, has recently come under question. Christine Froula in her 'When Eve reads Milton: Undoing the canonical economy', compares early Christian canonists to the Gnostics, staking out a very different economy between these two parties from the one represented in Bloom's later work. Froula uses the inclusion/exclusion polarity to argue that the Gnostics, like contemporary women writers and critics, did not seek to repossess the canon or to enter its portals, but rather to highlight and then to disrupt the very logic (economy) of the rhetoric of inclusion/exclusion, order/excess, centre/periphery, culture/anarchy predicated by the very concept of canonicity.[26]

Arguments concerning canon-formation appear to depend on a rhetorical opposition between order and excess, authority and anarchy, the centre and the margins. Reading through the proliferating interventions into this debate we begin to recognise the positions available to authors: radical valorisations of plurality over order stand in contrast to conservative attempts to protect standards of authority, while a good many critics attempt to negotiate their way through the opposition, recognising the practical and discursive limitations set by the basic polarity. In Bloom's comparisons between the 'liberating burden' of the anxiety of influence and contemporary cultural excess, we see one side of the current rhetoric of canon-formation. We also begin to see, I would argue, the ideological implications and motivations behind Bloom's construction of a theory of poetry on a rigorously intratextual, intrapsychical process of agonistic revisionism.

Such an account of rhetorical structures represents the kind of approach I would advocate as a revision of Bloom's work. As a method it argues that the *meaning* of Bloom's texts (and of the 'poetic' texts he interprets) cannot be contained within an intratextual process of (mis)reading, but is also determined by their inclusion within a contemporary discursive structure which exists in a dimension beyond any particular textual articulation. Such a discursive structure is specifically social and historical in its contribution to the very manner in which we currently can know and mean. Before this revision can be developed any further, however, we need to move on to the complex issue of critical (mis)interpretation foregrounded in *The Anxiety of Influence* and made the central subject of inquiry in the works which succeeded it, beginning with Bloom's next text, *A Map of Misreading*.

CHAPTER THREE | *Maps of misreading*

## Ant-agon-ism and the question of misreading

There are two principal features of Bloom's conception of critical interpretation, the first of which concerns its place within literary history. Bloom writes that the 'remedy for literary history' lies in a conversion of its concepts 'from the category of being into the category of happening'. He adds: 'To see the history of poetry as an endless, defensive civil war, indeed a family war, is to see that every idea of history relevant to the history of poetry must be a concept of happening' (KC, p.63).

Bloom's assertion that the critic exists *within* the tradition of which s/he writes has been a much praised aspect of his critical approach. It is this aspect of Bloom's work which leads Frank Lentricchia to assert: 'Anyone who desires to write on the theory of literary history must henceforth wrestle Bloom' (Foreword to BV, p.xii).

The other feature of Bloom's approach to misreading emerges when we attend to the outline he provides in his 'The map of misprision' of the formal characteristics of 'what has been the central tradition of the greater modern lyric' (MM, p.96). Bloom's view of this 'greater modern lyric' is indebted to the work of his former teacher M. H. Abrams.[1] Indeed, Bloom's map combines Abrams's description of the typical Romantic crisis-lyric with the revision of Northrop Frye's analysis of the quest-romance mode I have already discussed. Romantic and post-Romantic poems, in Bloom's approach, become internalised quest-romances founded on various systematisable moments of 'break-through'. This tradition, which stretches from Spenser to the poetry of John Ashbery, is predicated by Bloom on the discovery of a recurrent triadic pattern within such poems (MM, p.96).

With these two aspects of Bloom's approach to the reading of poetry, we are presented with two distinctive and apparently contradictory conceptualisations of the critical text and its interpretative function: criticism as event or act and criticism as description, representation and systematic (inductive) totalisation. With this apparent conceptual divergence, a question, naturally enough, arises: is Bloom attempting to have his cake and eat it too? How can a critic who styles all criticism as 'prose poetry' and all poetry as misinterpretation of prior poetry write of the 'pattern' that *truly* exists in all Romantic lyrics?

The example of Harold Bloom has become so debated and discussed in the contemporary English-speaking critical arena because he brings the issues of critical representation, totalisation and misreading to an intense, polemical, frequently paradoxical and often sublimely pitched focus. This is illustrated by the number of articles and reviews dedicated to the work of Bloom that have focused on the issue of critical map-making and its relation to the central trope of misreading. A comment by Robert Scholes is typical: 'If there is no "understanding" then there can be no "misunderstanding" either. We cannot have "deliberate misinterpretation" without the possibility of correct interpretation, from which this "deliberate misinterpretation" departs in some intelligible way.'[2] Commentators such as Scholes would highlight comments like this one from 'The necessity of misreading' to exhibit Bloom's ultimate reliance on the epistemological concept of reading: 'The strongest of poets are so severely mis-read that the generally accepted, broad interpretations of their work actually tend to be the exact opposites of what the poems truly are' (KC, p.103).

Here Bloom's insistence on the necessity of misreading 'strong' poems appears to conflict with his suggestion that he in fact does possess the capacity to *know*, somehow, through his reliance on the process of misreading, 'what the poems *truly are*'. Gerald Graff sums up this response to this particular passage: 'Here Bloom seems to be disagreeing with himself by implying that we *can* know what a poem "truly" is. For that matter, the very concept of a *mis*reading seems to presuppose that there is such a thing as true reading and that we know how to recognize it.'[3]

The objections of Scholes and Graff are typical in that they are presented as logical objections. Both critics highlight the manner in which epistemology returns in Bloom's apparently anti-epistemological practice of misreading. Yet such objections do not really engage with the true significance of the concept of misreading.

Joseph N. Riddel points to the strange relation Bloom's schematics appear to possess with regard to such concepts as systematic lucidity and methodological stability. He writes: 'Bloom's first system of terms . . . reduplicates and predicates the system which, as Hillis Miller has said, becomes a labyrinth, every repetition of the system amplifying and complicating it rather than giving us a definitive reading and thus a "way out".'[4] This is a useful representation of a map-making practice, which culminates, not in a settled, teachable pattern, but in the creation of a defensive system, a map grounded in repression and critical 'warfare'. A poetics of conflict is thus predicated on vital conflicts with rival and alternative critical theories and methodologies, in the spirit of what Riddel calls 'ant-agon-ism'.[5] Such an account of the motivations behind Bloom's schematic 'ant-agon-isms' requires an analysis of his response to Paul de Man's critique of *The Anxiety of Influence*.

## Forms of totality

I

Paul de Man, in his review of *The Anxiety of Influence*,[6] presents Bloom's study as a radically unstable or volatile kind of text in which such staple terms as literature, poetry and criticism undergo what we might call a crisis of identity. This representation of *Anxiety* allows de Man to submit the theory presented in that book to a radical requestioning and revision. De Man begins his review with such a revision in mind: 'Like most good books, Harold Bloom's latest essay is by no means what it pretends to be'.[7] Having made this observation, de Man can then suggest what *Anxiety* 'really' is.[8] In other words, de Man endeavours to supplement *Anxiety* with principles and insights it is thought already, in a negative way, to possess: these principles or negative insights can be grouped under three interrelated subheadings.

To begin with, we would do well to refer to de Man's treatment of the revisionary ratios. The principle which de Man highlights within this central area of Bloom's theory of poetry is that of rhetorical substitution, the notion of poetic meaning as the product of the poet's revision of pre-existent figurations and modes of linguistic signification. However, de Man asserts that 'from the moment we begin to deal with substitutive systems, we are governed by linguistic rather than by natural or psychological models: one can always substitute one word for another, but one cannot, by a mere act of will, substitute night for day or bliss for gloom'.[9]

This point leads de Man into a major re-evaluation, stating that it is possible 'to transpose Bloom's six ratios back to the paradigmatic rhetorical structures in which they are rooted'.[10] De Man associates ratios such as *tessera* with synecdoche and *apophrades* with metalepsis, in a manner which clearly forms one of the vital motivations behind Bloom's creation of his map of misreading. The important point for us here is the implicit critique such a translation contains, particularly with regard to the psychopoetic theory of poetic influence Bloom's six revisionary ratios are meant to substantiate. This leads to the second major element in de Man's review.

In an earlier review of *The Visionary Company*, de Man had analysed Bloom's construction of an anti-natural or 'antithetical' theory of Romanticism on a highly personal or idiosyncratic reading of the poetry of William Blake.[11] In his review of *Anxiety* de Man takes up Bloom's description of Romanticism once again, showing how his antithetical portrayal of the poetic imagination relies on an apparently outmoded language of psychological naturalism and historical geneticism: the language of temporality, originality, priority, poetic desire and the poetic 'subject'.

What Bloom refuses to do, as far as de Man is concerned, is accept that his antithetical claims concerning Romantic poetry deconstruct not only the myth of the Romantic imagination but also the Romantic 'subject' itself. Bloom has gone half way, according to this reading, and then stopped short, because to proceed any further would lead him into a privileging of language over 'psychological naturalism'. The full import of de Man's projection of 'paradigmatic rhetorical structures' *within* Bloom's revisionary ratios begins to be recognisable at this point.

De Man wishes us to understand that, by relapsing into a 'subject'-centred language of psychological desire and anxiety, Bloom evades the true nature of belatedness, which is not, after all, a temporal, historical and psychological phenomenon, but an aspect of the epistemological uncertainty which persists in every reading of a literary text. This insistence on the primacy of linguistic substitution over 'psychological naturalism' reinstates the question of epistemology, of the truth or falsity of the literary text, as the cardinal issue in critical interpretation.[12]

*A Map of Misreading* is dedicated to Paul de Man. It is not unreasonable to view it as an answer to de Man's critique of *Anxiety*; an answer, moreover, to the post-structuralist tendencies of thought that critique encapsulates. The review is crucial to our understanding of Bloom's subsequent development, because, in positing language as prior to Bloom's poet-as-poet, de Man appears to have elicited an extension of the Bloomian theory of poetry; an extension which contains a degree of complicity and reversal. *A Map of Misreading* certainly reads like an apology for Bloom's brand of criticism: an *apologia* or defence of Bloom's version of the Romantic 'subject', of the Romantic tradition of imaginative pathos and desire, of critical map-making and the drive towards interpretative totality, and of the critical reconstruction, rather than deconstruction, of meaning. Attending to de Man's review focuses our sights on the manner in which Bloom's critical map-making and his theory of the relationship between criticism and poetry is inextricably related to his complex defence of the Romantic strain in poetry and in thought generally.

The chapter in which Bloom engages with de Man's brand of criticism most directly is entitled 'The belatedness of strong poetry'. Bloom's answer to de Man here is to incorporate into his map de Man's insistence on rhetorical, linguistic structures, but then largely to reverse the implications of such an inclusion. Instead of de Man's assertion of the priority of language over the naturalistic criterion of the poetic 'subject', Bloom establishes the interdependence of trope and defence, an interdependence which reasserts the validity of the language of poetic psychology over the deconstructive criterion of language. Bloom rejects the de Manian argument in which 'the linguistic model usurps the psychological one because language is a substitute system responsive to the will, but the psyche is not' (MM, p.76). In opposition to this position, Bloom asserts that the criticism of 'strong' poetry discovers that 'a trope is just as much a concealed mechanism of defense, as a defense is a concealed trope' (MM, p.77). Such an assertion transforms de Man's focus on the 'epistemological moment' in literary texts into what we might term a *category mistake*. 'The burden for readers', Bloom argues, 'remains that poetry, despite all its protests, continues to be a discursive mode, whose structures evade the language that would confine them' (MM, p.77). Poetry, according to Bloom, 'is a discursive and not a linguistic mode' (MM, p.68).

Bloom's move is to contain the destructive features of language by merging trope and defence. He states that if we were to follow de Man in his privileging of the linguistic over the psychological model, 'Influence would . . . be reduced to semantic tension, to an interplay between literal and figurative meanings' (MM, p.77). We might say that while de Man's form of deconstruction is still concerned with exhibiting the negative, self-defeating aspects of meaning as a mimetic term, Bloom's view of meaning in poetry rejects the very category of mimesis in favour of what he calls 'super-mimesis'. Super-mimesis is to be understood here not in terms of the relations between a text and some criterion of 'literal meaning', but, rather, in terms of the meaning which is produced by a text's defensive revisionism of a previous text or texts. Meaning happens *in-between* poetic texts.

To put this in a form more pertinent to this study's preoccupation with the question of literary history, de Man and Bloom differ over the nature of the hermeneutic circle. De Man reduces Bloom's theory of the poetic anxiety of influence and the critical and poetic necessity of misreading to a deconstructive version of the hermeneutic circle between text and reader. Bloom, on the other hand, seeks to defend his theory of poetry by reincorporating the precursor into such a circuit of reading. Bloom, in fact, moves from a dyadic to a triadic version of the hermeneutic circle, and so allows for a reinscription of the language of poetic psychology and also for a form of literary history.

II

Poetry is a discursive rather than a linguistic mode, for Bloom, because its tropological swerves are pitted not solely against literal meaning but defensively against past instances of poetic language. Such a radical reassessment of poetic meaning produces an equally radical reassessment of the nature of critical interpretation. Since our current interests lie in Bloom's theory of critical misreading, this issue requires careful examination. We can get a little nearer to an understanding of Bloom's reassessment of poetic meaning by returning to the difference between his own brand of interpretation and that of de Man and his deconstructive colleagues. Bloom writes:

Reading, despite all humanist traditions of education, is very nearly impossible, for every reader's relation to every poem is governed by a figuration of belatedness. Tropes or defenses (for here rhetoric and psychology are a virtual identity) are the 'natural' language of the imagination in relation to all prior manifestations of imagination. A poet attempting to make this language new necessarily begins by an *arbitrary act of reading* that does not differ in kind from the act that *his* readers subsequently must perform upon him. In order to become a strong poet, the poet-reader begins with a trope or defense that *is* a misreading, or perhaps we might speak of the trope-as-misreading. A poet interpreting his precursor, and any strong subsequent interpreter reading either poet, must *falsify* by his reading. Though this falsification can be quite genuinely perverse or even ill-willed, it need not be, and usually is not. But it must be a falsification, because every strong reading insists that the meaning it finds is exclusive and accurate. (MM, p.69)

In this passage we can observe Bloom utilising de Man's reading of such authors as Nietzsche and Rousseau in order to mark a significant divergence from the theory of reading de Man abstracts from such interpretative engagements. For de Man, the critic must 'falsify' because of an aporia within the constitution of all texts. This aporia is the central subject of de Man's seminal study *Allegories of Reading* and is discussed in that text's opening essay in terms of the relation between rhetoric (as the figural, tropological aspect of language) and grammar (as the systematic, epistemologically oriented account of trope and figure).[13] The play of these two functions of discourse, which any theory of accurate reading would require to remain distinct from each other, is shown to animate all literary and critical writing. Such a situation produces a deconstruction of the inside/outside antinomy which traditionally structures critical interpretation. Criticism's drive towards total explication produces a reliance on the object-text, which disqualifies any assertion of anterior or objective understanding at the very moment that the text is most properly 'understood'. Such a scenario necessarily involves the critic in falsification and error whenever s/he attempts to represent the 'insights' s/he has discovered *within* the object-text. The drive towards totalisation is thus, for de Man, one side of language's characteristic bifurcation, the other side denying the very possibility for the success of such a drive.

What we are coming to focus on here are two very different versions of what it means to write intrinsic criticism and, as a consequence, two different accounts of critical totality. What critics such as de Man and Hillis Miller suggest is that, although the drive towards the closure of the reading activity seems a prerequisite of all interpretative practices, an adherence to the (deconstructive) logic of the text itself produces a total reading only as negativity. That is, the object-text comes to be seen as containing its own negative, its 'linguistic moment' as Miller puts it, in which the myths of unity, self-coherence and autonomy are destroyed or demystified in the undecidability of the text's own status as text.

The most important aspect of this deconstructive practice of reading, this negative hermeneutics, is that the critical text is inextricably tied and reliant on the reading or 'allegory of reading' which the object-text provides for and in itself. As Hillis Miller puts it: 'any cultural expression in our tradition, such as a literary text, is undecidable in meaning, though the choices the text offers (among which the reader cannot except arbitrarily decide) may be precisely defined.'[14] What such a reading practice provides is totality as the precise location and expression of a text's undecidability. What such a reliance and intrinsicality also dictate is the impossibility of critical systematisation or totalisation. There is, in other words, no possibility of a simple movement from hermeneutics to poetics, since they cannot be maintained as separate functions.

Bloom's insistence on critical reading as misreading appears to bring him into line with his deconstructive colleagues; yet, as I have suggested, his map of misreading equally appears to reinscribe the criterion of empirical verifiability, the objective, anterior perspective of the critic who founds his or her interpretative machine or model on an inductive, empirically based, survey of literary texts *as in themselves they really are*. The first thing to say about these appearances is that at best they are starting-points and at worst they are considerably wide of the mark. We must remind ourselves that de Man and Bloom are, in effect, interpreting very different things. De Man interprets the epistemological status of a text's statements. Bloom, however, does not interpret a text at all. As we have already observed, for Bloom there are no texts but only relations between texts. He explains his use of the word 'influence' as representing 'the whole range of relationships between one poem and another', going on to explain that such a conceptualisation makes of influence 'a highly conscious trope, indeed a complex sixfold trope that intends to subsume six major tropes: irony, synecdoche, metonymy, hyperbole, metaphor, and metalepsis, and in just that ordering' (MM, p.70).

The map is Bloom's personal hypostasisation of this trope of influence, which functions as Bloom's personal chart of the possible roads through which meaning can be said to 'wander' between texts. A personal chart, we should say, which makes use of a number of discursive structures including the tradition of Kabbalistic interpretation. Bloom describes his method as converting the 'Lurianic dialectics of creation' into a 'map of misprision, a charting of *how meaning is produced* in post-Enlightenment strong poetry by the substitutive interplay of figures and images, by the language strong poets use in defense against, and response to, the language of prior strong poets' (MM, p.87). The most significant aspect of the Lurianic triad comes once it has been converted into the analogical form of limitation, substitution and representation. Such a triadic system allows Bloom to relate three of his leading tropes (and their corresponding defence mechanisms, ratios and images) to the principle of limitation and the other three tropes to the principle of representation; thus adding two 'higher' tropes (hyperbole and metalepsis) to Kenneth Burke's 'four master tropes'.[15] In this way, Bloom can postulate a dialectical shuttle in poetic rhetoric and defence between the limitation of meaning and the representation of meaning; a dialectic grounded on the cardinal principle of rhetorical substitution. 'Strong' poems, on this model, are mini-apocalypses, which brew gradually to a persuasive but temporary minor victory over past time, past Words. The Romantic ideal of an apocalypse of personal vision is re-enacted by each 'strong' poem's re-rehearsal of the map of misprision.

One could of course object that such a trope (map) depends on the possibility of abstracting, from an empirically based survey of the poetic tradition, a mimetically accurate, universally valid model or paradigm. Bloom, however, heads off such objections when he writes of his use of 'influence' as 'an act of interpretation' and as 'a trope antithetical not only to all other tropes but to itself in particular', a conception based on the realisation that 'as de Man says, all criticism is a metaphor for the act of reading'. Bloom adds: 'If all tropes are defenses against other tropes, then the use of influence as a composite trope for interpretation may be that it will defend us against itself' (MM, p.74). Such a description of his use of the term influence constitutes a defence of the map of misreading as one critic's personal representation of the nature of both poetic and critical misreading. As Peter de Bolla writes:

> All interpretation in this scheme of things is necessarily a misreading, since we uncover the poet's stance to a previous text which itself is

determined by the poet's own misprision of his relationship to his precursor. We note that this description of interpretation is completely consistent within its own terms: the Bloomian map of misreading functions as an exhaustive account of its own description of the production and interpretation of poetic texts.[16]

The map is a defensive trope, yet as a map of the ways in which trope and defence can be said to interrelate in texts it can be be said to 'defend against itself'. Bloom, at the conclusion of his presentation of the map, writes: 'What matters is not the exact order of the ratios, but the principle of substitution, in which representations and limitations potentially answer one another. The strength of any poet is in his skill and inventiveness at substitution, and the map of misprision is no bed of Procrustes' (MM, p.105). This account of the map as a defensive trope would appear to answer criticisms of it as a reification and thus as a deterministic machine imposed on poetry.

If the interpretation of poetic texts is a defensive act – the 'interpretation of [a] poem's interpretation of other poems' (MM, p.75) – it is so because of the undecidability of the nature of poetic meaning, where *meaning* is conceived as the product of the relationships between a poem and past poetry. The map represents 'six tropes' which are 'six interpretations of influence' and 'six ways of reading/misreading intra-poetic relationships . . . which means six ways of reading a poem'. These six tropes combine into 'a single scheme of complete interpretation, at once rhetorical, psychological, imagistic, and historical, though this is an historicism that deliberately reduces to the interplay of personalities' (MM, p.71).

The map of misreading is one critic's multifaceted *interpretation* of influence as an element in poetic texts and poetic meaning. Indeed, in that recognition of deliberate reductionism, Bloom alerts us to the foundation of his brand of critical misreading. This foundation lies, not in the totalising tendency itself, though for some this will continue to be a problem, but in the positive reconstruction of intra-poetic relationships. Given that the uncertainties of meaning lie *in-between* texts rather than *in* a single text, the moment of reductionism, which is equally a moment in which the critic reverts to the language of empirical verifiability and mimetic validity, will occur for Bloom in the reconstruction of the presumed misinterpretation or revisionary misprision which is involved in any text's apparent meaning.

In 'The necessity of misreading' Bloom explains:

Every act of reading is an exercise in belatedness, yet every such act is also defensive, and as a defense it makes of interpretation a necessary misprision . . . A *strong* reading can be defined as one that itself produces other readings – as Paul de Man says, to be productive it must insist upon its own exclusiveness and completeness, and it must deny its partialness and its necessary falsification. 'Error about life is necessary for life'; error about a poem is necessary if there is to be yet another strong poem.   (KC, p.97)

When we remember that, for Bloom, a poem continually strives to negate or revise its dependence on prior poems, so that no explicit surface echo or allusion to a specific past poem need be discernible when reading the poetic text, then we recognise that the presentation of Bloom's reconstructions of the revisionary relations *between poems* is accurately described by Bloom himself as an 'exercise in belatedness'. It is this rejection of traditional, positivistic source-study, in fact, which explains the importance of Bloom's Kabbalistic paradigm in the establishment of the map of misprision. If 'strong' poetic texts do not exhibit the intratextual agonism on which they depend for their production of meaning, then the only way in which such intratextual modes of affiliation and revision can be recuperated is if the antithetical reader can find a 'pattern in the dance' of trope, defence and image. Bloom affirms that there is such a pattern (see PR, p.270) and that it finds its best manifestation in Kabbalah. The tradition of Kabbalah thus grounds Bloom's interpretative paradigm; a paradigm through which he can map the pattern or dance of tropes, defences and images in all post-Enlightenment poems and by so mapping them locate the *places* at which 'strong' poetic texts wrestle agonistically with their prime precursors (see KC, pp.86–92).[17]

Bloom's argument now begins to manifest a disturbing circularity, however. The pattern is based on the intratextual relations between 'strong' poems, but the only way he can discover and interpret and thus verify those relations is by depending on his antithetical deployment of the Kabbalistic 'pattern' (map). If we return to de Bolla's assessment we will see this circularity quite distinctly.

In 'The necessity of misreading' (KC, pp.93–126), Bloom asserts that poems are 'apotropaic litanies, systems of defensive tropes and troping defenses, and what they seek to ward off is essentially the abyss in their own assumptions about themselves, at once empirically reifying and dialectically ironizing' (KC, p.111). Bloom goes on to justify his own brand of criticism by alluding to its 'poetic' vacillation between empirical and dialectical assumptions. Such a self-assessment is an extremely appropriate representation of the paradoxical nature of Bloom's restitution of poetic meaning: restitutions of intratextual relations which are presented as exclusive and accurate and yet which are motivated by a theory in which the impossibility of total reconstruction, and indeed the perpetual deferral of origins and sources and thus meanings, is recognised.

This, then, is the fundamental interpretative context within which Bloom presents his theory of critical misreading; a context which incorporates the apparently paradoxical play or vacillation between dialectical and empirical modes of critical representation into a theory, which begins to turn criticism into as discursive (tropological and defensive) a mode of discourse as poetry itself. To criticise Bloom for relying on an outmoded empiricism is, then, not to recognise the manner in which such an aspect is contained within his theory and practice of misreading. As Bloom writes:

> *All interpretation depends upon the antithetical relation between meanings, and not on the supposed relation between a text and its meanings.* If no 'meaning' of a 'reading' intervenes between a text and yourself, then you start (even involuntarily) by making the text *read itself.* You are compelled to treat it as an interpretation of itself, but pragmatically this makes you expose the relation between its meaning and the meaning of other texts. As the language of a poet is his stance, his relation to the language of poetry, you therefore measure his stance in regard to his precursors' stance. (MM, p.76)

This is a persuasive representation of the belatedness of all poetic and critical texts and of the paradoxical vacillation inscribed in Bloom's theory of misreading or misprision. Yet in this very representation of the necessity of misreading, we begin to recognise the area of Bloom's critical approach which may justifiably be questioned. For the reference to the 'precursor's stance' in this passage is not sanctioned by anything Bloom has stated concerning the necessary reductions or acts of reconstructive framing practised by the antithetical critic. The reference depends on the theoretical connection Bloom would have us register between the modes of revision encapsulated by and through the map of misreading and Bloom's theory of the primal scene of instruction. If every reconstruction of an intratextual relationship between poems involves an arbitrary act of misinterpretation *qua* reduction and framing on the part of the belated reader/critic, then such references to a poet's precursors would surely have to be understood as originating from and remaining under the sign of such a critical form of belatedness.

Bloom attempts to resolve this difficulty, in his 'The necessity of misreading', by placing tradition itself, as a concept, within the map of misreading. Rhetorically conceived, 'tradition is always an hyperbole, and images used to describe tradition will tend to be those of height and depth' (KC, p.97). Such a conception makes tradition an 'uncanny' or 'daemonic' term: 'Tradition is itself then without a referential aspect, like the Romantic Imagination or like God. Tradition is a daemonic term' (KC, p.98).

If influence can be said to constitute the dialectic between a poem and the past poems which affect it and which it misreads, then tradition, as a substitute trope for influence, becomes the product or effect of the act of misreading. Tradition, or poetic history, in this sense, becomes the product of the misreading event carried out by the poet or by the critic. Indeed, in this essay, Bloom makes it clear that if misreading is to be conceived as the creation of meaning through acts of interpretation of past texts, the troping of past tropes, then 'reading' can also be said to be at one not only with literary history but with the practice of canon-formation, the process of revising tradition.

The critic, like the poet, cannot step outside the dialectic of tradition, and so there can be no 'definition' of tradition, and no literary history properly speaking: a history, that is, of literary production and meaning composed from a perspective outside the play of misreading. What there can be is a description of 'how tradition makes its choices, how it determines which poets shall live, and how and when the chosen poet is to become a classic'. More importantly still, Bloom argues: 'we can try to describe how the choosing and classicizing of a text itself results in the most powerful kinds of misreading' (KC, p.98).

Such a position leads us back to Bloom's characterisation of misreading in criticism as an act or event positioned within the poetic tradition. It leads us, in fact, towards his account of the reading process as an act of Thirdness – the effect of the misreading event between text, reader and the text's 'strong' antecedents. 'A single text has only part of a meaning', which means that 'it is itself a synecdoche for a larger whole including other texts. A text is a relational event, and not a substance to be analyzed.' Such recognitions lead Bloom to the following self-description:

> Though I acknowledge from the start that poems are dialectical events, I still take up a relatively empiricist stance in regard to poems, though with a peculiar epistemological twist in my empiricism. Emerson denied that there was any history; there was only biography, he

said. I adapt this to saying that there is no literary history, but that while there is biography, and only biography, a truly literary biography is largely a history of the defensive mis-readings of one poet by another poet. (KC, p.106)

The empirical stance of the critic emerges as the attempt to trace the play of meaning between texts; the 'epistemological twist' occurs when we realise that such an empiricism is the product of that critic's own misreading of the texts in question. 'There are weak misreading and strong misreading, just as there are weak poems and strong poems', Bloom announces, 'but there are no right readings, because reading a text is necessarily the reading of a whole system of texts, and meaning is always wandering around between texts' (KC, pp.107–8). The empirical stance of the 'strong' reader is located in his or her reconstruction of the intratextual relationships between texts, a projection of meaningful relationships or revisionary interpretations s/he erroneously (defensively) asserts is exclusive and accurate. Epistemologically speaking, however, such a determinate reconstruction, which is at once the interpretation of a poem, the construction of a history supposedly relevant to that poem (although perhaps more relevant to the assumptions and desires of the critic) and an act of evaluation akin to canon-formation, only serves to make the reader part of the history of malforming interpretations s/he is attempting to describe.

We are left with a vision of critical reading as an act or event within the tradition itself; an act or event which might lead us into insights concerning how the processes of misprision work but which always pulls us back from any definition of what tradition is itself. What Bloom calls 'our bewilderingly perverse revision of a hermeneutic circle' (KC, p.112) encloses precursor, poem and critical reading and, as Bloom states, negates the possibility for a definition of tradition, for a literary history, and for anything more than a strategic employment of the language of empirical representation. Such a theory of misreading forms the basis for Bloom's postformalist reduction of the dialectics of poetic tradition to the 'interplay' of 'strong' 'personalities'.

What such an approach does not resolve, however, is the tension between the act of (mis)reading itself and the various assumptions, presuppositions and theoretical paradigms which help structure and frame such readings. Bloom clearly would describe such elements as necessary reifications of the principles perceived in the process of misprision. He would justify them in terms of their reliance on the 'triadic relations' of the reading process. However, such elements are as much a source of the meanings produced in the misreading event as they are the products of such an event. Just as importantly, such elements have meanings which remain resistant to a simple recontainment in and through a return to the interpretative triad.

Bloom frequently steps out of the circle of misreading in order to establish his theoretical representations of the nature of tradition, influence and poetic meaning. Such a process drags the Bloomian approach back towards the kind of dyadic relation to tradition he himself has disallowed. Bloom's texts continually offer up definitions of the *essence* of tradition, rather than simply remaining with descriptions of how it works.

Bloom's defence of his approach to poetic meaning is, as we have seen, founded on his belief in criticism's position within a triadic process of misinterpretation. It is this constant referral to the 'bewilderingly perverse . . . hermeneutic circle' which allows him to justify the tension, within his work, between 'empirical reification' and 'dialectical ironization'. While paying full attention to the persuasive insights produced by this approach, we need to recognise that it allows Bloom to sidestep the issue of the relationship between his critical positions (theories, presuppositions) and the wider, intertextual dimensions of social and cultural practices and formations; as well as sidestepping the issue of the relationship between poetic texts and their own sociocultural contexts. By subsuming the whole issue of influence within the enclosed circuit of misprision, Bloom refuses to acknowledge the interpenetration between what we might call the intratextual (or poetic) and the intertextual (or historical) dimensions of discourse. If Bloom is correct in describing poetry and criticism as discursive events, he is correct not merely because such texts are revisions of specific past texts, but equally because they take their place within culturally significant formations.

Criticisms that highlight the apparent slips of logic within Bloom's account of misreading merely reflect, in a negative form, Bloom's own engagement with what he sees as a necessary tension between totalisation and agonistic defensiveness. To criticise and revise Bloom's theory of misreading effectively, we have to leave such objections behind in favour of an attention to the manner in which that theory is employed as a means of evading and of defending against the cultural and historical situatedness of every act of misprision.

## Critical persuasion

In the texts that immediately succeed *A Map of Misreading* and *Kabbalah and Criticism*, Bloom extends his account of the nature of poetic and critical reading in ways which bear directly on the issues we have traced so far. Indeed, through a renewed 'ant-agon' with de Man over the nature of rhetoric, Bloom can be said to transume if not resolve the tension between 'empirical reification' and 'dialectical ironization'.

In his essay 'Rhetoric of persuasion', de Man condenses much of his argument concerning rhetoric.[18] Focusing on Nietzsche's attempted deconstruction of logic and its reliance on the assumption of *a priori* truth, de Man indicates the manner in which, in Nietzsche's notebooks on rhetoric, the constative function of language is contaminated by the performative. The language of description and verifiability in Nietzsche's text is, de Man shows, not distinct from the language of rhetorical assertion and persuasion. Nietzsche attempts to deconstruct the very language of logic through a presentation of its reliance on prior assumptions, a situation which turns every assertion of *knowing* into an act of *willing*, and turns logic and truth into modes of metaphysical belief. Nietzsche can only construct and present such an argument, however, by having recourse to the very kind of logical language, the language of identity and non-contradiction, he is attempting to deconstruct.[19]

Such a scenario validates for de Man his insistence on the epistemological nature of reading, in that it proves that every negative (deconstructive) reading must necessarily reiterate the language it is deconstructing. We cannot 'go beyond' the language of epistemology into the realm of pure performativity. For our performative acts are always inevitably imperative in the act of reading and as such reinscribe the criteria of constative identity and proof.[20]

This vision of the contamination of constative and performative language should remind us of the processes we have observed in Bloom's map-making practice. Are we bound to accept the de Manian insistence on the negative hermeneutics of deconstructive practice? De Man understands the issues raised by such a situation within the reading process to be a symptom of the very essence and history of rhetoric itself. It is precisely on this issue of rhetoric that Bloom fixes his reaction to and defensive critique of the de Manian position.

An important representation of de Man's reading of rhetoric comes at the end of the essay I have been referring to. Here, de Man points to the aporia between rhetoric conceived as a system of tropes and as the art of persuasion.[21] De Man portrays rhetoric as a text which we are able to read, a situation brought about by the 'antithetical' history of the term. In the concept of rhetoric, as Peter de Bolla has illustrated, two mutually exclusive definitions reside. Rhetoric is defined both in terms of its 'substance' and in terms of its 'effect': it is defined as 'a system of tropes' and as 'the art of persuasion'.[22]

De Man takes up the bifurcated history of the concept and shows how the contradictory strains of substance and effect, of constative and performative functions, inhabit all manifestations of rhetoric in discursive texts. For de Man, the existence of these antithetical strands means that the aporia they produce, the 'figuration of doubt' created by any text's constitution as rhetorical text, transforms all effects of utterance, by which is meant the intentional dimensions of discourse, into aspects of the predetermining nature of language. The de Manian reader traces the contradictory play within a text of figural language as system and as performance back to the synchronic and semantic paradoxes of language. The aporia within rhetoric cuts off all texts from their historically projected contexts by illustrating the deconstructive negativity of their imperative statements, claims and assumptions. It is precisely this reduction to a synchronic conceptualisation of the aporia within rhetoric that Bloom finds so objectionable and sets out to challenge.

Bloom's first major confrontation with de Man's account of rhetoric occurs in his essay 'Emerson and Whitman: The American sublime' (PR, pp.235–66). In this essay Bloom asserts that 'what relates one trope to another in a systematic way, and carries each trope from evasion to persuasion, is that trope's function as defense, its imagistic maskings of those detours to death that make up the highway map of the psyche . . .' (PR, p.240). Bloom centres his confrontation with de Man on a re-evaluation of the very notion of meaning. This re-evaluation is dependent, in fact, on a distinction between 'significance' and 'meaning'. 'What holds together rhetoric as a system of tropes, and rhetoric as persuasion', Bloom writes, 'is the necessity of defense, defense whose aptest name is "meaning" ' (PR, p.240).

If we were to characterise the reading which de Man extracts from the 'text of rhetoric' it would surely be, as Ann Wordsworth puts it, a 'three-part movement (trope, persuasion, aporia)'.[23] De Man projects this three-part movement as the dialectic of constative and performative assumptions, leading not so much to a Hegelian synthesis as to an ironic Hegelian anti-synthesis (aporia), supplied by the reader and yet not so much imposed *on* as discovered *within* the text being read. Bloom takes up this reading of the text of rhetoric and, through a revisionary reading of the history of orthodox conceptions of rhetoric, produces a revised reading whereby the de Manian triad is translated into the apparently more traditional triad of ethos, pathos and logos. What this does is reject de Man's emphasis on the epistemological character of the poetic trope in favour of an emphasis on the trope as a combination of intention or wish and 'meaning', conceived as the product of rhetorical defence. Describing the deconstructive belief in the trope as a 'figure of knowing and not a figure of willing' and the deconstructive reader's attempt to find in any text 'a cognitive moment, a moment in which the Negative is realized, but only insofar as a postponing substitution becomes an approximation of the Hegelian Negative', Bloom writes:

> How can we speak of degrees of knowing in the blind world of the wish, where the truth is always elsewhere, always different, always to be encountered only by the acceptances and rejections of an energy that in itself is the antithesis of renunciation, a force that refuses all form?  (WS, p.387)

As David Fite reminds us, the Aristotelian definition of this triad, as it applies to classical oratory, associates ethos with the 'character' which the orator presents, pathos with the 'effect' of that presentation on the orator's audience, and logos with a form of discursive 'logic', 'encompassing all the means of representing the proof proper of an argument'.[24] Bloom, however, via a reading of the alternative or repressed understanding of rhetoric originating with the Sophists, going underground with the dominance of Platonistic rational enquiry, until it surfaces again with the rise of associationism, Romantic poetry and the combination of these innovations in Freudian psychoanalysis, transforms this triad into a play between action and desire, with logos representing the principle of rhetorical substitution in which the limitations of ethos (action) are replaced by the representations of pathos (desire).

I am skimming over Bloom's main argument here, although I intend to return to it in chapter 5. What is important here is the manner in which Bloom combines a revised reading of rhetoric with his already established utilisation of Kabbalistic and Gnostic terminology. What the association of the triad of ethos, logos and pathos with the Kabbalistic triad of limitation, substitution and representation allows Bloom to achieve is a tropism on the synchronic understanding of rhetorical tropes. This promotes a diachronic version of rhetoric which can manifest the interplay of linguistic with psychological principles.

For Bloom, deconstruction is caught in a version of traditional poetics, a synchronic attention to the trope as system. Deconstruction, for Bloom, fails to recognise the true nature of rhetorical tropes as persuasion. Once again, Bloom is acceding to deconstruction's undoubted ability to demystify the claims of any text, its ability to reduce or *limit* any text's assertion that it possesses coherent meaning, yet is also indicating its failure to recognise the full import of the restituting pathos of representation *as persuasion* (see WS, pp.386–7).

Bloom's meditations on the notion of rhetoric lead out from the synchronic abyss of deconstructive practice; they produce a privileging of persuasion over system which begins to turn every synchronic, systematic, critical hypostasisation (every articulation of a totalising map) into a strategic limitation, finally to be conceived as under the sign of a more primary motive of persuasion and performativity.

The manner in which Bloom achieves such a revision is to push the aporia between system and persuasion to its very limit, cutting the dialectical ties between one side and the other. By rejecting de Man's focus on trope as semantic error, a swerve away from literal to figural meaning, Bloom incorporates the systematic understanding of trope into a vision of the larger, rhetorical Will-to-Power and does this by deepening the gulf between system and persuasion. Bloom thus progresses to a redefinition of misprision as the manner in which 'the meanings of intentionality' either 'trope down to the mere significances of language, or conversely . . . [are] troped upward into the meaningful world of our Will-to-Power over time and its henchman, language' (WS, pp.394–5).

To trope down to 'the mere significances of language' is to follow deconstruction in its negative epistemology and, equally, to produce a systematic or map-like account of tropes: it is to produce a kind of poetics where every instance of poetic trope is related to its function in a system of organised tropes. Yet only to pursue such a reading of trope is to forget that we can also 'trope upwards into the meaningful world of our Will-to-Power'. To engage simply with trope on the level of epistemology or system is to remain blind to the persuasive motives behind the appearances of system. It is also to remain blind to the fact that one's own definition of trope, and thus one's own system, is itself a trope of the concept of trope, an instance of one's own will-to-persuasion, one's 'utterance within a tradition of uttering'.

Bloom, however, can not only move 'upwards' to the poetic will-to-power, he can equally justify his production of a synchronic map of misreading by assimilating it, through the movement from ethos to pathos which the troping 'upward' and 'downward' expresses, to the diachronic, eminently poetic, because rhetorically persuasive, will-to-power. The map is a synchronic limitation, the product of ethos, ruled ultimately by a diachronic tropism on the very concept of trope and thus the very concepts of poetry, tradition and rhetoric. The map may reduce poetry to *significance*, yet it works, through its function in a diachronic transumption of past systems, past meanings, to transform such significance into *meaning*.

What is even more important is the manner in which it can be said to resolve the disjunction between interpretation and theoretical presupposition. This redefinition of Bloom's theory of misprision in poetry and criticism depends on his redefinition of the trope. Bloom's new definition tears the trope away from the epistemological criterion of de Manian deconstruction and directs it towards the 'blind world of the wish' (see WS, p.393).

With this redefined conceptualisation of the trope as a figure of will, Bloom can go on to produce a persuasive defence of his own brand of misreading – a defence which begins to offer a final resolution of the tensions we have been studying in this chapter so far. Distinguishing his understanding of the 'trope' from Gerard Genette's, Bloom writes:

> a trope is a reader's awareness of a poet's willed error and results from a reader's *will to be lied to*, or to be repersuaded of persuasions already implicitly formulated that are crucial for the survival of the reader's internal discourse, the hum of thoughts evaded in the reader's own mind. I verge here upon the true outrageousness of Kabbalistic theory of rhetoric. (WS, p.394)

Here Bloom resolves the disjunction between the various levels of his discourse, by recognising that every critical interpretation of a specific text is informed by presuppositions and even 'definitions' which the critic possesses *before* the specific reading event begins. Such presuppositions inform any reader's interpretation of the poetic text and even predetermine the particular susceptibility the reader exhibits towards certain kinds of texts over others. Such presuppositions rule not only the *ethos* of reading but equally the *pathos* of reading. They determine not only how the critic will read, but what the critic will read. In this way, they inform the vision of tradition the critic will produce through his or her reading of poetic texts.

The pragmatic irony here, of course, is that Bloom's best defence of his own practice of antithetical practical criticism marks the most intense expression of the questionability of that discourse. Such a questioning can generate viable alternatives to the presuppositions brought to bear in Bloom's exercising of his own critical will-to-persuasion, and can help to produce alternative readings of the very nature of what I am here calling presupposition. For as we will see in our subsequent analysis of his work on poetic origins, poetic rhetoric and the relation between poetic originality and cultural history, despite this recognition of the determining influence of presupposition on the reading event, Bloom continually seeks to contain such an issue within an agonistic reduction to a 'history of personalities'. Once the recognition of the determining effect of presupposition upon the reading event has been made, however, it becomes questionable whether such a vision of the 'subject' outside historical and sociocultural contexts can be sustained. I have already established that it is this containment in and through a recourse to the 'pragmatics of (mis)reading' which must be questioned if we are properly to revise Bloom's critical approach. I want to proceed to such a revision by way of a specific counter-reading, a reading which can substantiate and extend, in a practical manner, the theoretical issues discussed in this chapter so far.

## Counter-reading: Bloom and the Comedian

In this analysis of his reading of 'The comedian as the letter c' (WS, pp. 68–87) I shall illustrate how Bloom's misreading, despite its undoubted strength, fails in its attempt to 'contain' that text interpretatively. In the introduction to his book on Stevens, Bloom asserts that 'Though Stevens read Emerson early and fully, and remembered much more than he realized, his Emersonianism was filtered mostly through Whitman, a pervasive and of course wholly unacknowledged influence upon all of Stevens' major poetry' (WS, p.10). Bloom's reading is of particular interest because it deals with a text which ultimately fails the Bloomian test of 'strength', the agonistic wrestling with the 'composite-precursor', Emerson–Whitman. Bloom's mapping of the poem is meant to establish just where Stevens goes wrong in this first major long poem in his canon, and as such it offers a particularly intense example of Bloomian misreading. There is a lot at stake in Bloom's mapping of the poem.

Written in 1921–2, the poem stands at the end of Stevens's first phase as a poet, immediately before the six-year silence between 1924 and 1930. Bloom, along with a number of other commentators, reads the poem as manifesting Stevens's particular crisis of form. The poem is represented as Stevens's attempt to complete, or overelaborate to the point of exhaustion, the European Romantic poetry of crisis and quest in favour of a new, thoroughly American style of poetry. Bloom echoes both Frank Kermode and Helen Vendler in foregrounding the apparently strained, overelaborate and finally indigestible style of the poem,[25] and, comparing two shorter poems – one from 1924 and one from 1930 –, writes of 'a transition from a mockery that knowingly mocks also the mocker to a painful searching out of the grounds for a reimagining' (WS, p.69). It is this self-mocking rhetorical style[26] which forms the starting-point of Bloom's diagnosis of the poem's limitations, and he writes, still comparing the two shorter poems rather than the 'Comedian' directly, that the difference between the 'Comedian' and Stevens's later style is the difference between a poetry which 'heightens rhetoricity for its own sake' and a poetry which 'seeks to heighten consciousness while maintaining a more controlled rhetoric that insists less upon its own status as rhetoric' (WS, p.69).

The logic of these remarks is far more flimsy than it might at first appear. It is hardly inevitable that the development of a form of allusiveness and rhetoricity which 'mocks itself' should be the equivalent to a heightening of rhetoricity 'for its own sake'. Bloom draws an identity between a certain self-mockery and a certain redundancy of rhetoricity because he cannot conceive of a form of poetry that attains 'strength' without warring agonistically against specific past poetry. Bloom confronts a kind of poetry in the 'Comedian' which sets a rather severe test for his particular brand of antithetical practical criticism. The 'Comedian' is not a text that will come out particularly well on the basis of his map.

The 'Comedian' began as a four-part poem entered for the Blindman Poetry prize in January 1922.[27] The first version, the four-part 'From the journal of Crispin', contains various important portions later edited from the six-part 'Comedian'.[28] Stevens, informing Harriet Monroe of his intention to enter the poetry competition, described the 'Journal' as 'a very rancid butter' (L, p.224). Bloom takes up this description as he outlines his interpretation of the poem's place within the tradition of the Romantic internalised quest-romance. Bloom describes the poem as 'in its form the least original and the least American major poem in *Harmonium*' and as 'the satyr-poem or parody that culminates and almost undoes the tradition of the High-Romantic quest-poem'. He goes on:

> I agree with Helen Vendler, as against most Stevens critics, that the *Comedian* is by no means primarily a comic poem. It is funny in places, it is bitter almost everywhere, frequently to the point of rancidity, and yet it shares fully in the obsessive quest that it only ostensibly mocks. That so outrageous a poem, the most outrageous in modern poetry, should be an authentic crisis-poem is surprising, but Stevens seems to have intended it as his farewell to poetry. (WS, p.70)

Whether or not Stevens meant the poem as his farewell to poetry, the 'Comedian' certainly reads like an intentional farewell to the kind of poetry Stevens had written so far. And yet, if the 'Comedian' is an epilogue of sorts, it seems rather strange to state that it 'shares fully in the obsessive quest that it only ostensibly mocks'. Bloom here is making the point that the poem *knows* more than its actual author; for certainly, Stevens's conception of the poem as 'anti-mythological' indicates his intention to 'mock' the quest voyage of his comedian. Bloom is rather uneasy when confronting a poem that mocks the quest for personal vision and voice.

Bloom writes: 'The *Comedian* is, conveniently, a poem in six parts, and it maps rather closely to the post-Wordsworthian crisis-poem model, which need surprise no one' (WS, p.72). That hint of self-mockery should alert Bloom's own readers to the arbitrary nature of his map-based interpretation. In Bloom's reading, the poem fails the test of the map while helping the map to succeed in its own test of validity: the map proves itself to be capable of containing the poem, while the poem both fulfils the dictates of the map's schematics and fails the test of 'strength' set by those dictates. Bloom's readers must, I would suggest, reverse that process, recognising that the excess of significance within the poem actually means that the map succeeds only by failing to represent (contain) the poem: the poem succeeds in mocking the map's pretensions to contain it.

These paradoxes are highlighted in Bloom's initial concentration on the figure of the sea. The sea that Crispin crosses in Part I of the poem is an excessive medium which produces, as Bloom's mapping stresses, a severe irony with regard to the intrepid quester Crispin.

As Bloom comments: 'The central irony (of Part I) is an epitome of the poem, which is that the Romantic Imagination cannot voyage unchanged to America, since any poet-quester is dwarfed by the Atlantic' (WS, p.72). This, I think, is a perfectly accurate reading of the irony of

Part I of the poem; and yet it depends on an insight Bloom cannot fully develop. The irony is precisely that the Romantic quester, seeking for a homeland, finds instead an excessive environment; a discovery which provides Crispin with the first in a series of lessons concerning the overdetermination of the supposedly 'new' world. The reaction of the quester to this first 'sundering' experience of a mocking excess is to become 'an introspective voyager'. Crispin internalises the quest and finds a 'newness' only, at this point, as potentiality:

>                    Severance
> Was clear. The last distortion of romance
> Forsook the insatiable egotist. The sea
> Severs not only lands but also selves.
> Here was no help before reality.
> Crispin beheld and Crispin was made new.[29]

Of this passage Bloom writes: 'The Atlantic severs the American Romantic Selfhood from its British precursor, and internalized romance becomes only internalization or insatiable egotism' (WS, p.74). This means that Crispin has escaped from the influence of the 'old' world, merely to discover a deeper, American influence: 'The American reality is sea and sky, the immensity of space, and like Emerson and Whitman, Crispin beheld and became that new man, the American' (*ibid.*).

This assessment takes the excessiveness, the 'magnitude' of the sea, and reduces it to the Whitmanian trope of ocean. Such a reading actually works directly against the meaning of the sea at this point of the poem. The sea severs 'selves' precisely by confronting them with a form of significance which is too large to be reduced to a name, a determinate representation, a 'myth'. I am leading up to a reading of the poem which would interpret it as mocking the Romantic quest for identity and home, while also mocking what Daniel T. O'Hara has called the critical romance of interpretation. The poem does this by focusing on forms of influence which are resistant to all modes of reduction. The poem, I am suggesting, is a mockery of the quest for determinate representation, for a total vision of reality, and it dramatises such a mockery through its excessive mode of word consciousness. Crispin, as romance-quester, is the object of the poem's mockery, but so also is any reader who would attempt the quest of total interpretation.

Far from being 'made new', Crispin's experience of the excessive environment of ocean sets him on the doomed quest for 'the essential prose': a stage of the quest which takes us into Parts II and III. Once again Bloom's map is highly enlightening in establishing the rhetorical figures which dominate these sections. The tropes of synecdoche and metonymy prevail here, figuring forth Crispin's quest for 'the essential prose' within environments which once again mock such a quest by their excessiveness and indeterminacy.

In Part III, Crispin discovers an America which, as Bloom puts it, has been 'troped to death' (WS, p.79). In other words, he discovers an American 'climate', which presents a parallel excessiveness and/or indeterminate mass of significances to that already experienced by Crispin in the Atlantic Ocean. Stevens's sense of America as a world of metonymic excess is made particularly clear if we look at the lines which he edited from the earlier version of the poem:

> A short way off the city starts to climb,
> At first in alleys which the lilacs line,
> Abruptly, then, to the cobbled merchant streets,
> The shops of chandlers, tailors, bakers, cooks,
> The Coca Cola-bars, the barber-poles,
> The Strand and Harold Lloyd, the lawyers' row,
> The Citizens' Bank, two tea rooms, and a church.
> Crispin is happy in this metropole.[30]

This seems to me a rather clear instance of poetic echo, the intertext being Wordsworth's description of his first impressions of London in Book VII of *The Prelude*. What is different in Crispin's reactions to the modern, American counterpart of Wordsworth's London, of course, is that while Wordsworth responds negatively to the experience of being made a metonymic part of a vast, babel-like city-scape, Crispin 'is happy' to be so reduced. Bloom describes the section as it appears in the final version as 'the *kenosis* or self-emptying of the poem, Crispin's knowing loss of his poetic heroism, or his metonymic reduction of imagination to "realism" ' (WS, p.78).

Bloom is undoubtedly right that Crispin's response to the vast 'metropole' is, at least temporarily, to relinquish his quest for what the 'Journal' calls 'the true poem .../... the simplifying fact,/The common truth ...'.[31] However, as Bloom reminds us, Crispin does not learn the lesson of his metonymic reduction, and clings to the ideal of the 'essential prose' (see WS, p. 79).

While I would agree with Bloom's assessment that what the poem shows is that the dream of an essential realism is 'simply metonymy', Bloom's reading begins to impose itself on the poem by demanding that it attain the poetic counter-sublime and by judging it adversely as it fails to do so. For what Part IV appears to illustrate is that Crispin's attempt to establish a 'colony', to bring to a sublime fulfilment his new realistic ethos, is shadowed by exactly the same form of false authority as his earlier Romantic objectives had been.

The world which the 'essential prose' would contain or colonise remains resistant, uncontainable: 'The plum survives its poems' (PEM, p.70). The recognition of excess which has led Crispin first to found his dream of an 'essential prose' now comes to exhibit the impossibility of such a form of representation and leads Crispin into the 'fatalism' of Part V, 'A nice shady home':

> Should he lay by the personal and make
> Of his own fate an instance of all fate?
> What is one man among so many men?
> What are so many men in such a world?
> Can one man think one thing and think it long?
> Can one man be one thing and be it long?
> The very man despising honest quilts
> Lies quilted to his pole in his despite.
> For realist, what is is what should be. (PEM, p.71)

However, even the position of 'fatalist' is marked by the romance of authoritative position. Such a position is shown to be untenable as Crispin is steadily absorbed into the realm of abundant domesticity.

The poem's last part, the at once comic and yet bitter 'And daughters with curls', promises to present 'Crispin's last/Deduction' (PEM, p.72), but merely shows us a Crispin drowning under the weight of his familial and quotidian existence. The 'doctrine' (PEM, p.74) Crispin finally wins through to is the final line of common 'indifference' in the poem's ostensibly bathetic and yet, on this reading, wholly effective conclusion.

In the consideration of its last three parts I have, as it were, taken over from Bloom's own reading of the poem, because it is important to acknowledge the possibility of a reading which would view these sections as a sustained achievement. Bloom's response is not so positive. Completing his interpretation of the middle section of Part IV, Bloom writes: 'Indeed, the *Comedian* as poem deteriorates very rapidly after this, and the conspicuous failure of most of the two remaining sections is a disconcerting instance of self-fulfilling prophecy' (WS, p.80). Bloom writes of the concluding part: 'One can even wonder if Stevens is attempting to write badly, though the sourness of human and poetic failure is so evident that any critic must hesitate before ascribing intentionality to some manifest poetic blots' (WS, p.82). Bloom overtly means that the poem's concluding two parts are stylistic failures; but his 'deep' meaning is that they fail to rise to true prophecy and cannot pass beyond *daemonisation* to *askesis* and *apophrades*. Bloom writes: 'The reader looks in vain for the transumption of this lateness into an ever-earliness, but that will not take place until *Ideas of Order* and afterward. It is because Stevens is blocked out from such a figurative reversal here that he ends in the bitterness of "So may the relation of each man be clipped" ' (WS, p.82).

Searching for the signs of poetic agon, Bloom does not see that the poem is concerned with a different form of influence-anxiety: not the anxiety produced by individual past poets, but the anxiety experienced in the face of a world of excessive forms and uncontainable, even indeterminate influence. Stevens, writing to Hi Simons, explains:

> I suppose that the way of all mind is from romanticism to realism, to fatalism and then to indifference, unless the cycle re-commences and the thing goes from indifferentiation back to romanticism all over again. No doubt one could demonstrate that the history of the thing is the history of a cycle. At the moment, the world in general is passing from the fatalism stage to an indifferent stage: a stage in which the primary sense is a sense of helplessness. But, as the world is a good deal more vigorous than most of the individuals in it, what the world looks forward to is a new romanticism, a new belief. (L, p.350)

By January 1940, when Stevens wrote that letter, he had discovered his own way of completing the cycle back from 'indifference' to 'romanticism' to 'belief'. At the time of composing his poem on Crispin's quest, Stevens had not found such a route. Instead, he composed at once a diagnosis and a dramatisation of the particular historical malady which he, hardly alone, saw as the cause of such a turn to 'indifference'. In his lecture 'The noble rider and the sound of words', Stevens produced a rather concise expression of that historical context when he wrote of the lack of 'distance' in a world in which 'We are intimate with people we have never seen and unhappily, they are intimate with us.' Stevens quotes I. A. Richards's observation on 'the wide-spread increase in the aptitude of the average mind for self-dissolving introspection, the generally heightened awareness of the goings-on of our minds, *merely as goings-on*', and then adds, 'This is nothing to the generally heightened awareness of the goings-on of other people's minds, *merely as goings-on*.'[32]

The 'Comedian', as an examination of this modern overwhelming of individual vision by an overdetermined yet contracting world, dramatises such an historical experience. By mapping the poem in terms of his intrapsychical, agonistic theory of influence, Bloom fails to establish the efficacy of his own statement that 'This is a poem "about" the anxiety of influence . . .'. The form of influence examined in the poem is precisely resistant to such a positive reduction.

CHAPTER
FOUR

Scenes of instruction: the
limits of Bloom's
psychopoetics

## The anxiety of choice

The primal scene of instruction, Bloom's psychopoetic paradigm for literary origins, plays a crucial role in the development of his agonistic version of literary history. The paradigm has an equally vital function in Bloom's particular repetition of the rhetorical polarity between tropes of order and tropes of excess, which I have suggested lies at the heart of modern forms of canon-formation. I shall deploy this polarity as a means of establishing the theoretical and ideological importance of the scene of instruction in Bloom's work.

In the following notorious passage from his essay 'The dialectics of poetic tradition' (MM, pp.27–40), Bloom utilises various traditional figures in order to set up the order/anarchy polarity in a particular way:

> I prophesy . . . that the first true break with literary continuity will be brought about in generations to come, if the burgeoning religion of Liberated Woman spreads from its clusters of enthusiasts to dominate the West. Homer will cease to be the inevitable precursor, and the rhetoric and forms of our literature then may break at last from tradition. (MM, p.33)

What Bloom finds disturbing here is the prospect of a plethora of traditions or 'canons' emerging from a number of competing, disparate perspectives, signalling the defeat of the notion of *the* canon's absolute centrality. An anxiety, that is, with regard to the prospect of cultural plurality, which, it must be said, is fostered by implications within Bloom's own theories concerning misreading. His theories, for example, have proved fruitful paradigms for feminist critics to appropriate and revise, helping, in this way, to extend our sense of existent and potential canons.

In 'The dialectics of poetic tradition', Bloom produces his most direct representation of what I am calling the anxiety of choice. In this essay, he discusses the place of the literary critic in modern society. Such a figure finds himself, Bloom argues, in an age in which 'our mutual sense of canonical standards have [sic] undergone a remarkable dimming, a fading into the light of a common garishness' (MM, p.36), and in which the central question is, in consequence: 'how is he to teach a tradition now grown so wealthy and so heavy that to accommodate it demands more strength than any single consciousness can provide . . . ?' (MM, p.39). Such a striking representation of the anxiety-inducing weight and wealth or quantitative excess of the inherited tradition allows Bloom to develop his revisionary critique of the Eliotic–Fryean conception of the inclusiveness of the literary 'order'. Bloom argues that 'There are no longer any archetypes to displace', a situation which means that 'For us, creative emulation of literary tradition leads to images of inversion, incest, sado-masochistic parody . . .' (MM, p.31).

The question remains, however, what historical forces have helped to bring about such a situation? Bloom describes Romanticism as being 'appalled by its own overt continuities, and vainly but perpetually fantasiz[ing] some end to repetitions'. Romanticism is thus a 'psychology of belatedness', and Bloom asserts that such a psychology 'is the cause . . . of the excessively volatile senses-of-tradition that have made canon-formation so uncertain a process during the last two centuries, and particularly during the last twenty years' (MM, p.36).

Despite the persuasive conjunction between Romanticism and what Bloom calls the 'psychology of belatedness', establishing this association and then presenting it as the 'cause' of our current senses of belatedness is a rather tautologous argument. Bloom appears to be stating that the cause of Romanticism's psychology of belatedness (including our own, as 'late' Romantics) *is* Romanticism. What creates such a circularity in Bloom's argumentation is his refusal to analyse the historical or *extra*poetic forces or influences which have helped to create what he calls 'the extension of the literary franchise' (MM, p.40). Bloom presents the issue as entirely incorporated into the question of continuity and discontinuity with a central canon, and ultimately with the inescapable claims of the scene of instruction. 'If we are human', Bloom asserts:

> then we depend upon a Scene of Instruction, which is necessarily also a scene of teaching and of priority. If you will not have one instructor or another, then precisely by rejecting all instructors, you will condemn yourself to the earliest Scene of Instruction that imposed itself upon you. The clearest analogue is necessarily Oedipal; reject your parents vehemently enough, and you will become a belated version of them, but compound with their reality, and you may partly free yourself. (MM, p.38)

Having established his version of the teaching process as a primal scene of instruction, and having projected such a scene as the only answer to the current anxiety concerning cultural continuity and direction, Bloom can explore the specifics of such a primal scene, while leaving the wider contexts of his subject underdeveloped.

Bloom's anxiety of choice means that a fundamental opposition between such a concept as *the* tradition and a projected discontinuous anarchy functions as a structural motif throughout his entire work. If *the* tradition cannot be sustained and somehow continued, then what takes its place is a meaningless babel of warring tongues, or 'blind mouths' as he put it in one review.[1] As Bloom writes: 'if tradition cannot establish its own centrality, it becomes something other than the liberation from time's chaos it implicitly promised to be. Like all convention, it moves from an idealized function to a stifling or blocking tendency' (MM, p.28).

In this chapter I will analyse Bloom's representation of tradition's establishment of its own centrality. In the last chapter I began to explain why for Bloom tradition is a daemonic term and 'the one literary sign that is not a sign'. We observed how, for Bloom, tradition is the product of the misreading event which is any 'strong' poetic text. If poems are intertexts, then tradition becomes the tropological swerve away from past poetic texts which every 'strong' text performs in its defensive revision of its relationship with specific past texts and to poetry in general. According to Bloom, however, poets are not free simply to trope against any particular past text or to trope against the poetic tradition in whatever manner they desire. In studying the map of misprision we observed Bloom representing the order or pattern in the dance of poetic acts of misreading; we also noted how such patterns ultimately depend on the theory of the primal scene of instruction. For Bloom, poets perform acts of rhetorical substitution in the context of a specific relation to a past poet or group of poets. From *The Anxiety of Influence* onwards, Bloom has employed the language of affiliation and obligation, of psychoanalysis (initially the 'family romance' and subsequently the terminology of transference, repression and repetition) and the rhetoric of precursor and ephebe, to represent this vision of the *intra*-textual nature of poetic influence and meaning. If tradition is a figuration or trope produced by any 'strong' text's revisionary misreading of past texts, then what Bloom continues to assert is that such acts of revisionism are generated by that poet's reliance on and revisionary repetition of the tropes of the precursor. Bloom's theory of the primal scene of instruction seeks to explain how the poet becomes possessed by the tropes and defences of the precursor. It is a theory of an originating moment of influx, a theory of poetic *election*, and, equally, a theory concerning the origins of the poetic sublime.

For Bloom no poet can become an authentic or 'strong' poet without first being elected by a 'strong' past poet. Before a poet enters into authentic poethood, we might say, s/he must seek for signs of election; signs which are met by a primal teaching scene.[2] This initial scene of induction is the poet's initial encounter with the poetic sublime; and its recreation of the poet (*as-a-poet*), and repetition in the poet's subsequent representations, means that, in poetry, tradition, that chain of 'strong' utterances into which the poet enters, is inescapably daemonic.

The scene of instruction, foundation of the daemonic relationship between precursor and ephebe, is an important, and frequently overlooked, element in Bloom's defence of the poetic 'subject'. Bloom's defence here is of what we might call human agency, and it depends on his understanding of the play between rhetoric and defence, between textuality and psychology. A number of critics have already remarked on the manner in which Bloom's theory of poetic psychology appears to be directly pitted against the anxiety-inducing indeterminacy of literary language, specifically as it has been defined in relation to the post-structuralist concepts of intertextuality and *writing*. Jonathan Culler argues that Bloom's employment of the language of psychology is a way of recuperating the rhetoric of origins, and thus of intentionality, in the wake of post-structuralist theories of language, meaning and the 'subject'. Neil Hertz employs a reading of the Kantian distinction between dynamic and mathematical varieties of the sublime, in order to represent theories, like Bloom's, of the daemonic or spectral nature of literary influence as strategic reductions or blockages of the potentially engulfing threat of intertextuality *qua* writing.[3] From this perspective critics like Bloom can be said to be involved in a modern, *critical sublime*; a confrontation with a textualised version of the mathematical sublime which prompts a return to the comforting determinacy of quasi-Oedipal structures.

In pitting his scene directly against Derrida's scene of writing, Bloom is attempting to enclose poetry in a determinate field, a field in which origins, although always open to further deferral and the effects of repetition, are pragmatically reconstituted. Just as in the last chapter, in which we saw Bloom self-consciously shuttling between empirical and dialectical assumptions about the reading process, such a reconstruction of origins is a literalising and a self-consciously rhetorical or tropological enterprise. A reader concerned with the historical dimensions of literary meaning and influence needs to interrogate this tension between literalistic and tropological representations of poetic origins, while also challenging the fundamental opposition between the scenes of writing and of instruction.

## Bloom, Derrida, Freud and the question of origins

I

Bloom's initial description of his theory of the primal scene of instruction comes in chapter 3 of the *Map*. Bloom begins his discussion with a meditation on the importance of origins in the context of Hebraic and Greek conceptions of speech, writing, interpretation and teaching. In the wake of contemporary demystifications of the quest for and valorisation of origins, Bloom declares: 'The prestige of origins is a universal phenomenon, against which a solitary de-mystifier like Nietzsche struggled in vain' (MM, p.46).

We are already well aware of the manner in which Bloom's theory of poetry and poetic meaning rests on this privileging of origins and, by implication, equally general anxiety concerning influence and belatedness. Yet stating the matter in this way can explain not only the centrality of the poetic scene of instruction but equally Bloom's choice of the two figures against which he wrestles in his endeavour to excavate this fundamental principle or paradigm. If Freud's theory of psychic development contains the twentieth century's greatest account of our origins as human 'subjects', then the philosophy of Jacques Derrida represents the apotheosis of the Nietzschean demystification of origins and beginnings. Bloom's 'The primal scene of instruction' becomes an agonistic conflict with the claims to priority of Freud's two primal scenes of the Oedipus and the slaying of the Totemic Father (Freud's individual and historical projections of origins) and the Derridean scene of writing, which, as a critique of the logocentric valorisation of speech, posits the non-originary *origin* before speech and its reifications: presence, autonomy, truth, being. To understand Bloom's complex argumentation for his scene, we must analyse his agon with Derrida; a critical 'ant-agon-ism' which incorporates much of his specific revision of Freud.

Derrida's account of Freud is useful for Bloom because it opens up Freud's great image of the unconscious to the phenomenon of influence, under the aegis of Derrida's prime concept of writing (*écriture*).[4] Derrida shows how Freud's constant desire to produce a mechanistic model for the unconscious and its functioning continually falls back on models taken from the realm of inscription. In his short essay 'On the mystic writing pad', to which Derrida devotes some considerable commentary, Freud defines the unconscious as a form of non-entropic memory, capable of being represented as a machine for writing.

Without becoming enmeshed in the spiralling implications of this reading, it is possible to state that Derrida generates by it a confirmation of his fundamental principle concerning the predominance of writing, standing as a figuration for differential structure, over the orthodox, metaphysical and logocentric emphasis on the primacy of speech. If the Freudian unconscious is structured like Derrida's *écriture*, then the psyche becomes a text within which memory traces, in a system of differential relations precluding the very possibility for stable structuration, cancel any orthodox notion of originary 'presence'. The question for Derrida becomes 'not if the psyche is indeed a kind of text, but: what is a text, and what must the psyche be if it can be represented by a text?'[5]

Bloom's reaction to Derrida's reading of Freud is to compound with its reality, only, in the long term, to diverge from it the more completely. Bloom begins by praising Derrida's emphasis on writing as a precondition for psychic articulation. He writes that 'Derrida has made of writing an intra-psychical trope, which is a making that necessarily pleases any reader who himself has made of influence an intra-psychical trope or rather a trope for intra-psychical relationships' (MM, p.49). In this initial identification, we observe Bloom equating *écriture* with his own notion of influence. He goes on: 'Such a reader can find supremely useful Derrida's conclusion that "writing is the scene or stage of history and the play of the world" ' (MM, p.49). Bloom's love-affair with Derridean *écriture* is, however, murdered in its infancy. Indeed, from such an initial convergence, Bloom comes to represent the difference between Derrida and his own brand of theory as a modern manifestation of an essential difference between Oral and Written Tradition dating back to biblical times. Having established the universal prestige of origins, Bloom asks: 'how do we pass from origins to repetition and continuity, and thence to the discontinuity that marks all revisionism?' His answer is to restore a 'missing trope' and a missing 'Primal Scene', a move effected by 'restoring the trope, which is technically the one that traditional rhetoric has called *metalepsis* or *transumption*' (MM, p.47).

The revision Bloom goes on to make of Freud and Derrida is, therefore, centred in an argument over the primality of rival tropes; an essential point which is clarified in Bloom's next statement: 'What makes a scene Primal? A scene is a setting as seen by a viewer, a place where action, whether real or fictitious, occurs or is staged. Every Primal Scene is necessarily a trope' (MM, p.47).

What Bloom is suggesting here is that if every primal scene is a rhetorical trope, or an interpretation of something ('real or fictitious') outside the realm of the literal, then what is required is a trope which will contain all other possible tropes. Such a trope will, so such logic runs, take priority over all other primal scenes conceived as tropes. What such a translation of the question of origins and priority allows Bloom to do is transume Freud's two primal scenes, which are, Bloom declares, 'both synecdoches' (MM, p.47). It also allows him to transume Derrida's 'third scene, more Primal than the Freudian synecdoches', which represents 'the more Sublime [trope] . . . of hyperbole' (MM, p.48). These tropes (synecdoche and hyperbole) are troped by the only trope that can be described as the *trope of a trope*, the sixth in the revisionary map of misprision, transumption or metaleptic reversal. Bloom writes: 'Derrida's Scene of Writing is insufficiently Primal both in itself and as exegesis of Freud. It relies, as Freud does, upon a more daring trope, a scheme of transumption or metaleptic reversal that I would name the Primal Scene of Instruction' (MM, p.49).

When we remember that the tropes of synecdoche, hyperbole and metalepsis are interpretations of the concept of influence, then we realise that the staged agon between tropes being conducted here is a dispute over the interpretation of the origins of influence and of tradition both historically and for the individual 'subject'. Bloom greatly intensifies what is at stake here when he gets down to the specifics of Derrida's *misreading* of Freud's notion of repression.

> For Derrida's interpretation of Freud to be correct – that is, for writing to be as primal as coitus – the inhibition of writing would have to come about to avoid a conflict *with the superego, and not with the id*. But *speech, not writing*, as Freud always says, is inhibited to avoid conflict with the superego. For the superego presides over the Scene of Instruction, which is always at least quasi-religious in its associations, and speech therefore is more primal. Writing, which is cognitively secondary, is closer to mere process, to the *automatic* behaviour of the id. Freud himself is thus more in the oral than in the writing tradition, unlike Nietzsche and Derrida, who are more purely revisionists, while Freud, perhaps despite himself, is a curiously direct continuator of his people's longest tradition. Freud, unlike Nietzsche and Derrida, knows that precursors become absorbed *into the id, and not into the superego*. Influence-anxieties of all kinds, with all their afflictions of secondariness, therefore inhabit *writing*, but not merely so much the oral, logocentric tradition of prophetic speech. (MM, p.50)

Any reader of Derrida will feel compelled to object here that the notion of writing is being malformed by Bloom. The Derridean notion of *écriture* is intended to *contain* both speech and writing and thus to remain immune to the charge of secondariness; a charge which depends on the reduction of the concept to mere marks on a page. Yet what is occurring in this passage is a reappropriation, first of Derrida, and then of Freud, into Bloom's vision of the Hebraic tradition; particularly the Kabbalistic tradition of speech and writing. The rather stark appearance of misinterpretation marks a clash of conceptual registers, and behind that of traditions, in which a concept such a writing, which for Derrida is a concept which deals with questions of epistemology and ontology, becomes a concept concerning influence and Bloom's active, discursive version of meaning. This translation of Derridean writing has already been established at the beginning of Bloom's essay, where he compares the Hebrew word for 'word' with its Greek counterpart and proceeds to suggest that the Derridean notions of *writing* and the *trace* belong as much to the former as to the latter. This distinction between 'words' (see MM, pp.42–3) lies at the heart of Bloom's distinction between significance and meaning, between philosophy and poetry, and ultimately between the Written and the Oral Traditions. Such a distinction forms the basis for our understanding of the realm of discourse towards which Bloom conjures the work of his two rivals. Bloom's vision of poetic texts as acts of persuasive misinterpretation means that poetic 'words' are discursive acts rather than mere signs on a page.

Bloom's critique of Derrida on Freud depends on his association of writing with influence, both conceived as intra-psychical tropes, and on his continued assertion that the precursor's language becomes part of the ephebe's defences and drives; part, that is, of the poetic equivalent of the id-component. More importantly, Bloom's critique depends on the notion that before writing or influence can be absorbed into the id there must be an initial fixation on a prior instance of writing. This primal fixation is not itself involved in the play of repression and defence, which ensues when such influences are fully internalised. In his paper 'On narcissism: An introduction', Freud presents an account of an initial stage of primal autonomy or autoeroticism which requires to be disturbed through a fixation on an external object (the mother).[6] Bloom takes this idea, of an initially strong and overfull narcissistic ego wounding itself by a fixation on an external object, and applies it to what we might call the aetiology of the 'strong' poetic personality.

Before the internalisation of a precursor's language into the poetic id (the ephebe's own patterns of internalised defence and drive), Bloom is suggesting, there must be an initial fixation on a precursor. Given its status as an act of fixation and as a scene of teaching, this fixation, which can be also described as a primal repression, stops the wandering of signification associated with writing and provides a point of origin which leads us into the realm of speech, of action and of meaning. This vision of a primordial moment or scene of teaching allows Bloom to associate the Freudian language of psychoanalysis with the Kabbalistic language of revisionism and influence. Kabbalah teaches that all text, all writing (for the Kabbalists this means the written Torah), depends on an initial instruction (see MM, p.44). Kabbalism, as a rhetoric and psychology of belatedness uncannily close to the belated poetry of our own post-Enlightenment era, illustrates the need to trace all influence, all writing, back to an initial fixation on a divinely inspired act of oral instruction (see KC, pp.52–3).

What Kabbalah teaches us, according to Bloom, is that an epistemological understanding of meaning, and particularly the

Nietzschean/Derridean deconstruction of that tradition, does not adequately confront the peculiar logocentric tradition of oral instruction, of spoken utterance. To go back to our analysis in the last chapter, Bloom takes Derrida's revision of Freud to imply that language, as a differential structure or, in de Man's terms, as a system of tropes, pre-dates any articulation of 'selfhood'. On epistemological grounds this might indeed be the case; yet for Bloom, every 'strong' text is a cut made into the synchronic level of language. Every strong textual utterance depends on a rhetorical defence which takes for its authority not some criterion of truth but its reiteration of a tradition of rhetorical, persuasive utterances. Attention to the poetic 'word' as *davhar*, to poetic meaning as the product of the 'beautiful necessity of defence', shows us, according to Bloom, that Derrida's scene of writing, as well as Freud's primal scenes, must be superseded by a primal scene of oral instruction, a reception of influence that marks a primordial point of origin for the wanderings of meaning. Having come this far, we have to ask the question: is Bloom presenting an imaginative necessity, even a 'necessary fiction', in the guise of a primary critique? Such a question takes us back once again to the status of Bloom's scene of instruction. This issue, in fact, is clarified by moving on to Bloom's employment of Kierkegaard and Vico as master theorists of such a paradigm and/or trope.

## II

Bloom writes that Kierkegaard is 'the inevitable precursor for formulating a Scene of Instruction' (BV, p.44). Explanations of Kierkegaard's importance are to be found in 'The primal scene of instruction' and also at the conclusion of chapter 6 of the *Map*. In this chapter Bloom asserts that 'In so far as a poet is and remains a poet, he must exclude and negate other poets. Yet he must begin by including and affirming a precursor poet or poets, for there is no other way to become a poet' (MM, p.121). The question remains whether such an inclusion is dictated by the poet or whether some form of necessity or determinism exists in such a scene. This problem is precisely what is captured by Kierkegaard's concept of *repetition*, which he contrasts to the more literalistic concept of recollection.

Kierkegaard's notion of 'recollecting forwards' is the essential element Bloom assimilates into his primal scene of instruction. The poet begins to be 'a poet' when s/he receives the teaching of a precursor. This primal scene of teaching represents the poet's 'birth' *as a poet*. The poet then internalises this teaching experience and reiterates it, in Bloom's terms repeats rather than recollects it, whenever s/he creates a new poem. Every poem is thus a recreation, a recollecting forwards, of a primary fixation on a precursor poem or poet. However, as the poet moves to full maturity, the primary fixation is steadily forgotten, so that it appears as if the poet were originating his or her own major tropes, images and meanings, rather than repeating the tropes, images and meanings of the precursor. Bloom writes: 'At the center of his [Kierkegaard's] idea of repetition is the problem of continuity for the individual, a problem that he believed could be solved only by first arriving at a decision, and then by continually renewing it' (PR, p.142). The Kierkegaardian notion of repetition can in fact be said to merge with Bloom's analogical utilisation of Kabbalism and Gnosticism, along with his continued employment of Freud. This merging of vocabularies produces Bloom's account of the primal scene of instruction as an initial fixation and repression, an account which dominates *Poetry and Repression* and the texts that succeed it. In the introduction to that text, Bloom considers 'the formula that a poem both finds its origins in a Scene of Instruction and finds its necessary aim or purpose there as well'. He goes on: 'It is only by repressing creative "freedom", through the initial fixation of influence, that a person can be reborn as a poet. And only by revising that repression can a poet become and remain strong' (PR, p.27).

The primal scene of instruction is the element which marks the cleavage between the poet-as-man and the poet-as-poet. It forms the basis of the poet's transcendence of an anxiety inducing 'creative "freedom" ' via an entry into the realm of intratextual agonism. We wish to know, however, precisely what is meant by 'creative "freedom" ', and equally what it means to call what appears to be an arbitrary decision primary when it depends for its motivation and even its meaning on such a prior context. The answer is clearly that the primal scene *is* primal only if we retain a notion of the poet-as-poet, of a 'rebirth' into authentic poethood after a natural/psychological maturation. Such an answer uncovers the true nature of such a scene: it is a fiction or trope that the poet, and after him the critic, passes upon him- or herself in order to facilitate an ascension to such an antithetical state. The primal scene is not classifiable as a literal cause but, rather, represents what we might call a strategic response to the inescapable recognition of belatedness and ignorance of causes. Such a description is highlighted and extended in Bloom's references to the philosophy of Vico, as his other great instructor into the paradoxes of poetic origins.

In the essay I have just been referring to, Bloom, in order to clarify the status of his primal scene and its relation to the poetic sublime, focuses on Vico's distinction between the gentile nations and the Hebraic-Christian traditions. While the latter is concerned with 'knowledge of the true God', the former bases its knowledge on the principle that 'we only know what we have made'. This principle depends on the belief that our knowledge and our poetry are 'identical with our fallen state of being in the body'. 'To be in the body', Bloom explains, 'is to suffer a condition in which we are ignorant of causation and of origins, yet still we are very much in quest of origins.' Vico's 'insight' is that poetry 'is born of our ignorance of causes, and . . . that if any poet knows too well what causes his poem, then he cannot write it, or at least will write it badly' (PR, p.5).

Bloom links Vico with the terminology of Kabbalism in order to produce a vision of poetic crossings between ignorance and identification, parallel to the already established pattern of crossings between limitation through substitution to representation: 'poetic image, trope, defence', writes Bloom, 'are all forms of a ratio between human ignorance making things out of itself, and human self-identification moving to transform us into the things we have made' (PR, p.8). If limitation equals ignorance equals the primal repression of something characterisable as 'creative "freedom" ', then representation equals identification equals a transumptive presentation of origins through a troping on particular past tropes. As Bloom himself is aware, such a perspective makes of the scene of instruction an equivalent of what in Freudian terminology is styled the 'primal scene fantasy', a fiction of origins rather than the origin itself. The primal scene becomes a recreation of origins by and for the benefit of the poetic 'subject'. Vico's dialectic of ignorance and identification certainly appears to clinch the secondariness of such a scene. As Bloom declares: 'Since poetry, unlike the Jewish religion, does not go back to a truly divine origin, poetry is always at work *imagining its own origin*, or telling a persuasive lie about itself, to itself' (PR, p.7).

Bloom's dispute with Derrida and Freud has led him, it would appear, to offer up not a more primal scene, but rather a persuasive defence of poetry's need to project for itself a more primal scene than Freud's or Derrida's versions of primality. The finest expression of this understanding of his paradigm comes, appropriately, near the conclusion of 'The primal scene of instruction', in which he states that 'Every Primal Scene is necessarily a fantasy structure' and that 'the idea of the most Primal scene as being a scene of Instruction goes back to the roots of the canonical principle and insists that "In the beginning was Interpretation." ' Bloom goes on to argue that 'a young Blake or a young Wordsworth had to know a possibility of sublimity in the self before he could know it in Milton and go on to be elected by Milton.' In other words, the initial scene of influence must be an interpretation that the new poet makes of himself. The first two stages in the scene of instruction (Election-love and Covenant-love), Bloom asserts, 'are imposed by the new poet upon himself, and both are therefore his interpretations, without which there would be no *given* whatsoever' (MM, pp.55–6).

Despite this passage, it is clear that there is far too much at stake in the issue of poetic origins for Bloom to remain completely faithful to the tropological implications of the primal scene *as interpretation*. The process of interpretation outlined above prompts us to question what it is that allows for the new poet's initial sense of 'sublimity'.

For Bloom, the scene of instruction is primal and equally a literal origin because it represents the birth, the moment of individuation, for the 'poet-as-poet'. However, it must be recognised (somewhat against Bloom's description) that because the poet (before becoming an authentic poet-*as-poet*) is already a being caught within language, within the scene of writing, which equally means within socially symbolic systems or signifying practices, this literal scene of origination is at the same time tropological, a scene of interpretation. The poet interprets him- or herself into full, authentic 'poethood'.

Putting the matter in this way foregrounds the question at the heart of Bloom's theory. If the poet is already a being caught up in the play of language, of socially specific signifying practices – the scene of writing, which, if we remember, Derrida styles as 'the scene or stage of history and the play of the world' – then what stops us from understanding Bloom's primal scene in terms of psychology and in terms of language or writing conceived as social symbolisation and practice? Bloom's desire to assert the priority and primacy of the scene of instruction would appear to remain eminently reversible. The kind of approach we find, for example, in the work of Julia Kristeva, in which poetic production and individuation are understood in terms of the relationship between psychology and social symbolisation, would appear to be capable of transuming the Bloomian theory of poetic origins.

Bloom constantly attempts to posit an initial, originary, primal scene of interpretation for every 'strong' poet. The notion of the poet-as-poet, the canonical projection of a tradition of 'strong' poets and the concomitant desire to insure such an intratextual sphere from all considerations of an apparently *extra*poetic nature, all lead Bloom into reiterations of a totalising language which, at least rhetorically, at least on the synchronic level of Bloom's discourse, threaten to turn that scene itself into a *given*. The place of this vacillation between Bloom's dialectical awareness of the tropological nature of his scene and his movement towards empirical reification of that scene occurs where that scene itself takes place: in the passage of the poet into full, antithetical 'poethood'. This process is nowhere more apparent than in Bloom's attempt to insure his own account of that pre-scene stage of development as a period of subjective autonomy, comparable to Freud's account of auto-eroticism, or primal narcissism. Bloom refers to Piaget's account of the gradual de-centring of the infant's sense of 'self' and 'space', a process in which these initial conceptualisations are gradually given up to a sense of communal space and time (history). He adds:

> Having assimilated much of the Not-Me, the child at last accommodates his vision to the vision of others. Poets, we can assume, as children *assimilated* more than the rest of us, and yet somehow *accommodated* less, and so won through the crisis of adolescence without totally decentering. Faced by the Primal Scene of Instruction even in its poetic variant (where the Idea of Poetry first came to them), they managed to achieve a curious detachment towards crisis that made them capable of a greater attachment to their own wavering centers.   (MM, pp.52–3)

It is possible to view the entire thesis of the scene of instruction as being threatened here by a literalising employment of the language of psychoanalysis. If the ascension to full poethood depends on a pre-scene excess of 'assimilation' yet deficiency of 'accommodation', then such an unusual, primary psychic economy and development would become open to a direct psychoanalytical explanation. Such a situation, indeed, would return Bloom's conception of the poet-as-poet to the Romantic ideal of a highly sensitive and exceptionally imaginative psyche, Wordsworth's 'more comprehensive soul', for instance. It would equally seem to reinstate the Freudian versions of primality as the inevitable basis of our critical investigations.

Why does Bloom feel the need to literalise his use of the language of psychoanalysis, projecting a 'psychological' rather than a 'poetic' aetiology for the fixation upon the precursor? The immediate answer to such a question must be that Bloom's argumentation, his attempt agonistically to trope both Derrida and Freud, requires a covering over of the basic discrepencies or analogical disjunctions in the discourses he is bringing into conjunction. A process which is not always quite successful. More specifically, I would suggest that Bloom's recognition of the tropological and defensive nature of his scene, its inevitable belatedness, includes the recognition of its amenity to further contextualisation. A recognition which is at odds with the fundamental purpose of such a scene.

Bloom, interested only in the 'aboriginal poet', and the various patterns of revisionism discernible within a select canon of 'strong' poetic texts, wishes to draw an equivalence between poetic 'beginnings' and the poetic fixation on the precursor. The primal scene, however, cannot establish such an equivalence and continually alerts us to a pre- or extra-scene context not necessarily consonant with Bloom's perspectives.

An informative parallel to the suggestions I am making here can be found in Bloom's approach to the work of Jacques Lacan. To comprehend the relevance of this parallel, we need only remark on the possibility of substituting Piaget's scheme of gradual maturation, as described by Bloom, with Lacan's scheme of the subject's progress through the mirror-stage, the Imaginary and the Symbolic Order. Just as the Lacanian *infans* becomes involved in an initial specular identification with a double (daemon), an image of the 'self' which is not the 'self' and yet which allows the 'self' to be constituted by the consciously distinguished and distinguishing 'I', so Bloom's poet-as-poet is constituted in the moment of recognition and differentiation which erupts into the previously perfect autonomy of the narcissistic poetic ego. The play of identification and difference which is established in the Lacanian 'mirror stage' continues until, with the period associated with the Oedipal crisis, the Symbolic Order is entered. In this phase, as Elizabeth Bruss states, 'the object itself no longer appears as a fixed (chimerical) image but as a freely interchangeable sign'. This progression to the Symbolic Order, in which, as Anika Lemaire states, 'socio-cultural and linguistic symbolism impose themselves with their structures as orders which have already been constituted before the *infans* subject makes his entry into them',[8] is the point at which Bloom's conception of a distinctly 'poetic' maturation requires a revision of Lacan (see PR, p.145).

Bloom reiterates his revision of Freud through his swerve away from Lacan, in which he reinsures his account of poetic origins and poetic aims as an agonistic play of identification and difference with the principal precursor. He does this by blocking off any outlet into the symbolic dimensions of language, of historical and social conditioning. Lacanian psycholinguistics becomes, like the language of Freudian psychoanalysis, analogically (*qua* figuratively) suitable for the 'poetic' processes Bloom wishes to reconstruct.

Although nothing stops Bloom from pursuing such analogical appropriations, they cannot in any way prove or insure his version of poetic origins. Indeed, the fact that Bloom feels the need to utilise such schemes in his 'poetic' constructions, while criticising Freud, Derrida, Lacan and others for being self-contradictory or partially 'blinded' *on their own terms*, leads to the kind of complaint brought to bear in Bruss's analysis: 'If the theorist insists upon remaining in the Imaginary, or refuses to see the fruitlessness of inverted polarities, it is not because he has failed to understand their demystification. Rather, it is because to abandon them would be to lose their satisfactions'.[9]

Bloom's theorisation of the primal scene can usefully be described as a 'remaining in the Imaginary'. It can be described as a presentation of the necessity of the poetic fixation on precursors which modulates continuously into a repetition of that 'fiction', or, in other words, a form of literalisation. Bloom achieves his finest assessment of the validity of his theory when he writes: 'The true use of a Scene of Instruction comes where true use must, as an aid to the pragmatics of interpretation' (MM, p.60). The scene of instruction works because it allows us to understand the manner in which certain poets trope against past poetic tropes and construct fictions of origination out of such a tropological practice. However, as Bloom reminds us, the theory has an ideological or ideational function as well:

> The first use then of a Scene of Instruction is to remind us of the humanistic loss we sustain if we yield up the authority of oral tradition to the partisans of *writing*, to those like Derrida and Foucault who imply for all language what Goethe erroneously asserted for Homer's language, that language by itself writes the poem and thinks. The human writes, the human thinks, and always following after and defending against another human, however fantasized that human becomes in the strong imaginings of those who arrive later upon the scene.   (MM, p.60)

While acknowledging the positive nature of Bloom's defence of the human 'subject', it is justifiable to assert that such a defence can only be strengthened if we attempt to reconstruct the historical contexts which inform, motivate and decisively affect the intrapersonal myths of origination poets apparently seek to construct. However, as is already obvious, such a contextualisation must be developed against the grain of Bloom's intentions and perennial perspectives. This is confirmed by attending to Bloom's most recent reimagining of his paradigm in his 'Wrestling Sigmund: Three paradigms for poetic originality' (BV, pp.43–70).

Bloom begins this essay with the astonishing claim that he has 'shied away from developing, until now' (BV, p.43) his paradigm of the scene of instruction. This assertion alerts us to the real objective of this essay: a massive revisionary re-reading of his own earlier account of the primal scene. Such a misprision, or transumptive troping on his own previous trope, indicates how uneasy Bloom is about the exact status of and the potential justification for his theory concerning poetic 'origins'. Having noted Wittgenstein's 'curious mistake in believing Freud had not distinguished between the Primal Scene and the somewhat later Primal Scene fantasy', Bloom takes up a criticism of his own work made by a former student, Cathy Caruth, and admits to having made a similiar mistake to Wittgenstein's. He points to the fact that his own earlier representations of the scene of instruction make that scene a primal scene fanstasy rather than a primal scene proper. He goes on to make the following distinction between an 'oral' scene – 'the topos or Primal Scene proper, the negative moment of being influenced, a perpetually lost origin' – and a ' "written" scene [or] trope or Primal Scene fantasy'. He concludes: 'As a Primal Scene, the Scene of Instruction is a Scene of Voicing; only when fantasized or troped does it become a Scene of Writing' (BV, pp.60–1).

Cathy Caruth's point is that in this essay, as well as in the essays on Freud collected in *Agon*, Bloom appears to be performing an act of self-wounding which mirrors a similar process of self-revision observable in Freud's *Beyond the Pleasure Principle* and the important papers which succeed that work. Caruth suggests that this revision of the scene is highlighted in Bloom's juxtaposition of the two 'uncanny' passages from the J writer (Jacob's wrestling with the Angel) and from Freud (the infant's suckling at the mother's breast). She suggests that the move from the Oedipal scene implicit in the first passage to the maternal scene presented by Freud marks Bloom's transcendence of the Oedipal theory of origins formerly grounded in the scene of instruction. This movement begins to place the primal scene, or what

Bloom now calls the scene of voicing, in a stage of development prior to any object consciousness.[10] What this process of revision allows Bloom to suggest, however, is that Freud, in the later stages of his work, moves towards a poetic theory of origins (see BV, p.69). Thus, in a complex reversal, Bloom's 'wounding' of his own trope for poetic origins becomes a reinforcement of that trope via a 'wounding' of the basis of Freud's whole psychoanalytic discipline and discourse (see also *Agon*, p.117).

In relinquishing the language of determinate origins, through his revision of his employment of Freudian terminology, Bloom gains a new form of justification for his primal scene; a justification based on Freud's apparent reinforcement of the theory of catastrophic origins. Such a 'strong' (mis)reading of Freud is, of course, an illustration of Bloom's power (*pathos*) as an interpreter. It will hardly be surprising, however, when I suggest that the revision equally illustrates the fact that Bloom cannot stop his psychoanalytic appropriations from foregrounding the secondariness of his scene of instruction.

Once again, what I have been criticising is the essentialistic element in Bloom's theory of poetic origins; the fact that he posits a primary element in poetic production and meaning which remains constant, fundamental and thus immune to the vagaries of history. We need to take the paradigm of the scene of instruction and reverse this a- or transhistorical interpretation. This means that we need to understand how a changing rhetoric of instruction within literature affects and is in turn affected by changes within the sociocultural field. If literature itself is a concept which has a history, which contains and reflects transformations in social and cultural practices, institutional organisations, national and/or ideological structures, then the rhetoric of authority, influence and instruction which attaches itself to such a paradigm or trope will itself reflect such historical changes. To utilise Bloom's paradigm or trope we need to place it *within* the history of literature – a history which forms part of History – rather than following Bloom in his attempts to position it at the centre of and thus, in a process made familiar by Derrida, outside the play of history. We need ultimately, taking up that Derridean reference, to explore the interimplication, rather than the opposition, of the scene of writing and the scene of instruction, of intertextuality with intratextuality, of the Symbolic (social) and the Imaginary (poetic/daemonic) Orders. In order to begin such an exploration, I wish to move on to an engagement with Bloom's pragmatic use of the scene: his reading of the poetry of Wordsworth.

## Counter-reading: Milton, Wordsworth, Bloom

Peter de Bolla has written a commentary on Bloom's 'Wordsworth and the scene of instruction' (PR, pp.52–82) in which he shows how, in his reading of 'Tintern Abbey', Bloom distances himself from the Derridean concept of *writing*.[11] Bloom's chapter achieves such a distancing by focusing on Freud's and Wordsworth's conceptions of memory. Bloom states that memory, for Wordsworth, is 'a composite trope, and so in Wordsworth what is called memory, or treated as memory, is also a composite defense against time, decay, the loss of divinating power, and so finally a defense against death, whose other name is John Milton' (PR, p.53). Bloom's 'antithetical' reading of the poem asserts that, as a result of 'the preternatural strength of Wordsworth's unconsciously purposeful forgettings of Milton', memory becomes the subject of the poem. The meaning of the poem, Bloom argues, 'is in its relationships to Milton's invocations . . . the poem becomes, despite itself, an invocation of Milton. Memory deals with absence, and the crucial or felt absence in "Tintern Abbey" is Milton's' (PR, p.56). I want to test the critique carried out in this chapter with regard to Bloom's theory of the primal scene of instruction by questioning this association of memory, writing and that important Romantic construct, the Miltonic sublime.

Through an exegesis of the central images in 'Tintern Abbey' Bloom uncovers a dialectic between what he calls voicing and writing (associated with hearing and sight respectively). Wordsworth wishes to celebrate a restoration of poetic voice (PR, p.56), a restoration bound up with a desire to hear the experiential world just as the blind bard John Milton had heard it. Wordsworth, however, cannot help *seeing* the environment to which he has returned and such a seeing becomes interconnected with that repressed *writing* which is the sublime of Milton's poetry. Voicing represents a desired poetic autonomy and election: writing represents a feared dependency on the precursor. The high point of voicing in Wordsworth's poetry, according to Bloom, comes in the 'Prospectus' to *The Recluse*, where the poet takes on 'Jehovah – with his thunder, and the choir/Of shouting Angels, and the empyreal thrones', as well as the sublime poetry of Milton, and defeats them all. For Bloom this is Wordsworth's great manifesto transformed, in poems such as 'Tintern Abbey', into a testament of defeat, a declaration of intent too severe for its producer to sustain. For Bloom, '*Power* is being repressed in "Tintern Abbey", a power so antithetical that it could tear the poet loose from nature, and take him into a world of his own, restituting him yet more sublimely.' Bloom adds: 'Wordsworth defends himself against his own strength through repression, and like all strong poets he learns to call that repression the Sublime' (PR, p.76).

Such a judgement depends for its interpretative power on Bloom's critique of the traditional understanding of Wordsworth as a nature poet; an argument which takes us back to Bloom's early work (see VC, pp.124–98). The modern heir of that tradition is Geoffrey Hartman, and Bloom's essay argues against what Hartman calls 'the phenomenology of literary allusion' in Wordsworth. In such a mode of revisionism, Hartman argues, the poet internalises the play of intratextuality in order to present himself as freed from cultural time and as existing in 'the personal and mortal experience of time' (Hartman, quoted in PR, p.58). Bloom takes up the issue of internalisation and gives us a Wordsworth who enters not into a phenomenological relationship with nature, nor into a position freed from the anxiety of influence, but into a severe repression of past instances of the sublime. Bloom writes that "Tintern Abbey" is a Scene of Instruction in which the poet brings a Sublime response to a place or state of heightened demand, but the genius of the state counts for more than the genius of place, which means that Milton counts for more than nature does, both here and in *The Prelude*' (PR, p.81). Wordsworth, according to Bloom, limits his poetic power by reverting to a myth of the saving function of memory. A kind of transparency of self-presence is replaced by the familiar and now almost all-pervasive Wordsworthian subjectivity. In the majority of his most sublime texts, Wordsworth cannot get beyond Milton. To be made by such a preternatural voice is to hover always on the wrong side of the voicing/writing divide.

Bloom writes that ' "Tintern Abbey" is at once the most enigmatic and perhaps the most influential of modern poems. Among much else it begins that splendidly dismal tradition in which modern poems intend some merely ostensible subject, yet actually find their true subject in the anxiety of influence' (PR, p.57). The intended subject of 'Tintern Abbey', for Bloom, is the Coleridgean and Wordsworthian combination of seeing and hearing. Bloom's point is that the intended subject of the poem is a complex marriage between sight and hearing, a poetic recognition scene in which the poet discovers in nature signs of his own election. However, because of his severe repression of his own poetic 'strength' in the poem, because of his purposeful forgetting of the Miltonic sublime, what Wordsworth sees in nature are certain 'inscriptions' which constitute projections of his own repressed dependence on Miltonic writing. Wishing to see and hear confirmation of his own identity in nature, Wordsworth unconsciously inscribes onto nature the repressed 'memory-traces' which are Miltonic writing. Bloom here, arguing against Hartman and the tradition that culminates with him, radically revises the conventional understanding of Wordsworth's engagement with the *genius loci*.

Far from discovering an 'answering spirit' in nature, Bloom's Wordsworth mixes what in traditional rhetoric were styled *loci* (or 'places') with *topoi* (or 'commonplaces'). The point Bloom is making is that in poems such as 'Tintern Abbey' Wordsworth's ostensible subject – the celebration of a reciprocal relationship with the natural world – conceals an actual estrangement from nature. A radical anxiety principle in the poet 'usurps voice in all the poems, and substitutes for voice various memorial inscriptions, various traces of Miltonic anteriority' (PR, p.59). In 'Tintern Abbey', Wordsworth does not see and hear nature, but rather sees and hears the repressed writing of his Miltonic precursor. Such a reading explains for Bloom the greatness and the limitations of Wordsworthian poetry. It also explains why Wordsworth is the inevitable precursor for all subsequent poetry. Bloom writes: 'The problem of surpassing Wordsworth is the fairly absurd one of going beyond Wordsworth in the process of internalization' (PR, p.60).

In Bloom's reading, Wordsworth becomes the great internaliser, the great estranger of the natural world, substituting for it a kind of phantasmal recognition scene in which the rejected dependence on prior script or writing cuts the poet off from all relationship and from all meaning, save for his own desire for self-presence. There is a great absence for Bloom in Wordsworth's poetry; an absence of the 'self' and an absence of an object-world. The meaning of his poetry becomes its defence against the recognition of the usurpation of 'self' and nature by Miltonic writing (see PR, p.81).

Bloom argues that his 'antithetical practical criticism' of 'Tintern Abbey' radically deidealises the poem. He asserts that only his 'antithetical practical criticism' of the poem allows us to avoid following 'the poet in his own self-presentation' (PR, p.67). He claims a superiority for his own brand of critical deidealisation over all rival readings of Wordsworth, but particularly the 'powerfully revisionist or deconstructive one implied by Paul de Man' and the 'powerfully canonical one . . . which culminates in Hartman's *The Unmediated Vision*' (PR, p.79). Bloom's own readers, however, must question whether he does actually deidealise Wordsworth's 'own self-presentation'.

90  *Harold Bloom*

The sections over which Bloom takes most pains are the poem's opening 57 lines and the conclusion, from line 112 onwards. Having mapped the first section of the poem as a *clinamen*, a reaction-formation against the knowledge of the passing of time, Bloom styles the next section – from around line 42 to line 57 – as 'a remarkable instance of thinking by synecdoche'. Such an estimate is confirmed for Bloom by Wordsworth's sudden shifts (line 42) from the first person to collective pronouns. This alteration lasts until line 49, after which Wordsworth's synecdochic identification gives way. At this point the poet falls back to 'being a solitary or mutilated part of a universal whole'. Bloom adds: 'This passage into and out of the universal is determined, in my interpretation, by the poem's largely hidden, revisionary struggle with two great precursor-texts, the invocations to Books III and VII of *Paradise Lost*' (PR, p.70).

Bloom finds confirmation of this intratextual, hidden agon with Milton in what he calls 'the curiously placed figuration of the Hermit' (PR, p.70). Bloom associates the solitary hermit with the hermit who 'appears at the close of *Il Penseroso*', a poem Bloom describes as 'the true start for Wordsworth as Pilgrim and Wanderer' (PR, p.71). He adds that 'This Hermit [Milton's] first *hears* an immortal music and only then has a vision of heaven', and this structure of emphasising the faculty of visionary hearing over sight is greatly reinforced in the next important figuration of the poem, contained in lines 23–5. Bloom associates the mist which Wordsworth sees rising from above the woods with the 'mist that Milton prays be purged from his mind'. This connection is strengthened as Bloom moves on to Wordsworth's figuration of memory in terms of the antithetical image of 'a landscape to a blind man's eye'. Bloom asks: 'Need we question who this blind man is?' (PR, pp.72–3).

Through an intratextual association between this solitary hermit, the figure of blindness and the blind bard of the Invocations in *Paradise Lost*, Bloom is able to unravel a host of issues revolving round the fear-of-writing/desire-for-voicing oppositions. Wordsworth, Bloom argues, wishes to return to a scene of instruction in which he can be 'taught or re-taught primarily through the ear (as the later Milton was)' (PR, p.76). The figuration of blindness, as a trope for Miltonic voicing, confirms this desire. Yet the poem shows Wordsworth submitting to a written landscape: a landscape which throws back to him his own rejected dependence on Miltonic writing, and thus instills a *fear of writing* in the poet (see PR, pp.76–7).

Bloom goes on to assert that, in the concluding section of the poem, as he turns to his sister Dorothy and thinks of her future, Wordsworth retropes the blindness/insight opposition:

> If I should be where I no more can hear
> Thy voice, nor catch from thy wild eyes these gleams
> Of past existence.[12]

The result of this retroping of the trope of blindness, and the opposition between voicing and writing it generates, is that Wordsworth completes the repressive process whereby memory comes to replace self-presence and the presence of the object-world. 'The power of Miltonic transumption is worked again', Bloom argues; 'defensively Wordsworth introjects the past, projects the future except as a world for Dorothy, and utterly destroys the present moment, the living time in which he no longer stands' (PR, p.78). Bloom's account of the poem concludes with the sense of a final movement away from a natural world which has become overwritten by the writing of the Miltonic sublime. Projecting into the landscape before him his repressed desire to supplant the blind bard Milton, Wordsworth has become blind. The 'strength' of the poem is located firmly in its negative power, the absence within it of any subject save for Wordsworth's own future poetic power.

Having followed Bloom's reading through to its end, I want now to turn to its most crucial section: the interpretation of the trope of blindness and its relation to what Bloom calls Wordsworth's fear of writing/desire for voicing. I want, in fact, to concentrate on two startling instances of *blindness* in Bloom's own reading.

Readers of my account of Bloom's interpretation of lines 15–25 will have already noted a striking omission. Where, in Bloom's reading, are the 'hedge-rows', the 'pastoral farms', and most importantly, since they are an equal candidate for the 'wreaths of smoke' made so much of by Bloom, 'the vagrant dwellers in the houseless woods'? The answer, of course, is that they have disappeared from Bloom's account.

The second striking blindness in Bloom's reading involves an earlier textual problem in any interpretation of 'Tintern Abbey', namely its title: 'Lines written a few miles above Tintern Abbey, on revisiting the banks of the Wye during a tour, July 13, 1798'. Bloom remarks: 'Wordsworth's title for the poem is deceptively casual, or rather this immensely ambitious poem is deceptively left untitled, since the title proper is the throw-away *Lines*' (PR, p.68). Why does Bloom feel the need to evacuate from his reading so much of the actual imaged landscape in lines 15–25, and why does he need so blatantly to reduce the title to the deceptive one-word 'Lines'?

Addressing the question of the poem's title, Marjorie Levinson, in her 'Insight and oversight: Reading "Tintern Abbey" ',[13] highlights the set of anniversaries which are at once invoked and yet deferred in the dating of the poem. She reminds her readers that the date of the poem, 'July 13, 1798, marked almost to the day the nine year anniversary of the original Bastille Day (the eight year anniversary of Wordsworth's first visit to France), and the five-year anniversary of the murder of Marat, also the date of Wordsworth's first visit to Tintern Abbey'.[14] The five years which separate Wordsworth's first and second visits to the Wye valley mark the period of Wordsworth's and Coleridge's loss of commitment to revolutionary politics. They mark a period of general alienation and government-led persecution of those British radicals who had supported the revolution; years which mark the crushing disappointment of the declaration of war with France, as well as the equally crushing disappointments of the turn of events in France itself. Despite the upturns in Wordsworth's personal life, with respect to financial matters and his friendship with Coleridge and life with Dorothy, the five-year period represents a time in which it became extremely dangerous for authors with radical ideals to write.[15]

Levinson's point in referring to the various personal and public anniversaries which collected for Wordsworth around the dates 13/14 June 1798, is to recuperate the historical contexts within which Wordsworth's return to the Wye valley occurs. She argues that it is only when we remember these historical contexts that we will understand what it is that the poet is seeking for in the landscape.[16]

Such a reading offers up an alternative understanding of what it might mean to style it as Wordsworth's staged scene of instruction. As she writes: 'Before embarking on an estrangement that would objectify his political status at home, Wordsworth would secure his birthright as an Englishman – the paternal blessing, so to speak'.[17]

That impending literal estrangement is, of course, the planned voyage with Coleridge to Germany; a voyage from which, at that point, neither poet could know whether they would return. This impending departure determines much of the meaning of the last section of the poem: a section which, once again, displaces sociopolitical contexts – Coleridge and Wordsworth were departing because of political pressures – into a scene of election within an aestheticised nature. More importantly still, Levinson's interrogation of the title begins to reactivate the specific socio-political contexts which determine Wordsworth's figuration of nature and his place within it. Wordsworth, after the tempestuous years since 1789, and particularly after the spiritually and politically disturbing five years within counter-revolutionary Britain, seeks for confirmation of his relationship to a realm of truth and identity outside of the scene of writing, the contemporary world of ideological conflict. What Wordsworth actually finds in the Wye valley near Tintern Abbey, however, is a nature radically *marked* by social and political conflict.

Levinson, concentrating on the first section of the poem, emphasises the fact that behind the apparent images of natural beauty lies a landscape scarred by industrialisation and by socioeconomic displacement.[18] Wordsworth, as in the opening book of *The Prelude*, having escaped 'from the din/Of towns and cities', returns not to a scene of natural 'restoration', but to a nature exhibiting dramatically the marks of social and political crisis. Wishing to escape from the scene of writing (the social world symbolised at this time by London), Wordsworth discovers the scene of writing in nature. Whereas, for Bloom, the poet's eyes are met with the anxiety inducing writing of the repressed precursor, in Levinson's reading they are met with the anxiety inducing 'writing' of sociopolitical struggle and crisis. In both readings, Wordsworth's reaction is to embrace a form of blindness; a blindness (repression) of external nature which the poet wishes to convince its readers brings a compensatory and more lasting insightfulness. In both readings, the poem's adoption of memory as its dominant motif represents a defence against the disturbing writing inscribed onto the phenomenal surface of nature. Levinson suggests that 'a land stripped of its sacred spots offers the individual no escape from the social body and the historical moment'.[19] Wordsworth rededicates (refigures) the Wye valley through a series of poetic acts of exclusion and 'memorialisation'. He does this, according to Levinson, through an act of blindness which transforms the scene of writing into a scene of instruction and election. From this perspective, Bloom would have to be seen as more fundamentally blind than Wordsworth, since, although in Wordsworth's text the scene of writing remains negatively articulated through its problematical title and its complex images and figures, Bloom's reading takes these images and figures at face value and then submits them to a further process of internalisation and 'memorialisation'. It almost seems as if Bloom's reading is a staged agon with 'Tintern Abbey'; a scene of instruction in which the critic attempts to achieve greater poetic 'strength' by internalising the meaning of the poem more severely than the author does himself.

Are Bloom's and Levinson's readings mutually exclusive? What happens if we do not completely reject the Bloomian assertion that the poem exhibits a scene of instruction in which Wordsworth negotiates a covert identification with and defence against Miltonic writing? My answer is that such a position begins to demonstrate the interimplication of the scene of instruction and the scene of writing. To explain what I mean by this and why it should be so I shall explore further the issue of the trope of blindness and its relation to the central opposition of a fear of writing/desire for voicing.

A major problem in assessing Bloom's reading of 'Tintern Abbey' concerns the fact that the figurations of the hermit and of blindness do not in themselves foreground their Miltonic source. To judge Bloom's reading of 'Tintern Abbey' we are inevitably led *outside* the text itself towards other texts, related either in terms of the date of composition or of subject-matter and/or figurative texture.

Bloom employs Wordsworth's 'Prospectus' to *The Recluse* as a textual confirmation of his reading of 'Tintern Abbey'. If we look at the 'Prospectus' we can see why it should substantiate for Bloom his 'antithetical' reading of the tropes of blindness and of the hermit in 'Tintern Abbey'. This text, composed soon after Wordsworth's arrival at Dove Cottage in late 1799, is, as Bloom points out, a great expression of internalisation. Wordsworth's subjects, as he tells us in the first two lines, are 'Man, Nature, and . . . human life', subjects contemplated 'in solitude'.[20] This declaration of internalised vision immediately leads Wordsworth on to a restaging of the scene of instruction with Milton ('Pros'. ll.12–40). One can understand why for Bloom this should be Wordsworth's greatest expression of poetic 'strength'. The Miltonic sublime, with its representation of the War in Heaven, is invoked by Wordsworth only in order to be superseded by Wordsworth's more sublime, naturalistic subject of the 'individual mind':

> The darkest pit
> Of the profoundest hell, night, chaos, death,
> Nor aught of blinder vacancy scooped out
> By help of dreams, can breed such fear and awe
> As fall upon me when I look
> Into my soul, into the soul of man,
> My haunt, and the main region of my song.
>
> ('Pros'. ll.23–9)

This whole passage appears to confirm how closely Wordsworth's sense of his election to poetry (Writing) was bound up with a figurative negotiation with Miltonic blindness. Miltonic blindness/insight is agonistically reversed here. Wordsworth presents himself, with his new, naturalistic subject, as more profoundly blind to external influences than Milton – who remained caught within a world framed by the *outward* forms of religion and myth. Yet this intenser form of blindness is predicated on a naturalistic ethos which allows Wordsworth to present his vision as more 'wedded to this outward frame of things' ('Pros'. l.39). Wordsworth is at once 'blinder' and yet possessed of more 'vision' than Milton. He is more profoundly isolated in his poetic stance than Milton; yet he is more profoundly connected to the naturalistic source of all true human values (see 'Pros'. ll.6–7).

A reading of the 'Prospectus', therefore, confirms Wordsworth's centring of his agon with Milton on figurations of solitude, and especially on the trope of blindness. We might also refer at this point to the episode, in Book III of *The Prelude*, of Wordsworth's drunken desecration of the sacred site of Milton's room at Cambridge. In this episode the young poet appears first to experience the complexities of poetic election, with its combined elements of veneration and rebellion. Before relating the episode, Wordsworth introduces Milton:

> Yea, our blind Poet, who, in his later day,
> Stood almost single; uttering odious truth,
> Darkness before, and danger's voice behind –
> Soul awful, if the earth hath ever lodged
> An awful soul – I seemed to see him here
> Familiarly, and in his scholar's dress
> Bounding before me, yet a stripling youth –
> A boy, no better, with his rosy cheeks
> Angelical, keen eye, courageous look,
> And conspicuous step of purity and pride.[21]

Once again Wordsworth presents us with a scene of instruction and election in which Miltonic writing inscribes itself on the phenomenal surface of his immediate environment. Wordsworth's quest for signs of his own poetic vocation are again bound up in a figuration of the Miltonic tropes of blindness and insight. Indeed, this allusion to the early visionary Milton, figuratively 'child' to the visionary 'father'-bard, is a transumptive reworking of Wordsworth's own personal history as presented in 'Tintern Abbey':

> And so I dare to hope,
> Though changed, no doubt, from what I was when first
> I came among these hills: when like a roe

> I bounded o'er the mountains, by the sides
> Of the deep rivers, and the lonely streams,
> Wherever nature led; more like a man
> Flying from something that he dreads, than one
> Who sought the thing he loved.
>
> (TA. ll.66–73)

The trope of blindness, as the relation between these two passages demonstrates, is Wordsworth's way of figuring forth what is particularly important for him in Milton: his visionary and prophetic isolation in a bad time. Milton, for Wordsworth, stands in an exemplary position, with literal 'darkness before' and 'danger's voice behind'. What is crucial is Milton's example as a republican poet who, in a dangerous time politically, shows all subsequent poets how to resolve the tension between a commitment to radical ideas and the very immediate dangers such a commitment holds. The resolution is centred in the opposition between blindness and insight. It involves a movement of the eyes away from the immediate world of ideological conflict to the timeless realm of Writing, as contained in Nature and 'the hearts/Of mighty poets' ('Pros'. ll.57–8). The trope of blindness is pitted directly against the blindness of contemporary society. A move from the scene of writing to the scene of instruction or Writing is figuratively presented as a passage from spiritual blindness to literal blindness, from externalised vision to internalised vision, from a vision of literal writing to a vision of Writing.

What is important in all this is both that Wordsworth's various stagings of a scene of instruction and election with Milton appear to be directly determined by what we must call a fear of writing – fear of his position within and fear of the actual nature of the scene of writing – and, equally, that in recognising this fact we begin to perceive a whole range of interrelated contexts and meanings related to the trope, or rather the tropes, of blindness.

Wordsworth's fear of writing is a complex subject, which I can hardly begin to do justice to here. Peter de Bolla alludes to the poet's literal fear of the activity of writing.[22] Wordsworth's 'Letter to the Bishop of Llandaff', written in 1793 but unpublished because of fear of prosecution, makes it quite clear what other fear, apart from personal attacks (physical or legal) and psychological eccentricities, an author should have for his and for others' writing. Discussing the effects of the bishop's published protest against the execution of Louis XVI, Wordsworth explains his reason for composing a counter-statement: 'Sensible how large a portion of mankind receive opinions upon authority, I am apprehensive lest the doctrines which they will find there should derive a weight from your name to which they are by no means intrinsically intitled.'[23] This issue, of the public's susceptibility to ephemeral or wrong-headed or simply pernicious writing, was one to which Wordsworth returned in the 'Preface' of 1800. Defending his attempt to 'follow the fluxes and refluxes of the mind when agitated by the great and simple affections of our nature', Wordsworth writes of the 'multitude of causes, unknown to former times, [which] are now acting with a combined force to blunt the discriminating powers of the mind, and unfitting it for all voluntary exertion to reduce it to a state of almost savage torpor'. Listing these 'causes', he begins with the 'great national events which are daily taking place', moves on to 'the increasing accumulation of men in cities' with its tendency to 'uniformity of . . . occupations' producing 'craving for extraordinary incident', before fixing on 'the rapid communication of intelligence' which 'hourly gratifies' such unnatural cravings. Having established this babel-like social context, Wordsworth then goes on to find the same disintegration of order and significance reflected in the literary scene. Shakespeare and Milton ('The invaluable works of our elder writers'), he writes, have been 'driven into neglect' by 'frantic novels, sickly and stupid German tragedies, and deluges of idle and extravagant stories in verse'.[24]

In his essay 'The historical text as literary artifact', Hayden White recollects hearing Geoffrey Hartman remark that he did not quite understand what literary historians wanted to do, but that he did know that 'history meant to place an event within a context, by relating it as a part to some conceivable whole'. As far as he [Hartman] knew, White continues, 'there were only two ways of relating parts to whole, by metonymy and by synecdoche'.[25] Such an opposition is in itself, of course, an ahistorical feature of language. However, as Raman Selden reminds us, discussing Jakobson's work on the clearly related opposition between metaphor and metonymy, such binary oppositions can become 'a valuable piece of conceptual equipment' when we begin to recognise the manner in which 'particular artistic forms [or in our case particular artists working within particular discursive formations] lean towards one or other figure'.[26] There is an increasing tendency in Wordsworth's 'great period' towards a representation of the scene of writing (the social realm) in terms of metonymic figures. Balancing this, we can discover a tendency to represent an alternative, synecdochic context: the scene of instruction, containing 'the invaluable works of our elder writers' (what we would nowadays call 'the canon'). The trope(s) of blindness plays a crucial role in such an opposition between writing and Writing. This opposition is not simply an opposition between modes of literary writing, but, as the 'Preface' passage shows, between alternative contexts (social contexts, particularly the city of London compared to Nature: scenes of political and social crisis contrasted to the visionary realm of timeless 'human nature'). Wordsworth cannot, despite his intentions, keep these contexts, these figured scenes, separate.

Wordsworth's most complete depiction of the scene of writing can be found in Book VII of *The Prelude*. As Neil Hertz has shown, Wordsworth represents London as a realm dominated by a repetitious mode of textuality.[27] In his essay on the sublime, Hertz concentrates on the following passage:

> Rise up, thou monstrous ant-hill on the plain
> Of a too busy world! Before me flow,
> Thou endless stream of men and moving things!
> Thy every-day appearance, as it strikes –
> With wonder heightened, or sublimed by awe –
> On strangers, of all ages; the quick dance
> Of colours, lights, and forms; the deafening din;
> The comers and the goers face to face,
> Face after face; the string of dazzling wares,
> Shop after shop, with symbols, blazoned names,
> And all the tradesman's honours overhead:
> Here, fronts of houses, like a title-page,
> With letters huge inscribed from top to toe;
> Stationed above the door, like guardian saints,
> There, allegoric shapes, female or male,
> Or physiognomies of real men.
> Land-warriors, kings, or admirals of the sea,
> Boyle, Shakespeare, Newton, or the attractive head
> Of some quack doctor, famous in his day.
>         Meanwhile the roar continues, till at length,
> Escaped as from an enemy, we turn
> Abruptly into some sequestered nook,
> Still as a sheltered place when winds blow loud!
>
> (P.VII., 1850, ll.149–71)[28]

The city is perceived as a 'vast' accumulation of impressions. The poet enters the city and is *struck* by a 'quick dance' and a 'deafening din'. Wordsworth is struck by a plethora of sensations which appear to 'flow' like water. The city, indeed, is a perfect example of Wordsworth's sense of the despotism of the eye: he is struck through the eye by an environment that is in a very real sense *all writing*. It is as much as the poet can do to offer some limited catalogue of impressions: the city is one vast accumulative writing, overwhelming and destroying any possibility of voice, of *voicing*.

The dominant metaphor in the last four lines of the passage is the familiar Wordsworthian image of a perceived 'roar' of 'rolling waters'; an image or trope which usually accompanies Wordsworth's temporary achievements of vision and which clearly relates to the emphasis on 'hearing' in such moments (see, for example, TA. ll.93–111 and the Snowdon ascension in P.XIII ll.45–65). The 'roar' that comes from the city is the antithesis of such a natural 'motion' and 'spirit'. It is neither 'anchor' nor 'guide' nor 'guardian'. Far from constituting an external power which can activate a 'correspondent' internal power, the city offers an external 'roar' or 'din' that floods, that drowns, that overwhelms. As Hertz writes: 'In London, more than in the country, everybody's experience is mediated by the semiotic intentions of others', so that 'it is not that differences disappear, but that the possibility of interpreting them as significant differences vanishes'.[29]

We seem, then, to have a situation in which the city threatens to destroy the poetic imagination in an antithetical manner to that restoration which is supposed to be offered by Wordsworthian nature. The timeless 'roar' of waters associated with the 'One mind' behind Wordsworthian nature is, as it were, mocked or parodied in London by a 'roar' emanating from a temporal, historical ocean of forms. As Hertz suggests, what Wordsworth learns in London is a process of reduction or framing – a fixation on a specular double or 'object' standing synecdochically for the 'Whole'. This process of reduction or framing parallels the kind of romance of identification Wordsworth practices in nature. Wordsworth begins to attain such an identification or framing in an episode which involves another complex deployment of the trope of blindness: the shocking and sublime encounter with the blind beggar.

The blind beggar is a human being who is all writing: he is at once the product of a scene of writing (London) and a written sign for the poet. He *writes* himself on the mind of Wordsworth. And yet, as the author of himself, as the writer of his own text (the text of his own 'self'), the figure possesses a form of identity, presence and knowledge which illustrates the ability of written signs to become a Sign. Such a sublime particular allows for a crossing from the scene of writing to the eternalised Writing (types) associated with voice or voicing (P.VII. ll.608–23).

Wordsworth's fear of writing in London involves a fear of being engulfed by a metonymic, repetitious realm in which no sign remains fixed, in which contingency reigns. Escape from this contemporary scene of writing to the realm of Writing is, once again, achieved with the aid of the trope of blindness. Such a structural movement from the scene of writing to the scene of Writing (Instruction) seems to be at the heart of the dream symbolism in Book V of *The Prelude*; Wordsworth's most sustained account of his fears concerning the material and temporal fragility of writing ('shrines so frail').

In his dream Wordsworth again experiences a scene of instruction/ election. The Arab or 'semi-Quixote', appearing out of the desert, seems without doubt to be 'a guide/To lead [him] through the desart' (P.V. ll.82–3). What this figure teaches Wordsworth can be said to be the importance of election or dedication to the protection of Writing. How Writing can be protected or saved is the 'lesson' of the dream: a dream which presents us with an act of continuity (burying the books) performed in the context of a lateral or synchronic apocalypse or catastrophe in which the 'fleet waters of a drowning world' (P.V. l.136) threaten to engulf the fragile continuity of textual tradition in an oceanic deluge.[30] Once again a polarity between a contingent or metonymic world (again, as in the written space of London, parodying the 'roar' of visionary Nature) and a transcendent world of synecdochic and/or metaphorical identification is mediated by figurations of solitude and the blindness/insight (hearing) opposition. Wordsworth sees the impending flood, while he hears the 'loud prophetic blast of harmony' coming from the shell-book. The act of burying the books is an act of internalisation, which hides them and protects them from the material, visible world. The entire dream rests on an ability to transcend the appearances of things towards a visionary perception:

> I wondered not, although I plainly saw
> The one to be a stone, th' other a shell,
> Nor doubted once but that they both were books.
>
> (P.V. ll.111–13)

This passage dramatises again the movement from a metonymic to a synecdochic and/or metaphorical context and concludes in a declaration of election to a state of visionary isolation from the contemporary world, the scene of writing (P.V. ll.153–65).

In all the passages I have referred to there is a general working through of Wordsworth's complex fear of and about writing. The passages demonstrate Wordsworth's development of a compensatory logic in which an anxiousness about his position within the scene of writing is mediated by the possibility of election to and protection within the scene of Instruction or Writing. Wordsworth, in *The Prelude* and the 'great period' poems, helps to inaugurate that 'Romantic' process in which the tradition is figured, to redeploy McGann's phrase, as a realm 'immune from the sufferings of history and time'. Such an ideology depends, of course, on the belief that the two contexts – the scene of writing and the scene of Instruction or Writing – can be kept separate. Wordsworth's greatest fear concerning his own writing seems to be that it necessarily belongs to both contexts at once. The only way in which Wordsworth can protect himself from the scene of writing is to write (to enter into that scene). This paradox is summed up in the theme of the fragility of 'immortal verse' in Book V, the dream passages concluding with an image of writing's simultaneous existence within the temporal and the timeless (see P.V. ll.161–5).

Such a recognition of the interimplication of the scene of writing and the scene of instruction or Writing is the principal subject of the second half of the 'Prospectus'. Contemplating the inevitability of a continuing perception of social (human) suffering in nature as well as in urban environments ('Pros'. ll.46–51), Wordsworth, again playing on the opposition between sight and hearing, develops a compensatory sense of his election to a timeless realm of 'wisdom'. A Bloomian reading seems particularly suited to the set of images and covert allusions through which this comparison between contexts is developed. The image of Wordsworth 'Brooding above the fierce confederate storm/Of sorrow' ('Pros'. ll.49–50) seems to mark, after the overt agon with Milton, an internalisation (transumption) of Milton's grand opening self-representation in *Paradise Lost*:

> Thou from the first
> Wast present, and with mighty wings outspred
> Dove-like satst brooding on the vast Abyss
> And mad'st it pregnant: What in me is dark
> Illumin, what is low raise and support;
> That to the highth of this great Argument
> I may assert Eternal Providence,
> And justifie the ways of God to men.[31]

Following Milton as Republican poet, Wordsworth's 'vast Abyss', becomes the 'confederate storm' of a counter-revolutionary age. Following his own construction of Milton as blind, prophetic instructor, his response is to attempt an ascension to a transcendent tradition of Writing, providing a permanent instruction to future generations. To retain his commitment to human society, Wordsworth must follow the example of Milton and become blind to its immediate appearance. The conclusion of the poem is a direct request for instruction and election, made to an ambiguous instructor first addressed as

> prophetic spirit, soul of man,
> Thou human soul of the wide earth, that hast
> Thy metropolitan temple in the hearts
> Of mighty poets.
>
> ('Pros'. ll.55–8)

and later 'O great God' ('Pros'. l.71) and 'Innocent mighty spirit' ('Pros'. l.73). A Bloomian reading would unmask this variously nominated instructor as Milton, taking this as evidence of Wordsworth's struggle for poetic 'strength' with his great poetic precursor. The allusions to the opening of *Paradise Lost*, and the dependence once again on the blindness/insight, seeing/hearing oppositions, would seem to confirm Wordsworth's covert revisionism of Milton. Yet attending to the juxtaposition of potential contexts – Wordsworth's request to be instructed in how to 'discern' beyond a realm of casual relationships to the permanent, inherent relationships and identities behind them – it is clear that what also determines the meaning is Wordsworth's negotiation of the position of his poetry within the socio-political realm, the scene of writing. The meaning of the passage lies in the attempt to sustain radical commitment to human liberty while defending against a specific and historically determined fear of writing. It is determined by Wordsworth's management of the relationship between literature and the sociopolitical realm, his negotiation between the scene of writing and the scene of instruction (Writing).

For a Bloomian reading of the passage to work we would have to take the impact of the Miltonic sublime as a given; beginning with the assumption that literary tradition is a pre-set realm into which Wordsworth is attempting to force his way. In this way we could attend to the scene of instruction without reference to the scene of writing. The passage itself, however, demonstrates the fact that Wordsworth remains less blind to the interrelation of the two scenes than his critical ephebe. The tradition is being constructed in texts such as the 'Prospectus', just as the social realm is being constructed through the deployment of various figurative frames. Indeed, the construction of the scenes of writing and instruction (Writing) depends on rhetorical oppositions which establish their mutual interdependence. Wordsworth's text presents us with perhaps the most complete image for the poet's position between writing and Writing, between the sociohistorical and the literary: the image of the borderer ('Pros'. ll.69–70).

To return then, at last, to 'Tintern Abbey'. Bloom may well be correct in his interpretation of the tropes of the hermit and of blindness as covert allusions to Milton. The trope of blindness does appear to be a dominant figure in Wordsworth's quest for signs of election, and it does appear to be specifically related to Wordsworth's conception of Milton as the exemplary member of the scene of instruction/ Writing. Where Bloom remains blind is in his insistence that the intratextual agon such covert (at times overt) allusions display determines the meaning of the poems. The scene of instruction or Writing to which Wordsworth constantly turns is at best half created and half perceived. It remains inextricably tied to Wordsworth's defensive responses to the scene of writing and has its significance in that context. Milton's blindness has significance for Wordsworth because of its symbolic relation to his fear of writing, his specific reaction to the historical moment in which he lived and wrote. The disturbing confrontation with social, economic and political crisis in the Wye valley which the opening of the poem negatively articulates seems to provide another example of metonymic figurations of the scene of writing. Which is to say that if, at the beginning of 'Tintern Abbey', Wordsworth encounters a nature marked and marred by visible inscriptions, they characteristically take the form of metonymic relations. The 'wreaths of smoke' signify to the poet two competing causes which have only a contingent relationship to each other and thus form an 'uncertain notice'. Once again, visible displays of the metonymic scene of writing provoke the necessity for an election, via the trope of blindness, to a scene of instruction or Writing. We should remember here Bloom's description of lines 36–49 as a 'remarkable instance of thinking by synecdoche'.

As Nicholas Roe has argued, it is important to understand the manner in which historical events and the public and private responses to such events affected Milton's reputation as a poet in Britain in the years prior to and subsequent to the French revolution.[32] Roe's account of Wordsworth's estimate of Milton runs from Milton's 'enhanced reputation as a republican during the revolutionary years and especially after the declaration of the French Republic in September 1792',[33] to the period 'Between 1793 and 1800 [when] Wordsworth moved from republican fellowship with Milton to creative competition in his "Prospectus" '.[34] Roe's account might be said to underplay slightly the ambivalence in Wordsworth's identification/ agon with Milton in this later period. However, it is generally a salutary reminder that Milton's importance to Wordsworth depends on the latter poet's responses as a writer to the political and social turmoil of his day and, also, that the figure of Milton was a socially significant one in Britain prior to and after 1789. If identification or antagonism towards Milton and the Miltonic sublime became a central facet of what we nowadays call Romanticism in Britain, then it did so, not because Milton was the inevitable precursor, but because the social and aesthetic significance of his poetry became a crucial point of convergence for modes of discourse (poetry, criticism, the novel) developing in the wake of counter-revolutionary Britain.

The figure of blindness is not simply a 'Miltonic trope' or a trope on the 'Miltonic sublime'. As a major figuration in Wordsworth's poetry, it mediates between metonymic figurations of the scene of writing and synecdochic figurations of the scene of instruction/Writing. It is at once intratextual and intertextual, and can manifest the meaning of Wordsworth's poetry between text and prior poetic intertexts and between text and historically specific discursive formations.

Wordsworth's poetry helps to inaugurate the Romantic emphasis on literature and the literary tradition as a saving realm of order. It helps to establish the concept of a literary tradition which can be juxtaposed to a world of contingency, that indeterminate social world which T. S. Eliot was later to describe as the 'immense panorama of futility and anarchy which is contemporary history'.[35] Wordsworth's studied *blindness* to the scene of writing as a means of election to the scene of instruction or Writing, constitutes a major precursor for the academic canon-forming tradition: the tradition of Arnold, Eliot, Leavis; a tradition, in fact, which finds, at least in this respect, its late apotheosis in Bloom. Bloom would not be happy with this identification of his work with the line of Arnold, Eliot and Leavis. But literary tradition in his work, however deidealised, still functions as a possible escape from a world characterised by excess, by partisan and incoherent textuality. Tradition, for Bloom, still functions as a transhistorical realm of order and *meaning*. Bloom's rhetoric of excess and/ or anxiety of choice represents his repetition of that Romantic opposition between writing and Writing, which gained a seminal articulation in the poetry of Wordsworth.

CHAPTER
FIVE

Lies against time:
transumptive allusion,
diachronic rhetoric and the
question of history

## Poetic echo: substance and effect

I

Bloom's revision of traditional conceptions of rhetoric means that when we interpret a poetic (or even a critical) text we are involved in two opposing directions of reading. One direction is the attempt to establish the precise meaning within ('inside') a text; that is to say, we attend to the play between literal and figural uses of language in the text in an attempt to get the poem right, to reproduce the exact structure of the text. This is the level which corresponds to rhetoric conceived as a system of tropes. Bloom points out, however, that every attempt to represent the synchronic significance of a text, every attempt to represent the 'inside', so to speak, of a text, involves us also in a movement 'outside' its specific linguistic structure. We recognise that every pattern of significance we can detect within ('inside') a text depends on a measurement between that text and previous texts. Tropes become echoes of earlier texts.

The movement from synchronic to diachronic dimensions is thus representable as a movement from 'inside' to 'outside'. Bloom shows, however, that such terms as 'inside' and 'outside' are fundamentally insupportable. Every text, due to its dependence for meaning on other texts, has no 'inside' but is rather the product of the relationships (more specifically our measurement) between chains of rhetorical tropes and chains of poetic and critical texts. What is truly 'inside' a text is its relationship to other texts: what traditionally is conceived as a text's 'outside', its ground or context. As Bloom writes: 'To study what poems are about is to interpret their outside relationships. A "subject" is indeed under something else, and a poem's subject thus subjects the poem' (MM, p.75).

A deconstructive reading of a poetic text tends to limit us to the synchronic play of that text's finite units of signification. It denies the possibility of fixing those units in a stable and meaningful structure. Bloom argues that texts exist in a vertical as well as a horizontal dimension of meaning. A text 'means' something because of its relationship with other texts (and because of the critical reader's measurement of this relationship). A text is, for Bloom, a concept of Thirdness, and the reading of a text is an event in which meaning hovers somewhere between the three nodes involved in that triadic relationship: the text itself, the tradition against which it tropes itself into being, the interpretation of this relationship by the 'strong' (mis)reader.

Bloom's point is that every poetic trope stands in a diachronic relationship with past tropes, a relationship which need not in any way be signalled on the surface level of the text. The question becomes then, confronting for instance the 'trope of the leaves' in Wallace Stevens's poem 'The course of a particular', to what past instance of this particular trope is the Stevensian example directing itself? In his essay 'Transumption' (BV, pp.73–107) Bloom renews his discussion of the poetic trope of the leaves, studied formerly in chapter 7 of *A Map of Misreading*.[1] According to Bloom, Stevens's poem represents a modern reiteration and revision of a tradition of troping the leaves which stretches back to Homer and the Old Testament.

To speak of the 'trope of the leaves' when reading 'The Course of a Particular' is clearly a rather strange use of the word trope, which traditionally has been associated with certain forms of language use, such as metaphor and metonymy. Yet, as Peter de Bolla explains in discussing the 'Aeolian trope' as located by Bloom in Coleridge's 'France: An ode', the word trope undergoes a form of substitutive transformation or tropism when employed by Bloom; a transformation which explains why Bloom asserts that 'Any critic necessarily tropes or turns the concept of trope in giving a reading of a specific poem' (BF, p.10). As de Bolla writes, the 'Aeolian trope' is 'a principle of organisation of poetic discourse, a trope in the sense of a principle of substitution which determines the specific language of this poem ["France: An ode"]'. He goes on to explain that Bloom 'wants us to understand that what "figures" this text is a trope in the same way that metaphor might be understood as determining the specificity of an utterance'.[2]

De Bolla's allusion to 'figure' is crucial here. The 'trope of the leaves' in the Stevens poem involves various traditional forms of trope as it progresses through the poem, passing from irony through metaphor and hyperbole to metalepsis, or so Bloom would have us understand the figurative process involved. Yet the only way in which we can associate the various occurrences of the cry of the leaves to the more traditional forms of trope (irony, metaphor, metalepsis) is to relate each instance to a prior use of the same trope of the leaves 'outside' of the poem. We have to proceed, in a movement now familiar, from a reading of the patterns of misprision 'within' the poem to the scene of instruction staged by the poem's act of misprision.

De Bolla explains that Bloom's use of trope, when discussing such issues as the 'fiction of the leaves' (to employ the phrase Bloom appropriates from Stevens's 'The rock'), pertains to what were traditionally styled 'figures of thought' as opposed to the various forms of 'figures of words'. This is a distinction which leads us to the difference between tropes as swerves from literal language (synchronic) and tropes as the products of willed acts of revision (tropes of tropes – diachronic). As a figure of thought, Bloom's notion of trope becomes an aspect of poetic desire.

De Bolla produces a scheme whereby the synchronic form of the trope is conceived as a 'first-order trope', while the diachronic form is understood as a 'second-order trope'. The difference between these two categories of trope is that while the first-order trope is a swerve from literal usage, the second-order trope is a swerve away from a previous trope.

When reading 'The course of a particular', particularly when reading the 'trope of the leaves' which constitutes its specific rhetorical mode of organisation, we are involved in a tracing of that trope in its various mutations back to a former instance of the 'trope of the leaves' on which it is performing its diachronic, second-order tropism or turning. A certain measurement between the trope in Stevens's poem and its appearance in the prior context is, according to Bloom's theory, *the meaning* of Stevens's employment of the 'fiction of the leaves' and thus, ultimately, of the poem as a whole.

Yet how do we discover the 'outside' (context) towards which Stevens' tropism is directed? This problem takes us back to the theme of the critic's vacillation between empirical reification and dialectical ironisation. Bloom's framing of the diachronic tradition within which the poem exists and has meaning, the list of poetic instances of the 'trope of the leaves' supplied by Bloom (Milton, Shelley, Whitman, *et al.*), is, no matter how persuasive it may appear to his readers, his own invention. As Hollander writes: 'like all phenomena of this sort, we must always wonder what our own contribution was – how much we are always being writers as well as readers of what we are seeing'.[3]

Another question emerges at this point. If the notion of a diachronic rhetoric, and the accompanying notion of transumptive allusion, necessarily involves the interpreter in an arbitrary (in the sense of belated) act of imposition, closure and/or critical persuasion, how is it possible to retain the element of intentionality in our assessment of such apparent acts of poetic rhetoric and allusion?

Hollander spends some considerable time in explaining why and how the notion of transumptive allusion relies on an interpretative assumption concerning intentional acts of poetic will.[4] In his discussion of 'Echo Metaphorical', Hollander distinguishes between quotation, allusion and echo, establishing a cline in which a steady decrease in what we normally would style authorial intention accompanies any progression from the former to the latter. The idea of 'echo' leads out towards the post-structuralist account of intertextuality, a concept which, in some of its guises, posesses a key role in the deconstruction of such traditional metaphysical ideas as the authorial 'subject' and authorial will or intent.

While 'allusion', in Hollander's cline, does not have the direct sense of intention which is traditionally associated with the concept of quotation, it appears to find its location *between* the traditional ideas of intentionality ascribed to quotation, the forms of uncertainty with regard to intention which inhere within the concept of 'echo', and the post-structuralist version of that term: intertextuality. Hollander states: 'one cannot . . . allude unintentionally . . . an inadvertent allusion is a kind of solecism'.[5] Clearly, the concept of intentionality in allusion and echo is inextricably tied to the ability to be able to fix the potential source of an allusion, the ability to interpret a potential intertext as *the* (intended) source. If we can so fix the source of a transumptive echo or allusion, we can equally reincorporate the language of intentionality, whether this has for its focus an author's conscious or various unconscious symbolic actions. Bloom's desire is directed towards such a fixing of origins and sources, and thus such a reassertion of the concept of authorial will and/or intentionality. Yet, as we are observing here, Bloom remains aware of the problems involved in such an interpretative procedure. Bloom states that a trope is 'either the will translating itself into a verbal act or figure of *ethos*, or else the will failing to translate itself and so abiding as a verbal desire or figure of *pathos*'. He adds: 'But, either way, the trope *is* a figure of will rather than a figure of knowledge. The trope is a cut or gap made into the anteriority of language, itself an anteriority in which "language" acts as a figurative substitution for time' (WS, p.393).

To cut the poetic trope loose from its relation to a specific past trope or determinate series of tropes denies the performative nature of poetic rhetoric, leaving the nature of that rhetoric open to the deconstructive assertion of the priority of language over the psychological and poetic will. Clearly a diachronic conception of the trope relies on a determinate chain of relationships between signifying units. As Hollander puts it: 'When we speak metaphorically of echoes between texts, we imply a correspondence between a precursor and, in the acoustical actuality, a vocal source'.[6] Yet, as Bloom recognises, the chain of tropes against which a poet such as Stevens can be said to be transumptively troping in 'The course of a particular' remains resistant to definitive determination, complete representation. This is why Bloom's examination of transumptive allusion in poets such as Stevens has led him to talk about transumptive criticism, to highlight the critical act of transumption which necessarily occurs in any interpretation of a poetic act of transumption. As Bloom writes: 'Reading a transumptive chain becomes necessarily a critical exercise in transumptive thought' (BV, p.75).

As Bloom suggests, the meaning produced in any act of diachronic rhetoric occurs in the work that such a troping performs: the *lie against time* which is diachronic rhetoric is produced by the *effect* rather than the *substance* of such transumptive chains. I want to illustrate how Bloom's theory of diachronic rhetoric relies on an understanding or interpretation of the performative *effect* produced by the determinate (and yet often, paradoxically, concealed) chain of tropes established in every poetic instance of what Bloom has called transumptive allusion. In order to do this, it is necessary to look more closely at Bloom's key concept, transumption.

## Transumption, Gnosticism, history

### I

In his essay 'Milton and his precursors' (MM, pp.125–43), Bloom associates transumption with the psychological defence mechanisms of projection and introjection. As Bloom explains, these processes are performed through the deployment of late words for early words or early words for late words. Bloom's clearest illustration of this process in Milton comes in his reading of *Paradise Lost*, Book 1, lines 283–313 (see MM, pp.130–8); a reading which provides a clear instance of the substitution of a 'late' word for an 'early' word in Milton's reference to the 'Optic Glass' of the 'Tuscan poet' (Galileo) famously discussed, before Bloom, by Dr Johnson. This form of rhetoric is, for Bloom, the most powerful weapon in the battle between the ancients and the moderns.

The manner in which transumptive tropes offer a final defence against the poetic tradition and thus against time, anteriority and otherness is encapsulated in the quotation from George Puttenham Bloom employs.[7] Puttenham defines metalepsis as the 'farrefetcher' and his notion of the fetching of further words expresses exceptionally well the rhetorical strategy Bloom discovers in *Paradise Lost* and in the poetic tradition that poem fostered. In such a strategy the poem's words are pitted against time, against all that comes between the *now* of the poet's own present moment and the origin or source of time and tradition projected by that poet. As Bloom puts it in one review: 'Such a poem swallows up an ever-early freshness as its own, and spits out all sense of belatedness, as belonging only to others.'[8] In other words, metaleptic reversal is a scheme designed to defend the poet against history.

Every poet after Milton, who is the poet in whose poetry 'temporality fully becomes identified with anxiety' (*Agon*, p.112), wishes to murder time. Bloom explains that 'Metalepsis or transumption can be described as an extended trope with a missing or weakened middle, and for Milton literary tradition is such a trope' (MM, p.139). The preternatural strength of Miltonic metalepsis resides precisely here, in the fact that the entirety of poetic tradition including the Bible itself is conceived of as a weakened middle between the divine origin and the divine, though exponentially darkened, moment in which Milton composes *Paradise Lost* (see MM, p.138).

The technique by which Milton 'murders time' depends on his transumption of particular past texts, particular past tropes; yet the effect of such a poetic practice is to defend Milton against all past text, against all tradition or fallen time. Transumption turns the orthodox and classical notion of *figura*, the form of interpretation which has its origins in the medieval development of a typological reading of the Bible, on its head. Figural interpretation, as exemplified in the work of Erich Auerbach and a number of more recent critics, works on the premiss that later writers can fulfil and complete their earlier precursors. It depends, in other words, on a fundamentally Christian notion of immanence, on the completion of the old by the new. The notion of transumption works on the basis of the inevitable priority and authority which attach to origins and the earlier manifestation of a word or thing.[9] Both *figura* and transumption are lies against time (PR, p.88); yet Bloom argues that transumption, because it foregrounds its own status as an interpretative lie against time, is a deidealised approach to the relationship between poetic texts. As Bloom puts it: 'In merest fact, and so in history, no text can fulfil another, except through some self-serving caricature of the earlier text by a later. To argue otherwise is to indulge in a dangerous idealisation . . . [to] refuse the temporal anguish of literary history' (RST, p.43). While transumption acknowledges and yet battles against what Derrida has called supplementarity, the necessary belatedness of all writing, figural interpretation remains trapped in an idealised vision, which continues to assert that texts can perform that impossible non-supplementary supplementation denied by the full recognition of the belatedness of all text.

What links Bloom's early work on transumptive allusion and his more recent development of a transumptive form of criticism is his engagement with the theory and practice of the ancient Judaeo-Christian heresy, Gnosticism. The reason why Gnosticism has proved such a suitable tradition for Bloom to plunder is perhaps clarified by Hans Jonas, Bloom's main guide in this area of ancient theology. Jonas, in his *The Gnostic Religion*, describes the unique form of interpretation engineered by Gnosticism in its reading of the sacred canon.[10] The Gnostic religion, built on the antagonism between an alien God and an evil demiurge, and paralleled by an agon between the Gnostic adept and the usurping, secondary deity of the natural universe, produces, according to Jonas, an interpretative practice, which can be designated as a form of 'shock tactics'. This interpretative practice, Jonas demonstrates, is pitted directly against the more traditional form of allegorical interpretation. The severity and audacity of this particular manifestation of the revisionary impulse is captured in the Gnostic association of Holy Scripture with the fallen and thoroughly corrupted demiurge.[11] For the Gnostics, to read the Bible is to read the work of the demiurge: to reverse the meaning of the Bible is to pass beyond the word of the demiurge back to the Alien, transmundane Godhead. It is this pattern of alien divinity, demiurge, Gnostic believer and its relation to a form of revisionary reading which so attracts Bloom. The demiurge and his texts can be said to be a 'weakened middle'; a fact which should illustrate the consonance Bloom discovers between the Gnostic worldview, Gnostic forms of misreading and his theory of transumptive criticism.

It must be said here that Bloom's analogy between Gnostic models of misreading and his theory of transumption is not a little tendentious (one must eventually say ideologically determined). Attending to the Gnostic parallels and paradigms employed by Bloom in his development of the theory of transumption highlights the manner in which he constantly seeks to pull his various critical insights into a theory of the essential, unchanging motivations for poetic utterance. A theory of motives orients Bloom's account of transumption: an account which, as the Gnostic analogies demonstrate, remains highly idiosyncratic, highly patriarchal and highly challengeable. To read Bloom's Gnostic account of transumption is, then, in a sense to read his interpretation of his own critical insight.

As we have seen, Milton's transumptive stance involves a skilful arrangement of precursor poets in a conceptual series. An arrangement of tropes which produces a kind of diachronic spatialisation of time forms the basis, in other words, for Milton's metaleptic reversals. As John Hollander remarks: transumption is that manifestation of 'interpretative or revisionary power which raises the echo even louder than the original'.[12] It is a process of interpreting past tropes which reverses the reliance (the scheme of causality) of the interpretative trope on previous texts and/or tropes. Transumption, at its most successful, produces what Hollander calls an 'ellipsis rather than a relentless pursuit, of further figuration'.[13] When made the exclusive means by which 'strong' poems achieve meaning, however, it necessarily creates a situation in which such an unnaming of the past begins to turn in on itself. The past (and nature) always seems to have the last laugh.

Certainly, if we read transumption as the process by which poems trope on past poetry, and if we read that process as the exclusive technique for the generation of poetic meaning, it becomes clear that there will eventually be far more trope than meaning. This, according to Bloom, is precisely the case and is the inevitable consequence of the kind of transumptive technique instituted by Milton. Bloom writes: 'what he [Milton] could do for himself was the cause of their [the Romantic poets] becoming unable to do the same for themselves. His achievement became at once their starting point, their inspiration, yet also their goad, their torment' (MM, pp.126–7). Transumption, as presented by Bloom, constitutes an internalised history of poetry: the history of poetry becomes equivalent to an intensification of poetic figuration and a decline in poetic meaning. This history, in other words, is centred on a dismal fact. Transumption in Bloom's hands is a phenomenon which could only be employed effectively once, at the moment of its inception. After this moment poetic history necessarily becomes a story of entropic repetition. We need to question Bloom's reading of his own critical trope of transumption. The best way in which we can do this is to look more closely at the internalised history it appears to generate and/or disclose.

II

I have referred to de Bolla's description of the Bloomian 'going beyond' of classical rhetoric as an attempt to bypass the deconstructive focus on the epistemology of the trope. As de Bolla demonstrates, this swerve from deconstructive approaches depends on making rhetoric work on both its axes. De Bolla, as I have stated, develops out of such an approach a description of the transumptive trope as a 'second-order' trope. Such a trope works within the context of a text itself (thus presenting itself as an example of one of the systematised tropes, such as metaphor, metonymy, synecdoche): it also works on a diachronic plane, being the transformation of a particular past trope, a 'first-order' trope.

A transumptive allusion or trope is a poetic lie against time, in that it transforms the tropes on which it is dependent for its meaning. As transumptive readers we, to employ de Bolla's useful terms, have to disfigure or decompose such tropes, measuring the transformations enacted between 'second-order' and 'first-order' tropes, between the transumptive trope and its tropological 'object' (the 'first-order' trope).[14]

Whenever we perform such a transumptive or disfiguring reading we are involved in the only form of literary history Bloom's own severely anti-historical criticism will sanction. Bloom's idea of what constitutes an authentic form of historicism, it should be remembered, depends upon a belief in the possibility of reading from *within* the poetic tradition. Such a mode of 'historicism' depends on a process of disfiguration or, translating the terms back into Bloomian ones, a misreading which is equally a defence and a rhetorical act of persuasion.

De Bolla does not merely help to unpack Bloom's approach to poetic rhetoric, he also helps clarify the implied transformation between Miltonic and Romantic or modern forms of transumption. It is in his distinction between metalepsis and catachresis that de Bolla offers the best opportunity for understanding the difference Bloom would have us observe between Miltonic and Romantic forms of transumption. De Bolla translates these two rhetorical terms into the opposition between *translatio* and *transgressio*.[15] He writes that the latter mode is a 'going beyond', 'a crossing in which the movement between the two domains, the proper and the improper, is only effected with some attendant disturbance'. This kind of 'crossing' or 'translation', he continues, 'cannot be carried out without supplying something that has been elided or erased in the initial crossing'. In such a situation a loss of the 'literal or primary figural base' inevitably occurs. As he writes: 'This in part explains why it is very difficult to isolate second-order tropes formed by catachresis'.[16]

Translating this distinction into the Bloomian account of Miltonic and post-Miltonic forms of transumption, we begin to understand why the trope of transumption undergoes a steady transformation in the post-Enlightenment tradition: a translation which moves such a trope from metalepsis to catachresis. From Milton's explicit arrangement of his precursors in transumptive chains, we move to the ellipsis of all precursors in modern texts. Such a movement can be seen as a translation of Bloom's earlier narrative concerning the history of poetry from pre-Enlightenment meaning to post-Enlightenment belatedness (Milton, and the steady decline after him) into a history of poetic language.

The characteristic feature of modern poetry, then, is its severity of repression, or negation; its generation of meaning through its unnaming of the tropes on which it is increasingly more dependent. No modern poem, according to Bloom, 'merely alludes to another, and what look like overt allusions and even echoes in strong poems are disguises for darker relationships. A strong authentic allusion to another strong poem can be only by and in what the later poem *does not say*, by what it represses' (BF, p.15).

What de Bolla's description of catachretic forms of figuration highlights is that in the interpretation of such forms of rhetoric the reader must 'supply' something to such poems if their transumptive tropes are to be 'disfigured' and so interpreted. This 'something' to be supplied is not merely a reconstituted first-order trope, for such a recuperation of previous tropes merely places the text within a potential or a latent, internalised history. The act of interpretation only properly begins when a measurement is made between the trope and the presumed precursor (first-order) trope. Interpretation only begins, that is, when the interpreter judges the effect of such a relationship between differently context-specific tropes.

The characteristic Bloomian interpretation of such transumptive *histories* – an interpretation which restores them to the psychology of intrapoetic relations – is in no way an inevitable interpretation of such tropological relationships. We cannot escape from the fact (the liberating fact, I would suggest) that the recuperation of such transumptive histories are the product of what Bloom, after Emerson, calls 'the reader's freedom to read'. De Bolla, for example, in analysing the relationship between the trope of desire and the trope of the body in Donne's 'A nocturnal upon St. Lucy's day' and Wordsworth's 'A slumber did my spirit steal', does not, rightly, feel the need to resort to a theory of primary precursorship and intrapoetic agonism in order to explain the relationship between these two poets and their utilisations of these two interrelated tropes.[17] Indeed, pushing the Bloomian theory of diachronic rhetoric towards a theory of properly historical rhetorics, de Bolla emphasises the historical, social and ideological contexts within which specific tropes are troped again. Such contexts, he argues, remain the fundamental criteria for a judgement of the histories internal to any specific second-order trope.[18]

De Bolla brings out the fact that, to judge the meaning of second-order tropes, we must understand the synchronic contexts within which they exist and *mean* before proceeding to compare the differences between them on the basis of such an understanding. The intratextual axis is inextricably linked to the intertextual dimension. Indeed, in making such judgements, the reader enters into the frame of such an interpretative process. The manner in which we perceive these diachronic and synchronic relationships is dependent on the relationship between our discourse, the historical (synchronic) context within which we are positioned, and the influence on that context and thus on our discourse of prior contexts, prior texts.

Bloom's refusal to historicise the *history* of transumptive allusion leads him into an interpretative impasse. Not only do his various theories appear to predetermine the entropic history of language and meaning which takes us from transumption proper to catachresis; without an ability to historicise such a process of intensifying repression and negation, Bloom is forced back on a certain literalisation of his terms. A literalisation, specifically of catachresis, which has led Bloom, in his more recent work, back towards the idealising category of originality.

Before moving on to this area, however, I shall test the points I have made concerning Bloom's account of poetic rhetoric, and particularly transumption, by examining the manner in which Bloom employs the concept in his interpretation of the poetry of Shelley.

## Counter-reading: transumption and/in history: the figure of the poet and the figure of the future in Shelley

In this section I shall demonstrate the manner in which Bloom's ahistorical understanding of his own concept transforms it from a potentially useful and incisive interpretative tool into a principle which blinds Bloom to important elements in Shelley's approach to the issue of poetic influence. I wish through this reading to argue not only that we need to use the concept of transumption to recover the historical dimensions of poetic meaning, but also that if such a concept is to be of use we must understand it as a representation of something – poets' positioning of themselves in relation to tradition – which changes radically through time. Transumption is not merely a technique for understanding the historical dimensions of literary texts, it is a literary technique which is itself subject to historical change.

Bloom's most sustained examination of transumption in Shelley's poetry comes in his 'Shelley and his precursors'.[19] Here Bloom concentrates on what he describes as 'the transumptive image proper' (PR, p.85), the Judaic trope of God as or in a chariot. This trope, the Merkabah, has its greatest representation in Ezekiel, is taken up in Revelations and then enters into a long series of revisions in the poetic tradition, from Dante through Milton to Shelley. Bloom's implicit argument is that the tradition of 'strong' poetry manifests the primacy of transumption over *figura*. This approach also allows him to produce a reduced account of the overall pattern of Shelley's poetry.

What Shelley does with the trope of the chariot comes to symbolise the complete pattern of his poetic career.

Bloom argues that Shelley's failure to revise Milton's priority with regard to this trope in *Prometheus Unbound* finally taught him the true use of such a trope – the transumptive reversal of temporal priority, the effective lying about his position (belated) within tradition. This lesson allowed him, in 'The triumph of life', to attain a limited, highly qualified, agonistic victory over his true precursor, Wordsworth. Accounting for Shelley's engagement with the transumptive trope of the chariot in this way, Bloom is able to produce a developmental narrative of Shelley's career, which hinges on his reading of Wordsworth during the winter of 1814–15 (see PR, p.105).

Bloom's reading functions as a revision of his own earlier readings of Shelley's poetry. Shelley's breakthrough into authentic poethood may come with his acceptance of Wordsworth as precursor, but Bloom argues that Shelley ultimately refused to employ the transumptive trope of the chariot against that precursor (see PR, p.109).

Bloom justifies his reading of Shelley's relation to Wordsworth by moving on to the grand conclusion of *A Defence of Poetry*, a passage I shall turn to at the conclusion of this reading. What needs to be considered here is the basic implication of Bloom's revision of his earlier estimations of Shelley's poetry. Bloom's reading asserts that poetic 'strength' must be judged in terms of the way in which poets succeed in developing a transumptive style, the manner in which they manage to transume their precursors. Bloom's reading suggests that although Shelley attained a degree of control over the trope of transumption, he never managed to exercise it successfully over the poetry of Wordsworth. However, the reader of Shelley's poetry should question this judgement. Reading 'Shelley and his precursors', we are forced to entertain the possibility that Bloom may actually be demanding something of Shelley's poetry that it cannot, indeed that it expressly will not, provide.

Such a possibility is bound up with the issue of Shelley's development of what Judith Chernaik calls 'the figure of the poet'.[20] Chernaik writes that 'The emotional power of his [Shelley's] poetry lies in his recognition of the imperatives binding upon the human being powerless to fulfil them, and dependent for what power he has on others of similar frailty'.[21] Shelley's poetry, as Bloom's own reading emphasises, centres on the question of what we might call the positionality of the figure of the poet: an ongoing analysis of the relation between the 'power' that figure is represented as having over itself, the 'power' that outward forces are represented as having over it, and the possible 'power' such a figure might exert over the world. The question which Bloom's account of Shelley and transumption raises is what kind of 'power' does Shelley come to claim for the poet and his work. G. Kim Blank, following Bloom's approach, has reasserted the benefit of analysing Shelley's 'problematic identification with the figurative authority of Wordsworth' in attempting to answer such a question.[22] Blank relies on a narrative of Shelley's career similar to the one provided by Bloom. He writes of Shelley's career as moving from 'ceremonies of baptism (the rights of admission to Wordsworth's sublime)' to 'exorcism' '(possessed by the "spirit" of Wordsworth, Shelley must free himself from Wordsworth)'. Blank continues: 'The former can be found in Shelley's earliest poetry ... the latter ... is evident in some of the poems written in his *annus mirabilis*, from autumn 1818 to early 1820'.[23]

Despite Blank's adoption of Bloomian stances, his comments reaffirm that an analysis of Shelley's direct engagements with Wordsworth's poetry provides the best answers to the question of Shelley's imagining of poetic power and poetic positionality. They also suggest that a useful strategy is to compare and contrast such textual engagements from the period of Shelley's initial reading of Wordsworth's poetry with his later return to the authority of Wordsworth.[24]

If the period around 1814–17 was a transitional one for Shelley then, as Blank demonstrates, a central text in this period becomes Shelley's 'To Wordsworth':

> Poet of Nature, thou hast wept to know
> That things depart which never may return:
> Childhood and youth, friendship and love's first glow,
> Have fled like sweet dreams, leaving thee to mourn.
> These common woes I feel. One loss is mine
> Which thou too feel'st, yet I alone deplore.
> Thou wert as a lone star, whose light did shine
> On some frail bark in winter's midnight roar:
> Thou hast like to a rock-built refuge stood
> Above the blind and battling multitude:
> In honoured poverty thy voice did weave
> Songs consecrate to truth and liberty,–
> Deserting these, thou leavest me to grieve,
> Thus having been, that thou shouldst cease to be.[25]

Although Bloom has not mapped this poem, it is possible to guess what a Bloomian reading of it would be. Such a reading would begin with a mapping of the text's play of image, defence and trope; indeed, the poem does appear to fit within the map of misprision.

The poem starts with images of presence and absence which, in their direct imitation of Wordsworth's characteristic opening move – the recognition of a missing gleam or glory – and yet their implied or latent irony, can be said to be a swerve away from the source, a *clinamen*. Focusing on the images and the rhetorical tropes, a Bloomian reading would remark on the move to synecdochic images of parts for wholes ('Childhood and youth, friendship and love's first glow'), followed by the metonymy of 'One loss' – a metonymy which forms a fine instance of what Bloom calls *kenosis*: an act of self-humbling which humbles the precursor more than the ephebe. The poem then moves on to the striking use of images of 'height' and 'depth' in lines 7–10, a hyperbole of tradition (in terms of the canonical status of the precursor) which begins to create problems in terms of the poem's management of the full movement to poetic 'strength'. Shelley's hyperbolic figuration of Wordsworth ('lone star' shining down on Shelley as ephebe within or actually as the 'frail bark in winter's midnight roar', and then again as a 'rock-built refuge' above 'the blind and battling multitude') leaves Shelley in a rather uncertain position. Shelley positions himself ambiguously between the 'multitude' and the sublime heights of the Wordsworthian precursor. His position between these two extremes ('multitude' = depths, precursor = heights) rules out, from a Bloomian perspective, a description of these lines as Shelley's attainment of a counter-sublime, since Wordsworth's pre-eminent position as guide/teacher remains unquestioned.

The reading at this point becomes rather similar to Bloom's reading of Wallace Stevens's 'The comedian as the letter c'. Failure to manage the *daemonisation* stage of the process of misprision successfully leads to an inconclusive completion of the final two stages in Bloom's map. Passing through the metaphorical (inside/outside) image of the 'weave' of 'Songs consecrate to truth and liberty', Shelley concludes his sonnet not with a final transumption of the precursor – introjecting Wordsworth's power as a property Shelley himself will now take into the future – but with a resistance to such a projection. Blank, who does present a detailed reading of this sonnet, stresses the fact that the conclusion exemplifies that element in 'Shelley's poetry about Wordsworth' in which he 'portrays the older poet as if he were dead',[26] and even more importantly stresses this as only the first stage in Shelley's ultimate resolution of the problem of Wordsworth's poetic authority. Blank describes 'To Wordsworth' as a 'clearing [of] the ground for individual expression'.[27] As a clearing of the ground

120  *Harold Bloom*

the poem may be seen as a preparation for Shelley's ultimate achievement of transumptive 'strength', but in terms of the map of misprision it does not offer us an example of that 'strength' in itself. Shelley, at the end of the poem, is left grieving for the 'dead' Wordsworth in a present moment in which his own positionality is uncertain.

This is, of course, only the first phase of a Bloomian reading of 'To Wordsworth'. Having mapped the poem we should move on to a reading in terms of Shelley's scene of instruction with Wordsworth: a reading which would involve a recuperation of the Wordsworthian tropes Shelley is retroping. Such a reading would depend on an 'antithetical' comparison of 'To Wordsworth' with various texts by Wordsworth: these would include *The Excursion*, including the 'Prospectus', and perhaps most significantly Wordsworth's own sonnet to *his* principal precursor, 'London, 1802':

> Milton! thou shoulds't be living at this hour!
> England hath need of thee: she is a fen
> Of stagnant waters; altar, sword, and pen,
> Fireside, the heroic wealth of hall and bower,
> Have forfeited their ancient English dower
> Of inward happiness. We are a selfish men;
> Oh! raise us up, return to us again;
> And give us manners, virtue, freedom, power.
> Thy soul was like a Star, and dwelt apart;
> Thou hadst a voice whose sound was like the sea:
> Pure as the naked heavens, majestic, free,
> So didst thou travel on life's common way,
> In cheerful godliness; and yet thy heart
> The lowliest duties on herself did lay.[28]

Attending to the manner in which Shelley tropes the major tropes in this sonnet helps in understanding the precise criticism Shelley is bringing to bear in his own sonnet. His transumption of Wordsworth's figuration of the positionality of Milton (the redeployment of the figures of the 'star', its separation from and yet influence on the world) establishes Shelley's play on the idea of the tradition of instruction. As Milton was Wordsworth's precursor, so Wordsworth is Shelley's. However, the other major feature of 'London, 1802' taken up by Shelley raises an issue with which the hypothetical Bloomian reading developed so far cannot adequately deal.

Wordsworth's sonnet praises Milton for his occupation of two distinct positions. Milton fulfils the role of the poet as a solitary 'star' and yet he also is praised for his active involvement in common life. Milton, for Wordsworth, is the exemplary poet because he is at one and the same time 'high' and 'low', separate from the common world and yet an active participant within it. Shelley praises the earlier Wordsworth for occupying just such a dual ('high' and 'low') position. Wordsworth was once a teacher and influence (a 'lone star') and yet equally a common man ('honoured poverty'). Examining the Wordsworthian intertexts behind 'To Wordsworth' helps us recognise that Shelley is criticising the later Wordsworth for losing this exemplary dual positionality. Wordsworth has become isolated from the social world and has thus lost his influence upon it.

Hazlitt's similar critique of the 'Lake School' poets some years later actually reverses the figurative structure of Shelley's sonnet. In his chapter on Coleridge in *The Spirit of the Age*, Hazlitt argues that Wordsworth has locked himself up in a watery refuge away from the desert wilderness of contemporary politics and society: 'They [the 'Lakers'] are safely inclosed there. But Mr. Coleridge did not enter with them; pitching his tent upon the barren waste without, and having no abiding place nor city of refuge.'[29] Shelley's earlier account of this retreat reverses the images, placing Wordsworth in a refuge away from the watery realm of contemporary history. What emerges from a comparison between Shelley's and Hazlitt's descriptions of this process is that when we ask where Shelley himself is positioned we find that he occupies a rather similar position to Hazlitt's Coleridge. Shelley is neither in the refuge nor part of the historical ocean/desert. He is neither an influence (star) nor part of the common world of humanity ('blind and battling multitude'). Indeed, like the Poet in *Alastor*, who also is figured being driven along within a 'frail bark', he appears to be the passive victim of influences from both figured realms: he is influenced by the 'star' (precursor) and equally by the sociohistorical realm (rocked within 'winter's midnight roar'). Why the latter source of influence needs to be read as a figuration of the sociohistorical realm becomes clear when we break from Bloom's mode of intratextual reading to an analysis of its intertextual relation to similar figurations in Shelley's work.

P. M. S. Dawson has done much recently to develop our understanding of just how ambiguous Shelley's position was as an intellectual radically committed to social and political revolution. He writes: 'The equivocal class situation of the intellectual stems from the fact that the very logic of the intellectual project will lead him (or her) to prefer the ideals of his class to its practice, but will then leave him to pursue these ideals in a social vacuum.'[30] In the transitional period represented by the *Alastor* volume and the poems immediately succeeding it, Shelley can be said to be working through the implications of and the possibilities available within such an 'equivocal' position. What is most significant for us here is that this developing recognition of and intellectual engagement with his poetic and social position in the poetry of this period appears to depend on or at least construct itself on the same figurative pattern we have located in his sonnet to and about Wordsworth.

In the three translations Shelley composed in 1815, two of which were published in the *Alastor* volume, Shelley extends the themes of 'To Wordsworth',[31] investigating the theme of the community of poets and its relation to the 'multitude/Of blind and maddening men' ('Cavalcante to Dante', ll.5–6) through the same figurations of poetic solitary and watery/stormy social world. In his translation from Moschus, Shelley writes:

> Whose house is some lone bark, whose toil the sea,
> Whose prey the wandering fish, an evil lot
> Has chosen . . .
>
> (ll.10–12)

The vision of earthly tyranny and oppression gained by the 'pure Spirit' at the conclusion of the first part of 'The daemon of the world', also published in the *Alastor* volume, is achieved from a position ('Serene and inaccessibly secure') somewhere in-between the heights and the depths:

> Stood on an isolated pinnacle;
> The flood of ages combating below,
> The depth of the unbounded universe
>     Above, and all around
> Necessity's unchanging harmony.
>
> (ll.285–91)

Moving out from the *Alastor* volume itself we can see at least three major examples of the figurative pattern in the following texts written soon after the poems in that volume. The famous description of Prince Athanese returns to the theme of the ideal, dual positionality of the poet, and does so through a redeployment of the figurative pattern I am extracting from 'To Wordsworth':

Although a child of fortune and of power,
Of an ancestral name the orphan chief,

His soul had wedded Wisdom, and her dower
Is love and justice, clothed in which he sate
Apart from men, as in a lonely tower,

Pitying the tumult of their dark estate. –
Yet even in youth did he not e'er abuse
The strength of wealth or thought, to consecrate

Those false opinions which the harsh rich use
To bind the world they famish for their pride;
Nor did he hold from any man his dues,

But like a steward in honest dealings tried,
With those who toiled and wept, the poor and wise,
His riches and his cares he did divide.

(Poems. ll.29–42)

These lines encapsulate the main features of Shelley's ideal of the figure of the poet. Prince Athanese, replacing the privileges of 'fortune and power' with 'Wisdom', has a sensibility which distinguishes him from common men. Yet his relations to these men is one of pity, instruction and, importantly, involves material as well as spiritual assistance. The image of the Prince 'in a lonely tower' above and yet pitying 'the tumult of their [common men] dark estate' echoes the figures I have examined in 'To Wordsworth', making more explicit the sociohistorical connotations of that poem's version of the 'dark estate', 'winter's midnight roar'. In the two narrative poems of 1817, both of which contain fictional treatments of the French Revolution, *Laon and Cythna* and *Rosalind and Helen* (finished in 1818), the respective poet-figures, Laon and Lionel, are also represented in terms of the twofold position between secluded tower and storm-blown ocean. And yet in these two figures we begin to observe a change in this figurative pattern, the two poet/revolutionary-figures coming to possess a tower-like strength amid the storm environment.

Dawson refers to the passage in which Laon is portrayed 'amid the rocking earthquake steadfast still' standing 'on high Freedom's desert land' like 'A tower whose marble walls the leagued storms withstand'.[32] The truly striking case for our purposes, however, is the following portrayal of Lionel:

> He passed amid the strife of men,
> And stood at the throne of armed power
> Pleading for a world of woe:
> Secure as one on a rock-built tower
> O'er the wrecks which the surge trails to and fro,
> 'Mid the passions wild of human kind
> He stood, like a spirit calming them;
> For, it was said, his words could bind
> Like music the lulled crowd, and stem
> That torrent of unquiet dream,
> Which mortals truth and reason deem,
> But is revenge and fear and pride.
> Joyous he was; and hope and peace
> On all who heard him did abide,
> Raining like dew from his sweet talk,
> As where the evening star may walk
> Along the brink of the gloomy seas,
> Liquid mists of splendour quiver.
>
> (Poems. ll.629–46)

Lionel here occupies that desired dual position of separation from the 'passions wild of human kind' and yet direct engagement with the social world. His embodiment of these two interrelated roles make him a 'star' (influence–teacher–guide) to all those around him.

At this point we are perhaps faced with an interpretative decision which takes us to the heart of our response to Bloom's reading of Shelley. Are we to follow a Bloomian reading and interpret these other instances of the figurative pattern we first observed in 'To Wordsworth' as being determined by and having their meaning in Shelley's poetic agon with his precursor, Wordsworth? It is clear that one of the principal sources for this frequently reproduced image-complex in Shelley is Wordsworth's poetry.[33] Indeed, we should go further than this: Wordsworth is crucial for Shelley in this period, both as a major example of poetic authority and as an example or warning of the way not to go as a poet. Wordsworth, in other words, is an ambivalent factor in Shelley's attempt to work through to a proper positioning of himself as a poet.

My brief survey of this image-complex should have demonstrated that the meaning of such a pattern in Shelley's poetry of the period 1814–17 cannot be contained within such an agonistic, intratextual account. The pattern manifests Shelley's personal attempt to confront and find a method of resolving the problematic position of poetry and of the poet him- or herself within contemporary society. What attention to the pattern actually demonstrates, in fact, is that in this early transitional period of his work Shelley was slowly coming to the recognition that, for the poet committed to social revolution, the historical period in which he lived represented a particularly unpropitious time. If the figurations of the desired dual position (the role of influence combined with social rootedness) leave Shelley strangely unpositioned in 'To Wordsworth', this problem is only partially resolved in *Rosalind and Helen*, a poem in which a poet/hero is imagined within the context of a revolution which, with hindsight, had not fulfilled its promise.

The meaning of this figurative pattern might well be interpreted as the impossibility of proper *presence* or *position* (in the sense of radical *influence*) in the present. The present moment does appear to be, to employ Bloom's own phrase 'experientially darkened' in Shelley's poetry of this period. Yet if this is so it is not so much because of Shelley's attempt to transume his precursor; rather, it appears to emerge from that characteristic Shelleyan recognition of the gulf between his ideals and the means to their attainment – the irreconcilability between 'good and the means of good'.

Jerome J. McGann, in his account of the 'second generation' phase of British Romanticism, attempts to revise Bloom's account of the belatedness of these poets by switching the meaning of that term from what we might call a post-formalistic to a properly historical definition.[34] In his 'Shelley's poetry: The judgment of the future', McGann writes: 'From "Alastor" (1816) to the uncompleted "The Triumph of Life" (1822) Shelley's work is marked by a poetic commitment to social melioration and by a reciprocal sense that circumstances seemed forever conspiring against such commitments'.[35] What McGann calls 'Shelley's futurism', which he describes as Shelley's poetic response to such an equivocal position, can usefully be described as his version of transumption, since it is a mode of poetry which does indeed appear to introject the past and project the future at the expense of the present moment. I have not space enough here to analyse the already well-trodden ground of Shelley's utilisation of the Godwinian idea of perfectibility and the education of opinion so fundamental to such an approach. What does need to be stressed is that although such an approach is intricately bound up with an examination of the nature of influence, as a reading of the prefaces to *Laon and Cythna*, *Prometheus Unbound*, along with the *Defence* will amply show, what is being introjected and projected is not a 'power' which can be originated or possessed by any single individual, any particular 'personality'.

Poetry, for Shelley, came to be defined as a medium by and through which the never-to-be-completed drive towards social perfection is channelled. Poets channel this 'power', as Shelley states in the preface to *Prometheus Unbound*, by clothing it in the 'forms' made available by 'the peculiarity of the moral and intellectual condition of the minds among which they have been produced'. The manner in which poets can introject the past and project the future is, in other words, determined by the influence on them of past and contemporary authors; but what is introjected and projected is neither the property of these past writers nor of the poet being influenced.

All this becomes particularly significant when we move on to Bloom's account of the conclusion of Shelley's *Defence*:

> An unacknowledged legislator is simply an unacknowledged influence, and since Shelley equates Wordsworth with the *Zeitgeist*, it is hardly an overestimate to say that Wordsworth's influence creates a series of laws for a world of feeling and thinking that went beyond the domain of poetry. Very strong poet that he was, Shelley nevertheless had the wisdom and the sadness of knowing overtly what other poets since have evaded knowing, except in the involuntary patterns of their work. Wordsworth will legislate and go on legislating for your poem, no matter how you resist or evade or even unconsciously ignore him. (PR, p.111)

Bloom, in his final estimate of the shape and significance of Shelley's work, reduces it to the determining influence of Wordsworth. The final paragraph of Shelley's greatest essay on poetry becomes the greatest example of Shelley's inability to turn his transumptive powers on the Father. Wordsworth remains pre-eminent and is reaffirmed as the influence which 'legislates' the meaning of his poetry. Wordsworth remains beyond transumption, which means that he remains beyond reversal: he is the 'unmoved mover' who controls whatever power Shelley's poetry manages to convince its readers it possesses.

In order to achieve this final assessment Bloom needs to produce a massive revision of what is perhaps Shelley's most famous line: 'Poets are the unacknowledged legislators of the world.' Rejecting the usual interpretation in which the line is read as an assertion that poets are the communicators of a 'power' they may not themselves recognise, Bloom redistributes the lack of acknowledgement (we might say 'blindness') to Shelley himself, thus returning the 'insight' and the 'power' to Wordsworth. Bloom's misreading of the line works to reidentify power with the poet. It also works to impose his theory of the intratextual nature of poetic meaning on a text which, as I have been attempting to assert, rather more conventionally perhaps, attempts to keep separate imitation and influence; attempts, that is, to distinguish between the power poets may exert on one another and the power which 'they may deny and abjure' but which 'they are yet compelled to serve'.

If transumption is an appropriate concept by which to understand Shelley's achieved poetic stance or position, and I would argue that it is, then this is so not because it is the inevitable means by which all post-Miltonic poets gain power or 'strength' but, rather, because it represents effectively the particular response Shelley brought to what he, among others, styled *the spirit of the age*. This spirit of the age included Wordsworth's influence, yet it cannot be reduced to that influence. Wordsworth himself, for Shelley, was at once the creator and, in another sense, the creation of his age. Poets like Wordsworth, in Shelley's transumptive terms, are products of history as well as being potential producers of future history, and the history of this process is not the history of the 'inter-play of personalities' so much as the inter-play between personality, time and that timeless force Shelley called power. To get closer to Shelley's particular brand of transumption it seems necessary to consider the notion of a form of influence which, because it is directed towards the communication of a mode of social power which each new age must reimagine in its own terms, depends ultimately on the dissolution rather than the imposition of personality on the future. Such an idea, which I believe is Shelley's final position on the issue of influence, allows me to conclude where many accounts of Shelley's work have previously concluded, with the final lines of the 'Ode to the West Wind'. In these lines, Shelley does not project his own 'personality' (in Bloom's sense) into the future, but rather his 'personality', his *voice*, becomes a time-bound medium through which a specifically social 'power', although figured as elemental, is passed on to the future. The 'power' may be constant, akin to the unchanging force behind natural processes, but the medium, the 'words', by which it is communicated and re-embodied is ever changing. Shelley's 'prophecy' is not that his own 'words' will dominate and retain authority over the future, rather it 'trumpet[s]' (heralds – foresees) a future which, unlike the present time, might be capable of embodying the ideal. It seems appropriate to call this poetic stance transumptive; what does not seem appropriate is to call it agonistic:

> Drive my dead thoughts over the universe
> Like withered leaves to quicken a new birth!
> And, by the incantation of this verse,
>
> Scatter, as from an unextinguished hearth
> Ashes and sparks, my words among mankind!
> Be through my lips to unawakened earth
>
> The trumpet of a prophecy! O, Wind,
> If Winter comes, can Spring be far behind?
>
> (Poems, ll.63–70)

## Transumption, Emerson and the American difference

In his article 'Bloom, Freud and America', David Wyatt suggests that the most crucial 'turn' in Bloom's critical career has been his 're-turn' to an analysis of the American tradition in poetry and criticism.[36] Wyatt refers to various comments by Bloom himself which date this crucial redirection of focus to the period around 1965, a dating which makes it coincident with the first appearance in his work of the idea of the anxiety of influence.[37] On the most immediate level, it is possible to state that this attention to the American tradition afforded Bloom the final piece in the historical narrative which underpins his theoretical account of the anxiety of influence. It provides a terminal point in that narrative of the gradual westering of the muse which, in many respects, *is* the theory of the anxiety of influence.

We should remember, as Wyatt does, that a turn is also a trope. If Bloom's work on American tradition is a turn away from his earlier concern with British Romanticism, then it is also a trope. Indeed, it is a 'turn of a previous trope' or the 'trope of a trope': the earlier trope being previously established representations of American tradition. What such a remembering of tropology highlights is that Bloom's invocation of a still nascent American form of 're-centering' interpretation (MM, pp.174–6) has found its fullest expression in the theory of transumption and the idea of a diachronic form of rhetoric: in 'the Emersonian difference, which is to say, the American difference: a diachronic rhetoric, set not only against past tropes, as in Nietzsche, but against the pastness of trope itself, and so against the limitations of traditional rhetoric' (*Agon*, p.32).

It should already be quite apparent that Bloom's sense of the specificity of the American tradition stems from his reading of Emerson as the 'father' of all American writers, his sense of Emerson as the great American beginning. One could fill many pages with examples of Bloom's representations of Emerson as the 'father' of the American tradition: from statements concerning the literary tradition of America – 'an American writer can be Emersonian or anti-Emersonian, but even a negative stance towards Emerson always leads back again to his formulation of the post-Christian American religion of *Self-Reliance*'[38] – to statements concerning the wider cultural identity of America, such as the following: 'The mind of Emerson is the mind of America, for worse and for glory, and the central concern of that mind was the American religion, which most memorably was named "self-reliance" ' (*Agon*, p.145).

This estimate of the place of Emerson in the American tradition allows Bloom to discover within that author's work a variety of transumptive allusion and a form of defensive (and thus diachronic) rhetoric, which he can then style as authentically American. To capture the essence of the transumptive style of reading Bloom extracts from Emerson we should attend to the quotation from 'The oversoul' Bloom employs in his essay 'Ratios' (BV, pp.7–40), in which he presents one of his most sustained meditations on the power and influence of 'Wrestling Waldo'. The section from the quotation which concerns me at present reads as follows:

> The soul is superior to its knowledge, wiser than any of its works. The great poet makes us feel our own wealth, and then we think less of his compositions. His greatest communication to our mind is to teach us to despise all he has done. (Quoted BV, p.32)

What Emerson teaches his pupils, then, is that criticism is always prior to literature: the *reader's sublime*, not the *literary sublime*, is the true mode of American tradition. Emerson teaches that the truly seeing soul is, as he states in the famous 'bare-common' passage from 'Nature', 'part or parcel of God'. In the Emersonian scheme, all contexts give way to the priority of the truly seeing soul.

Emerson's strength and rather malforming influence lies in his refusal to choose from among any of the available modes of expression or belief, or at least to set himself against all prior manifestations of the human will. Emerson chose not to choose but rather to rely on his own innate spark, his own 'self'. For Bloom, such a decision makes

Emerson the rightful heir of the most extreme forms of revisionism Western traditions have known: Gnosticism and the Lurianic Kabbalah. This decision also tears him loose from the British tradition, Protestant and Romantic, to which he obviously felt most debt and thus most anxiety (see FCI, p.75). Emerson's stance, according to Bloom, has generated a subsequent anxiety of influence in the American tradition comparable to the influence-anxieties produced by Milton and Wordsworth in the British tradition.

Bloom finds in the American tradition a fundamental support for his version of literary history. American poetry, we might say, is the last twist in the transumptive chain which stretches from Homer and the Bible through European, post-Enlightenment poetry to the poetry of A. R. Ammons, Elizabeth Bishop and John Ashbery. American poetry, Bloom declares, presents us with 'the last Western Sublime, the great sunset of selfhood in the Evening Land' (PR, p.244). In his preface to *Agon*, Bloom announces that 'The first theologians of agon were the Gnostics of Alexandria, and the final pragmatists of agon were and will be the Americans of Emerson's tradition' (*Agon*, p.viii). In his 1975 review of poetry, Bloom writes that 'America is the evening land, or the last phase of Mediterranean culture, and this late in tradition all reading (and writing) is heavily shadowed by the past.'[39]

Readers of this study should recognise the problem in such representations of the American literary tradition. Bloom wishes to claim a specificity for the American tradition; he wishes, in fact, to retain the possibility of representing discretely different traditions, not merely literary but cultural and/or national. However, such a representation of the American cultural tradition depends on the kind of historical contextualisation which Bloom's version of poetic rhetoric, his Emersonian adherence to the transumptive *reader's sublime*, denies. What is the *cause*, we might ask, for America's place as *the* last great phase of Western culture? What makes the American tradition the culmination of and even the end-game in the history not only of Western revisionism but of Western culture? These questions hover around and within Bloom's whole engagement with American poetry and are continually met by the Bloomian invocation of the great American *beginning*: Wrestling Waldo. The 'peculiar relevance' of Emerson, according to Bloom, 'is that we seem to read him merely by living here, in this place still somehow his, and not our own' (MM, p.171). Emerson, particularly the Emerson of the Optative Mood, the celebrator of an Apollonian 'individualism', is 'the metaphor of "the father", the pragmatic image of the ego ideal, the inescapable precursor, the literary hero, the mind of the United States of America', and if Emerson faded out of view for a while between 1945 and 1965, then he has returned 'as he always must and will, because he is the pragmatic origin of our literary culture'. As Bloom puts it: 'Walt Whitman and Emily Dickinson, Robert Frost and Wallace Stevens, Hart Crane, Elizabeth Bishop and John Ashbery have written the poems of our climate, but Emerson was and is that climate.'[40]

Bloom can represent and analyse American culture because such an activity becomes for him synonymous with reading the work of Emerson, both directly and as it manifests itself in any 'strong' American author. Bloom, it would appear, wishes to remain faithful to what he views as the Emersonian legacy of transumptive criticism and rhetorical acts of *pathos* or persuasion; in other words, the defiant, rhetorical revisionism of all contexts, all prior texts. Emerson is beyond deconstruction (*Agon*, p.178) because his texts do not present us with *significance* but work to break through into *meaning*, where meaning is defined as 'survival' and 'defence' (PR, p.240). Emerson demands that his readers develop a properly American, transumptive mode of criticism, and Bloom would achieve this fideistic critical manoeuvre by developing his attack on all forms of epistemologically or historically oriented modes of reading. Yet, as we have observed, Bloom cannot perform such a critical and theoretical affiliation and, we must say, *repetition*, without presenting the Emersonian tradition as an historically specific tradition. Bloom's account necessarily relies on the language of historical process and contextualisation (the language of periodicity, cultural change and cultural value). Historical projections and presuppositions may be negated by the Bloomian theory of diachronic rhetoric, yet they are indispensable in the employment of such terms as tradition and the form of belatedness Bloom would ascribe to Emerson and his progeny.

Joseph N. Riddel highlights what he calls a 'caesura' in Bloom's presentation of the American tradition. Referring to both Bloom's and Gertrude Stein's projections of the paradoxical combination, in the American tradition, of continuity (last outpost of Western culture, etc.) and discontinuity (new land, virgin soil, etc.) he writes of a 'catachresis intervening at the crossing or chiasmus' between the 'old' and the 'new'.[41]

Bloom has done much to explain how the figure of catachresis works in the perpetual crossings American poets make in their discontinuous leaps away from and yet paradoxical swervings towards the tradition which engenders them. Riddel's allusion to catachresis, of the dis-membering of the Father, or the discontinuity between present and past states, begins to subvert that explanation, however. What his account can be made to highlight is that, in Bloom's employment of the language of historical specificity, a forgetting of the intertextual links between Emerson and the pre-Emersonian traditions, both American and European, a re-membering of Emersonian 'Giantism', in other words, necessarily threatens the very pitch and tenor of Bloom's whole approach to poetic language and meaning.

The unresolvable claims of discontinuity and continuity threaten either to ruin the specificity of the American tradition by denying it the authentic Father it requires, or to transform Emerson, as representation of that beginning, into a literalised, monumental beginning. In this latter movement, Bloom's work threatens to become a repetition of the Emersonian rhetoric of self-reliance and total discontinuity: de-idealising the American poetic rhetoric of self-reliance in Whitman, Stevens and Ashbery at the expense of a re-idealisation of the Emersonian rhetoric in its representation of Emerson himself (see MM, p.165).

Bloom's attempts to establish Emerson's place within and influence on both American culture and, within that, a still nascent American form of criticism, constitute one of the principal motivations for his recent redefinition of poetic influence. More precisely, we might say that Bloom, confronting an apparent aporia within his own approach, has found it necessary to develop a new theoretical principle in his terminological armoury. This new principle is the theory of historical facticity.

Bloom's interpretative reconstruction of transumptive links between 'strong' American poets reaches a necessary end-point in Emerson and cannot proceed beyond that point without wrecking its entire description of the specificity of that tradition. Bloom, of course, resists the temptation to literalise Emerson's originality and status as Father. For Bloom, Emerson was no literal 'father', no self-begotten original; and yet his 'strength' of repressiveness was so severe that he has become a father to all those Americans living in his wake. Bloom writes: 'But so subtle is Emerson, so much is he our mother as well as our father, that he becomes our child also, for only we can bring forth Wrestling Waldo . . . Emerson's contribution was to invite the gift' (BV, p.36).

What Bloom is attempting to represent in this passage is the uncanniness of Emerson, where the uncanny is that which lies somehow beyond interpretation yet already within every potential reader. The extent of the uncanniness (*originality*) Bloom is ascribing to Emerson can be gauged when we place by the side of this passage the following comment from *Ruin the Sacred Truths*: 'the sublime takes place *between* origin and aim or end, and . . . the only Western trope that avoids both origin and end is the trope of the Father, which is only to say that we do not speak of "Father Nature" ' (RST, p.120).

If Emerson is both Father and Mother, then he can be said to be both an antithetical and revisable trope for origins and yet also an unrevisable, unsurpassable trope for origins. Emerson, in this sense, is the Demiurge of American tradition. Emerson is a facticity, which may be equivalent to saying that he is a successful catachresis, a wholly successful unnaming of the past, and so a figure resistant to all contextualisation.

It is interesting to note that in his recent interpretation of the J-writer, Bloom again relies on the 'trope of the Mother' in order to represent the facticity of that, for Bloom, most uncanny and original of all writers. We are brought back to Bloom's 'catastrophe theory' of meaning here, his assertion that meaning can only get started by 'catastrophes at our origins' (*Agon*, p.43–4).

It would appear that Bloom, wishing to explain cultural history in terms of an agonistic process of (Oedipal) conflict and revision, is forced to rely on the trope (myth) of the primal Mother (literal meaning, origins, death) in order to set the whole process going and to redirect it at specific points along the way. Apart from highlighting the fundamentally patriarchal nature of Bloom's vision of poetry and culture, such a reversion to the 'trope of the Mother' also highlights the impasse built into his critical system, its inability to account properly for transformations in the literary and cultural tradition. Such an impasse is generated by Bloom's refusal to recognise the determining effects of historical contexts on textual traditions. The theory of facticity, as I have suggested, represents Bloom's most recent and most severe attempt to evade such a recognition.

CHAPTER
SIX

# Literary cultures: facticity and the return of originality

## Bloom and current critical trends

That Bloom's most recent work constitutes, in part, a defence against the post-structuralist rethinking of literary history currently known in America as New Historicism may not immediately be apparent. Texts such as *Ruin the Sacred Truths* and *The Book of J* contain no direct engagement with New Historical readings, and the names of leading theorists, such as Stephen Greenblatt and Louis Montrose, do not punctuate Bloom's discourse in the manner in which the names of Paul de Man, Jacques Derrida and J. Hillis Miller punctuated the work of the mid-1970s. A sign of Bloom's desire to oppose the movement known as New Historicism, however, can be found in various polemical asides in his recent work.

In *Ruin the Sacred Truths* Bloom dismisses the reading of Milton's 'power' offered by what he calls 'our current School of Resentment' (RST, p.91). The exact delineations of such a school are established when he writes of the current replacement of 'a secular clergy' of literary critics by 'a pride of displaced social workers' (RST, p.93).

For Bloom current literary criticism, dominated by a false translation of literary power into the problematics of social power-relations, exhibits a general resentment with regard to literature. However, despite his dismissive, rather ill-tempered tone, Bloom does not appear to be able to brush aside such 'young' perspectives as easily as he may wish. They re-emerge in his recent interpretations as false questions, false positions, which, despite their supposed inadequacy, remain 'strong' enough to require rebuttal. In his treatment of Shakespeare's history plays, to take another example, New Historicist, feminist and other historically oriented readings lurk behind Bloom's interpretation, without ever being named directly. Bloom feels the need to explain that 'Falstaff's power seems to me not at all a matter of class, sexuality, politics, nationalism', and goes on to assert: 'Power it is: sublime pathos, *potentia*, the drive for life, more life, at any and every cost' (RST, p.82). Whether or not Bloom believes his own interpretative power to have reached a level where opponents no longer need to be named and confronted *in person* is hard to gauge. What is not difficult to recognise is that in two typically aphoristic sentences a huge amount of important, contemporary criticism is being lumped together as irrelevant to the 'proper' reading of Shakespeare. What is even more apparent is that these alternative approaches cannot be so easily dispensed with, a fact reflected by their re-emergence a little later in Bloom's reading (see RST, p.85). Bloom's most recent work represents a renewed defence against history; a renewed attempt to ward off history as it emerges both within his own established critical positions and from powerful, alternative modes of contemporary reading practice.

Having analysed Bloom's work up to the mid-1980s, it should be apparent that a general transformation occurs within it with regard to the question of literature's relationship to what at this point we need to call culture. Bloom, as I illustrated at the beginning of this study, began his career by developing a version of the Fryean concept of the 'literary universe': a twentieth-century version of the Romantic ideology of literature's essential separation from history. Bloom, however, as we have seen, was never very happy with an approach which would limit him to a discussion of texts conventionally classified as literary or poetic. His characteristic solution to this problem — the desire to retain literature's essential autonomy and transhistorical nature, while not disqualifying himself from the opportunity of reading important extra-literary texts — was to develop an extremely particular and yet equally flexible definition of what constitutes 'poetry'.

Throughout Bloom's work of the 1970s there is a progressive extension of the poetic tradition and the definition of what constitutes 'strong' poetry. In the work of the early 1980s Bloom begins to write

136  Harold Bloom

of Western culture as a 'literary culture', a culture whose most authentic texts, whether they masquerade under the guise of theology, philosophy, politics, sociology or literary criticism, are in fact 'literary' or 'poetic'; examples of 'strong' acts of rhetorical persuasion. Bloom here consciously places his theory of diachronic rhetoric, poetic misreading and his complex account of intratextuality within the American pragmatist tradition, particularly as it has recently been redefined in the work of Richard Rorty. He makes this link with pragmatism most strongly in his essay 'Agon: Revisionism and critical personality' (*Agon*, pp.16–51), an essay within which, not surprisingly then, we find Bloom's most useful description of just what exactly constitutes 'modern literary culture':

> by 'a literary culture' I do mean Western society now, since it has no authentic religion and no authentic philosophy, and will never acquire them again, and because psychoanalysis, its pragmatic religion and philosophy, is just a fragment of literary culture, so that in time we will speak alternatively of Freudianism *or* Proustianism. The necessary dualism of a literary culture has usurped the spirit, pragmatically and materially, so that to question the moral efficacy of reading now inherits the shock once attached to putting into question the moral value of prayer, or of metaphysical speculation. (*Agon*, p.23)

Bloom moves from a post-formalist account of the autonomy of the 'literary universe' to a pragmatism which collapses culture and society *within* the perimeters of an all-encompassing literariness. Instead of the distinction between poetic and non-poetic modes of discourse, Bloom argues for the unrivalled pre-eminence of 'strong' acts of rhetorical persuasion in a culture irredeemably cut off from the Enlightenment boundaries of truth and meaning. As he writes elsewhere: 'A culture becomes literary when its conceptual modes have failed it, which means when religion, philosophy, and science have begun to lose their authority.'[1] Such a position has obvious similarities to various currently influential discussions of modernity or post-modernity. Bloom, however, unlike many other theorists of post-modernity, is eager, just as it appears that he has finally succumbed to the historicising impulse, to contain and ultimately erase the element of historicism from such descriptions of contemporary culture.

*Ruin the Sacred Truths* begins with his definition of modernity and proceeds to claim it as a characteristic of all 'strong' poetry 'from the Bible to the Present':

Poetry and belief, as I understand them, are antithetical modes of knowledge, but they share the peculiarity of taking place *between* truth and meaning, while being somewhat alienated both from truth and meaning. Meaning gets started only by or from an excess, an overflow or emanation, that we call originality. Without that excess even poetry, let alone belief, is merely a mode of repetition, no matter in how much finer a tone. So is prophecy, whatever we take prophecy to be. (RST, p.12)

In this passage, which is a kind of synopsis of the thesis of *Ruin the Sacred Truths* as a whole, Bloom reiterates fundamental positions first articulated in *The Anxiety of Influence*. Reflecting on the J writer's naming of God, he writes: 'Poetry and belief wander about, together and apart, in a cosmological emptiness marked by the limits of truth and meaning. Somewhere between truth and meaning can be found piled up a terrible heap of descriptions of God' (RST, p.4).

To say that Bloom refuses to give properly historical reasons for the emergence of what he calls 'modern literary culture' is not sufficient then. What is generated out of the combination of such a description of modernity and the theory of poetry reasserted in *Ruin the Sacred Truths* is a containment of cultural history within Bloom's own version of literary history. Bloom's special brand of monumentalism is, in his most recent work, extended, through the theory of facticity, to culture in its entirety. The thesis of *Ruin the Sacred Truths*, along with other works of the 1980s and now the 1990s, can truly be said to constitute a reduction of cultural history to the 'interplay of personalities'.

We have already observed this process at work in our analysis of Bloom's account of Emerson's influence on American culture. We see it even more distinctly in Bloom's account of the role Freud plays in the development of modern consciousness. As Bloom states: 'We have become Freud's texts, and the *Imitatio Freudi* is the necessary pattern for the spiritual life in our time' (BV, p.64).

The theory of facticity has allowed Bloom to place such an assessment of the influence of Freud within a wider history or genealogy. Freud, Bloom argues, is ultimately only a strong revision of Shakespeare, who himself is merely the major revision in Western civilisation of the most original of all authors, the Yahwist. Bloom states that 'A transference or metaphor takes place when we read J, or Shakespeare, or Freud, just as similar transferences took place when our ancestors read these writers.' And he continues: 'These transferences, on our part, echo or repeat earlier transferences, and what is transferred is our love for authority, our desire to be augmented by the authority we have invested in the Yahwist, Shakespeare, or Freud' (RST, p.8). Such assertions are based on 'the mere truism that the Yahwist ultimately influences our ideas of God, while Shakespeare shapes our sense of human personality and how it can be represented and Freud informs our prevalent map of the mind.'

Such a reduction of cultural history to the originating influence of three monumental 'personalities' or 'precursors' represents the apotheosis of the repetition of Romantic ideology I have endeavoured to trace throughout Bloom's critical career. Bloom, characteristically, insists that his theory of facticity is the direct outcome of his reading of 'strong' texts. Reasserting his experiential approach to the practice of literary criticism, and equally to the production of theoretical paradigms, Bloom insists: 'I am nothing but a critical pragmatist, and so I advance a working notion of facticity in order to account for a surprise in my own experience as a reader' (RST, p.8). Bloom's readers are hardly surprised that he should continue to insist on the literary and now the cultural influence of a few 'strong personalities'.

Far from substantiating his claims, Bloom's evocation of the 'pragmatics of reading' foregrounds his continued adherence to a pre-established ideology which seeks to disavow the historical dimensions of literary texts and their interpretations. Such an approach cuts off literary texts from historical concerns, or translates them into literary terms and so conceals them. The paradigm of facticity, however, far from substantiating the relevance of that containment of culture, and more broadly history, within the literary, actually serves to indicate Bloom's inability to rid either the 'strong' texts of his choosing or his own 'strong' readings of their historical and ideological positionality.

We return here to the reversibility of Bloom's refusal of history, and we can see this feature more clearly if we further develop the comparison between Bloom's more recent work and the current poststructuralist rethinking of historicism.

New Historicism is a term which covers a wide range of current critical approaches. In the introduction to this study I referred to the difference between American New Historicism and British Cultural Materialism. Even within a more strictly demarcated version of New Historicism, there are differences between those practitioners concerned with the study of Renaissance literature and culture and those, among others, concerned with the study of nineteenth-century, specifically Romantic, literature and culture. Majorie Levinson dates the emergence of the latter form of New Historicism to the mid-1980s.[2]

There are clearly a number of reasons why a 'new zeal' 'within Romantic studies . . . to position literary works within a historical domain' should have taken hold at that time: one of the obvious influences being the work of Jerome J. McGann, particularly his study *The Romantic Ideology*. In that work McGann highlights three distinct modes of criticism within the Romantic tradition. Following the work of Heine, McGann advocates a 'critical' approach to Romanticism, a method which offers 'neither a repetition of the subject's forms and ideologies (Romantic Criticism) nor a reification of such forms and their ideologies (Hegelian Criticism)'.[3] McGann reserves his greatest strictures for the latter of the two rejected modes, stating that 'The academy today, its scholars and teachers, tend to follow some variant form of the Hegelian synthesis, though certain figures – Harold Bloom in particular – manifestly pursue a Romantic approach to the subject of Romanticism and its works.'[4]

McGann's own form of criticism, one which attempts not only to position the reader in an appropriately critical relation to the literature of the past, but which equally strives for an explanatory and even productive effect on the present, has been styled as 'critical historicism' or 'objective criticism'. New Historicism has contributed to McGann's critical project a recognition of the difficulty of gaining a properly critical or objective relation to the Romantic ideology. New Historicism's attempt to read the 'concept of culture' dynamically is an attempt, Levinson argues, to recognise the manner in which, within historical work, the object of study is both constituted by the reader and, equally, how the reader him- or herself is constituted by the cultural traces manifested in the textual 'object' itself.[5]

This 'dynamic' response seeks to recognise the interimplication of McGann's three modes of criticism: the totalising, the repetitive and the critical. On a more simplistic level, we might say that such an approach highlights the impossibility of completely severing a certain repetition of the forms and ideology of Romanticism from a modern critique of those forms and ideological positions. Romantic ideology is, to employ the terminology of Raymond Williams, emergent in Romantic literature itself; one, but importantly only one, of the futures which the critical tradition has realised as a hegemonic present. Modern criticism of Romanticism cannot help but manifest its place within this unfolding history, but remains capable of realising alternative futures latent within the literary and cultural past. On an even more simplistic level, we might say that such a recognition of the interpretative creation and recreation of the Romantic ideology illustrates the relationship between McGann's critique and Bloom's repetition of Romanticism. Bloom's approach to the interpretation of Romantic literature and that of the New Historicism are profoundly related.

Louis Montrose has produced a clear account of New Historicist tenets. He argues that the New Historicism 'is *new* in its refusal of unproblematical distinctions between "literature" and "history", between "text" and "context"; new in resisting a prevalent tendency to posit and privilege a unified and autonomous individual – whether an Author or a Work – to be set against a social or literary background'.[6] He goes on to encapsulate this post-structuralist rethinking of historicism in the following, 'chiastic' relationship: 'The Historicity of Texts and the Textuality of History'.[7] To pursue only the second part of this relationship can be said, in the study of literary works at least, to repeat Romantic ideology. What is more crucial for us to recognise here is that Bloom's brand of Romantic criticism, his textualisation of literary history and now cultural history, not only rests on a strategic evasion and negation of the first part of this relationship, but equally fosters, despite his concern with the interpoetic nature of literary meaning, a constant reliance on a version of that privileging of individual, isolated sites of meaning. How and why Bloom's approach continually resurrects, in a theoretically sophisticated and pragmatically deferred form, what Greenblatt calls the 'originary moment, [the] . . . pure act of untrammelled creation' has been a major question throughout this study.[8] This issue attains a new degree of importance, however, when we come to consider Bloom's most recent work. What precisely is involved in this characterisation of Bloom's approach can be clarified by comparing his work to that of Greenblatt himself.

Greenblatt's best account of his own method, a method which strives towards the establishment of what he calls a 'poetics of culture', comes in his 'The circulation of social energy'.[9] In this essay Greenblatt describes literary texts and their interpretations as constituting forms of 'negotiation' and 'exchange': literary texts are 'negotiations' of social 'energy' and the interpretation of such texts are similarly 'negotiations' between contemporaneity and the cultural–textual past. What links past and present for Greenblatt is the 'social energy' originally encapsulated within individual works. As he puts it: 'We identify *energia* only indirectly, by its effects: it is manifested in the capacity of certain verbal, aural, and visual traces to produce, shape, and organize collective physical and mental experiences'.[10] Greenblatt's interpretative practice, in this sense, can be said to take its starting-point from a fascination with the continued *power* certain literary texts hold over the present; a starting-point significantly close to that from which Bloom's own work commences.

The desire to explain the cause of the continued power manifested by certain literary works leads the critic into a fundamental temptation, a temptation to explain and thus contain such power by 'finding an originary moment, a moment in which the master hand shapes the concentrated social energy into the sublime aesthetic object'.[11] It is at this point that the concepts of 'negotiation' and 'exchange' come fully into play: 'In place of a blazing genesis, one begins to glimpse something that seems at first far less spectacular: a subtle, elusive act of exchange, a network of trades and trade-offs, a jostling of competing representations, a negotiation between joint-stock companies'.[12] This rejection of individual authorial intention and/or 'genius' leads Greenblatt on to a series of theoretical principles, largely articulated through a taxonomy of negations.[13]

It is highly enlightening to compare Bloom's theory and practice to this programmatic list of negatives, because it is only when we come to Greenblatt's sixth point, his insistence that 'There can be no art without social energy', that a real difference between the two critics can be detected. His first five principles are fundamental reiterations of post-structuralist tenets; they are, in a sense, reiterations of the consequences of that recognition of the unsettling force of intertextuality shared by all post-structuralist critics. As soon as Greenblatt translates these into collective and thus social terms, however, a radical break with the Bloomian approach emerges. Bloom, as I have shown, wishes to restrict the 'collectivity' of literary language to an autonomous version of literary tradition, while at the same time claiming for that tradition a shaping power over cultural life. The only way in which such a position can be maintained is to dismantle the sense of the negotiation between literary texts and sociocultural formations in the name of a strictly poetic power or energy which threatens, despite Bloom's basic agreement with the first five negatives in Greenblatt's list, to reinscribe a form of what has been called 'essentialist humanism'. We can see this more clearly by turning to a central passage in *Ruin the Sacred Truths*.

Meditating on the implications of the lines from Marvell's poem which provide him with his title, Bloom writes: 'All strong poets, whether Dante or Milton or Blake, must ruin the sacred truths to fable and old song, precisely because the essential condition for poetic strength is that the new song, one's own, always must be a song of one's self' (RST, p.125).

In this study I have endeavoured to respect the positive dimensions of Bloom's defence of 'the human that thinks, the human that writes'. I have attempted to demonstrate the manner in which such a defence is pitted against certain trends in post-structuralist theory which project a reified form of language as the primary agent of literary meaning. However, a defence of human agency is not identical to a defence of 'essentialist humanism', and Bloom gravitates towards this position as he seeks to represent a universal motive behind all manifestations of literary power and/or energy. Characteristically, Bloom grounds this universal motive in the language of psychology: he writes of a 'poetic drive' beyond both the Freudian death drive and pleasure principle (see RST, pp.125–6). We could describe this 'poetic drive' as an essential motive (tragically cast) in all literary work to gain precisely that autonomous, self-reliant identity which is the fundamental goal of humanism.

We come back, at this point, to a problem which has engaged our attention throughout this study: the problem of the hermeneutic circle and its effect on the possibility of historical work and total, universally valid, theoretical positions. Bloom wishes to argue for an essential, transhistorical poetic drive, more primal than Freud's two cardinal psychic drives. He equally wishes to argue for his own inability to attain a position outside of the play of misreading which apparently constitutes the tradition of which he writes. Given the latter position, how can Bloom argue so positively for the former? Even more importantly, how can he evade the recognition that his theory of the 'poetic drive' manifests its author's place within and adherence to cultural and ideological assumptions which are eminently historical, temporally specific in their emergence?

The only way in which Bloom can sustain such a position is to revert at important moments to 'the pragmatics of reading', to the theory of experiential interpretation, and, second, by collapsing history within a consideration of precursors so 'strong' that they end-stop the perpetual deferral of meaning. Such an approach evades the constant possibility (necessity) of moving to historical explanations of the negotiations between aesthetic and cultural practices and formations.

Bloom's desire to establish a theory of poetry as revisionism, as a manifestation of an essential agonistic will-to-power, cannot be realised without the projection of certain strategically positioned, original or uncanny authorial figures (sites of authority and meaning), stationed, like Covering Cherubs, at the origins of culture, and thus capable of containing not only all interpretation but, equally, cultural history itself. Bloom's recent move towards a theory of literary originality or facticity is the logical development of that attempt to ground the whole of poetic history within a psychopoetic theory of determinate modes of affiliation and negation which I have been attempting to isolate and criticise throughout this study.

## Difference and power

It would be possible to conclude this study by focusing on the more eccentric features of Bloom's recent work, arguing that the critique I have developed is confirmed by the oddities of Bloom on Shakespeare or the J writer. It is certainly true that Bloom on Shakespeare is at times a rather depressingly unconvincing spectacle, especially when compared to the current vitalities in Shakespearean and Renaissance studies generally. Compared, for example, to the complex arguments concerning containment and subversion in Renaissance theatre, Bloom's statement that 'Our greatest difficulty in rereading or attending Shakespeare is that we experience no difficulty at all', a situation which arises because 'We cannot see the originality of an originality that has become a contingency or facticity for us', appears massively reductive. Bloom's following remarks seem less the product of revisionary irony than of critical need:

> To say that, after God, Shakespeare has invented most is actually to note that most of what we have naturalized in prior literary representation stems first from the J writer and his revisionists, and from Homer, but secondarily and yet more powerfully from Shakespeare. (RST, pp.53–4)

An argument which commences with an assertion that modern readers find no difficulty in rereading or attending Shakespeare appears extremely unconvincing in today's critical environment. To say that female readers find no difficulty in rereading or attending *The Taming of the Shrew*, for example, does not seem a particularly appropriate description of their critical experience. An argument which attempts to persuade us of the originality or facticity of Shakespearean writing by arguing that it is based in his invention of 'the representation of change by showing people pondering their own speeches and being altered through that consideration' (RST, p.54) seems naive in the light of current debates concerning the historical and cultural significance and position of Shakespeare's work.

Such an approach, at its worst, marks a revival of an orthodox mode of character analysis.[14] Bloom offers his readers a Shakespeare who quite literally has invented the modern world by inventing our naturalised modes of speaking both to ourselves and to others. Bloom at one stage in his essay on Shakespeare asserts that 'we know the ethos of disinterestedness only because we know Hamlet'. He continues: 'The tragic hero in Shakespeare, at his most universally moving in Hamlet, is a representation so original that conceptually *he contains us*, and has fashioned our psychology of motives ever since' (RST, p.58).

Given such a thesis, Bloom can bring forward the memorable assertion: 'Shakespeare . . . contains cultural history, Freud, and what you will, and has anticipated every move to come . . . the difference between the world that Shakespeare saw and ours is to an astonishing degree Shakespeare himself' (RST, pp.55–6).

Rather than contrasting Bloom on Shakespeare's facticity to more critically convincing readings of his relation to culture and history, I want to demonstrate why Bloom cannot in fact maintain this vision of the power of original authors such as the Yahwist, Shakespeare and Freud over the cultural domain. An interpretation of power or authority is indeed at the heart of the theory of facticity. Yet, despite Bloom's own theoretical assertions, the attempt to explain textual power by containing it within a representation of authorial originality breaks down at crucial and decisive moments. These moments represent the point at which Bloom's 'poetic history' can no longer conceal its place within the wider power-struggles over authority and meaning which we habitually call history. They equally represent, as I will demonstrate, the point where Bloom's utilisation of the Freudian family romance as an analogy for cultural history begins to fragment.

Bloom's 'Criticism, canon-formation, and prophecy: The sorrows of facticity' (PI, pp.405–24), represents his first and most sustained account of the theory of cultural facticity. At the heart of facticity, Bloom explains, is the fact that we cannot help but literalise the major figurations of our culture's most original and authoritative authors. Such a fact, Bloom argues, means that we cannot reduce the issue of facticity to a post-structuralist account of textuality. In *Ruin the Sacred Truths* and in his interpretation of *The Book of J*, Bloom has taken up this point, analysing the manner in which the figurations of factitious authors are transformed into articles of belief. Bloom's point is that it becomes impossible to read factitious authors because, having transformed their figurations into forms of belief, we are at one and the same time contained by and yet separated from the figurative meaning of their texts. A major intertext for Bloom here is clearly Blake's assertion that history is the progression from poetic animation to priesthood; that men have chosen 'forms of worship from poetic tales'. A still more important intertext is Freud's reading of the uncanny. Factitious authors are uncanny in the sense that they are absolutely familiar and yet remain absolutely unknowable: *heimlich* and yet *unheimlich*.

The force or power of facticity, Bloom argues, threatens to destroy all figuration, all trope, by leaving us in our world of literalisations, of unfounded beliefs. Facticity creates cultural history but cannot be reduced to an historical mode of understanding. The reason for this takes Bloom back to his theory of catastrophe creation. Our place within cultural history, on the theory of facticity, is determined by a mode of arbitrariness *qua* originality, which for Bloom finds its modern analogue in Freud's account of psychosexual history, the family romance. 'The facticity of erotic suffering is shockingly disproportionate to the apparent blunder of erotic venturing, a disproportion that is a clue to many quieter versions of cultural facticity' (PI, p.408).

Facticity, it would appear, demonstrates the analogy between the family romance and cultural history: both begin with a catastrophe in the sense of a random happening or event which has totally overdetermined consequences. This is as much as to say that if there were no originals, no Fathers, then there could be no cultural history. Bloom's prime instance of this process is the writing of the J writer. Bloom writes: 'J is *our* original . . . precisely because J *was*. J was and is, and J has authority over us, whether we are Gentile or Jew, normative or heretic, concerned or indifferent. This is the authority of brute contingency, of our being imprisoned by what we might call J's facticity' (PI, p.408).

Earlier in this study I employed the notion of an anxiety of choice, with its concomitant rhetoric of excess and order, as a means of foregrounding the profound nervousness in Bloom's work with regard to the centrality and continuity of tradition. The anxiety of influence, I suggested, was a theory designed, at least in part, to reinforce the notion of a central, select tradition (canon) against the flood-tide of writing ('weak' poetry) even while it urged on poets themselves the virtues of discontinuity, difference and a freedom to read. It would seem now that the theory of facticity marks a recapitulation of this basic motive in Bloom's work. It is a concept which is designed to demonstrate the centrality *qua* primacy and thus unavoidable authority of a few 'strong' 'personalities'. The Yahwist, as the original 'personality', still holds undisputed power and authority over us, whether we are believers or non-believers, secularists, or whatever.

As one reviewer of Bloom's *Book of J* states, such an approach gives us a Romantic historicism, a Carlylean 'biography of great men – and some great women'.[15] Yet it also works to control and to reduce difference, particularly in its social and ideological forms, but also as these determine aesthetic and literary differences. The motive is still to posit the social, political and ideological conflicts manifested in literary and now cultural texts as subservient to an essential, unchanging and ultimately ordered conflict over meaning *qua* priority. This motive is made clearer as Bloom relates the concept of facticity to the practice of canon-formation. 'Strong' critics, he argues, 'must protect and yet correct the canon while prophesying accurately the kinds of discernment appropriate to the time, time as it is breaking over and through us' (PI, p.413).

Bloom's argument would appear to require a mode of historicism and even ideological positionality for the critic, for it is difficult to see how a critic can assess the contemporary value of canonical works and the canonical status of contemporary works without addressing sociocultural value. Bloom heads off this implication or necessity, however. Without fully describing how and why the assessments he is describing can be made, he displays his resistance to critical self-reflexivity, to the possibility for critical understanding and explication: 'All those who seek for a method that is not themselves will find not a method, but someone else, whom they will ape and involuntarily mock.' He adds: 'Poetry and fiction share with criticism the mystery that post-Structuralist speculation seeks to deny: the spark we call personality or the idiosyncratic, which in metaphysics and theology once was called presence' (PI, pp.413–14).

We arrive here at the point at which Bloom's theory (description) of cultural history and his personal presuppositions merge; a familiar point at this stage of our study. Bloom cannot prove that cultural history depends on the factitious power and authority of various strong 'personalities'. Such proof would require a methodology perpetually out of reach of those (all of us) who are imprisoned within facticity. All Bloom can do is to argue that we are so imprisoned and recognise that his description of that imprisonment necessarily betrays his own misreading of that belated state and of the cultural gaolers: the J-writer, Shakespeare and Freud. Bloom's account of facticity necessarily modulates into a staged agon between his reading of the Yahwist as uncanny original and various competing interpretative traditions: from the Hebrew prophets through normative and non-normative exegetical approaches to Bloom's immediate precursors in the literary interpretation of the Bible, the criticism of M. H. Abrams and, more importantly still, Northrop Frye.

Bloom contrasts the deidealising strength of his own concept of facticity to the overspiritualisation and idealisation of literary tradition in Frye and in Abrams. Given what he has previously asserted about the facticity of the J-writer, Bloom produces a rather odd description of Frye's cultural position. Highlighting the difference between Frye's Christian and his own Hebraic approach, Bloom writes: 'Frye is curiously free of J's facticity, but this freedom is purchased by bondage to another facticity, the typological traditions of the Christian religion, which imprisoned even William Blake' (PI, p.417).

Given Bloom's earlier assertions concerning the unavoidability of J's facticity, such a statement seems curious indeed; the curiosity attaching itself rather more to Bloom's position than to Frye's. Focusing on the apparent contradiction contained in this passage may well remind the reader of a similar passage earlier in the essay in which Wittgenstein's critique of Freud is discussed. Bloom argues that Wittgenstein, in recognising the mythological nature of Freud's work, was free from the factitious authority of Freud, yet enclosed, like Freud himself, by the facticity of Schopenhauer (see PI, p.407).

Twice in his essay Bloom is compelled to bring forward examples which refute his claims for the cultural facticity of the J-writer and of Freud. On both occasions Bloom seems to be satisfied to argue that although these authors (Frye and Wittgenstein) may be free of the facticity of the J writer and of Freud respectively, they are none the less imprisoned by other strong precursors, other authors of factitious power. At the point where Bloom is willing to accept that there are figures in contemporary culture and the recent cultural past who are not imprisoned by the facticity of the Yahwist and of Freud, however, the whole point of the theory of facticity begins to be brought into question. What emerges, in fact, is a radical disjunction within Bloom's own work between what we might call a totalising view of cultural tradition ('the literary culture of the West') and Bloom's development of a theme which has been a constant feature of his work from its very beginning: the 'intellectual and spiritual conflict between Jew and Greek', which he describes as 'anything but illusory and indeed still . . . irreconcilable' (RST, p.146).

148  *Harold Bloom*

At this point it is perhaps incumbent on me to note that Bloom's work since the early 1980s has gravitated towards what he has recently come to call 'religious criticism',[16] a mode of criticism which combines the experiential, autobiographical elements of his work since *The Anxiety of Influence* with at times profound meditations on the relationship between Jewish identity and its past and present textual expressions. I refer to this element here, an element which promises to intensify in the future, because in one important respect it leaves that work untouched by the kinds of criticism I have been developing throughout this study and am currently attempting to bring to bear on the theory of facticity. One does not have to assent to Bloom's rather reductive juxtaposition between the 'Jewish version of negation' with 'the Hegelian mode of negative thinking' (RST, p.150) to recognise that an assessment of Bloom's contribution to literary theory and criticism as it currently exists must of necessity remain a somewhat separate exercise from the assessment of the benefits and verities of his meditations on the historical, contemporary and potential qualities of Jewish consciousness or the Gnostic solitude of the American spirit. However, the fact that literary criticism and theory are mixed in Bloom's work with such modes of religious speculation does require commentary, for its effect is to produce a distinctive combination of totalisation and what might be called personalism, a shifting between registers which has distinct effects on the critical subjects Bloom treats.

Bloom's most sustained analysis of Jewish culture and identity to date comes in the last chapter of *Ruin the Sacred Truths*, 'Freud and beyond'. The first part of this essay deals with the Judaic nature of Freud's thought and is a revised version of his earlier essay 'Jewish culture and Jewish identity' (PI, pp.347–67). In this essay Bloom explains that the 'psychic cosmos' of Judaism is characterised by the notion that 'there is sense in everything, because everything already is in the past, and nothing that matters can be utterly new' (RST, p.152). It is reasonably easy to see how the work of Freud might be incorporated into such a universe. As Bloom puts it: 'The theory of repression is coherent only in a psychic cosmos where absolutely everything is meaningful, so that a dream or a joke or a symptom or a transference can sustain a level of interpretative intensity akin to the rabbinical procedures for unpacking Torah' (RST, p.147). Such a view of meaning, according to Bloom, marks the difference between the Greek agon for spatial authority and the purely temporal agon of the Hebraic tradition (see BV, p.52). 'Historical time as such does not matter to Israel; what matters are the times when God intervenes and Israel responds' (RST, p.148). It is also evident how Bloom's theory of poetic influence as an agon in which meaning, authority and priority become synonymous fits within such a 'psychic cosmos'.

Whether Bloom is accurate in his account of Jewish culture and identity is not a question I intend or possess competence enough to answer. What does need to be questioned, however, is the manner in which Bloom shifts from a description of this peculiarly Judaic account of meaning, temporality and authority to descriptions of the literary culture of the West. In applying this view to what he styles as our literary culture, in Hebraicising Western culture and tradition, Bloom effectively rejects sociohistorical *qua* ideological difference as a meaningful element in our reading activity. Pulling Shakespeare and Freud into the Judaic agon over the temporal blessing – 'the Shakespearean view of man is the biblical and now the Freudian view' (RST, p.149) – and yet retaining their canonical authority over Western cultural tradition, Bloom effectively closes the literary canon and transforms both literary and critical meaning into rather hopeless wrestling bouts between factictious Father-Gods, their diminished but quarrelsome sons, and the vast mass of weaker, hopelessly lost, offspring.

In his essay 'What is an author?', Foucault writes: 'The author is ... the ideological figure by which one marks the manner in which we fear the proliferation of meaning.'[17] Bloom's theory of facticity is a means of reiterating a vision of poetic and cultural history as a purely intratextual, agonistic affair. If everything is meaningful because meaning is always past, contained within the uncanny texts of a few 'strong' 'personalities', then no amount of change in the sociocultural domain will be capable of affecting the ultimate meaning of either the canonical texts of the past or our interpretation of them. Such a vision of the total belatedness of meaning, as we have already observed, allows Bloom to represent the Yahwist and Shakespeare as mortal gods, who have 'anticipated every move to come'. Bloom, as we have also seen, makes similar claims for the work of Freud. At the conclusion of 'Criticism, Canon-Formation, and the Sorrows of Facticity', Bloom describes Freud as 'Our Elijah or Supreme Critic' and asserts that 'We literalize Freud's tropes every day of our lives, and we have no way of freeing ourselves either of the tropes or of our literalizations' (PI, p.422). A little later Bloom asserts that, like Shakespeare and the Yahwist before him, Freud has 'anticipate[d] all legitimate criticism' (PI, p.423).

I intend to take up this description of Freud in order to conclude this critique of Bloom's account of cultural authority and textual power. The reading I now move on to commences with a paradox which will form the basis of those two objectives. The paradox is capable of simple expression: Bloom is fundamentally wrong about the uncanny authority of Freud and yet his representation of Freud's cultural power and authority remains oddly convincing.

## Counter-reading: canny fathers and uncanny daughters: Bloom, Freud and the question of authority

Bloom's most important account of Freud's analysis of the uncanny comes in his 'Freud and the sublime: A catastrophe theory of creativity' (*Agon*, pp.91–118), originally delivered as an address to The William Alanson White Psychoanalytic Society in 1977. Bloom begins this essay by invoking the long-established opposition between Continental and American schools of psychoanalysis, declining finally to choose between them, since 'Freud is so strong a writer that he contains every available mode of interpretation' (*Agon*, p.92). The major objective of the essay is to suggest, in its absence, what a Freudian theory of artistic creativity would look like. By focusing on the later phase of Freud's work, from 'The uncanny' of 1919 to 'Analysis terminable and interminable' of 1937, Bloom argues for 'what might serve as a Freudian theory of the imagination-as-catastrophe, and of art as an achieved anxiety in the agonistic struggle both to repeat and to defer the repetition of the catastrophe of creative origins' (*Agon*, p.97). The theory of artistic creativity Bloom extracts from Freud's later works thus serves to confirm the Bloomian account of poetry as an agonistic battle for priority and authority in which a defence against belatedness takes on the function of repression. In this way Bloom can associate Freud's account of the uncanny with his own agonistic interpretation of the poetic sublime (see *Agon*, p.98).

The reason why Freud has anticipated 'all legitimate criticism' and 'contains every available mode of interpretation' reduces, then, to the fact that he has reiterated and extended the 'truth' that human instinctual and creative life is posited on a drive for priority and a repression of belatedness. Freud's uncanniness (facticity) is defined as his reaffirmation of Bloom's own agonistic theory of meaning, developed as it was from a revisionary reading of Freud's work.

I am less interested here in the circularity of Bloom's arguments over Freud's nascent theory of creativity than in his fundamental claims for the cultural authority and power of the Freudian text. Bloom represents Freud as a theorist of the sublime who himself attains the sublime. 'The uncanny' becomes, in Bloom's reading, an essay which has the sublime for its repressed subject matter: it is in fact, according to Bloom, 'the only major contribution that the twentieth century has made to the aesthetics of the Sublime' (*Agon*, p.101). It also becomes a major instance of the sublime itself, not least because within it Freud inaugurates that final phase of his career in which he begins to make the subject-matter of his work his own sublime drive for priority (see *Agon*, p.118).

In Bloomian terms it is this aspect of Freud's late phase, its breakthrough into a mode of sublimity in which all prior texts are both unnamed and then renamed in the terms of Freud's own choosing, that makes him an uncanny cultural figure. For Bloom, Freud is *the* figure of authority and power in modern cultural history.

Freud's paper 'The uncanny', published in *Imago* a year before *Beyond the Pleasure Principle* (1920), is perhaps his most interesting contribution to aesthetics and has understandably attracted much attention from theorists concerned with the relationship between psychoanalysis, fantasy and fiction.[18] As Elizabeth Wright points out, recent commentaries on the paper have focused on the manner in which Freud's own interpretation of the central literary example in the analysis, Hoffmann's 'The Sandman', seems itself to become involved in a circuit of transference in which the uncanny becomes located as much in Freud's interpretation as in the fictional narrative being interpreted.[19]

For Bloom, what returns in Freud's text is his repressed desire for priority. Bloom points to Freud's distinction at the beginning of the paper between the uncanny and the traditional concept of the sublime (which Freud, incorrectly, links to the beautiful and the attractive, that is 'feelings of a positive nature').[20] Bloom makes the point that Freud's rather odd and mistaken distinction masks a relationship between the two terms and thus has the function of clearing the ground for Freud, providing him with an illusory freedom from a tradition of writing on the subject he intends to take up. For Bloom the repressed phenomenon which returns in Freud's paper is his own drive for priority and authority. This point has been corroborated and extended by Neil Hertz in his commentary 'Freud and the Sandman', in which he highlights Freud's remark that his paper is 'presented to the reader without any claim to priority' (UnC, p.340).[21]

Although such a reading is persuasive and is taken up in one form or another by most of its recent commentators, Freud's drive for priority is not the only candidate for what causes the paper's failure of 'theory in practice', or what we might call the emergence of the uncanny as an aspect of Freud's own reading. Hertz, along with Samuel Weber, Hélène Cixous, Sarah Kofman and Wright, all point to a relation between the theory of repetition included in his analysis of the uncanny and the theory of the death instinct which was to be presented in *Beyond the Pleasure Principle* the following year.[22] Bloom states that the theory of the death instinct contained in that pathbreaking work has 'still not lost the force of its shock value, even to Freudian analysts' (*Agon*, p.104). Freud, it has been suggested, in his paper on the uncanny, may be defending himself against the shock generated by his own disturbing new interpretation of the compulsion to repeat in terms of the death instinct. Indeed, this defence against the death instinct can be related to a repression of the drive for priority, since, as Wright points out, as a theory it constitutes a disturbing 'threat to the ego's narcissistic desire for omnipotence, and hence immortality . . .'.[23]

A third level of repression begins to be suggested when we look at Freud's positioning of himself with regard to his chosen subject matter. Freud informs us that 'It is long since he [Freud] has experienced or heard of anything which has given him an uncanny impression, and he must start by translating himself into that state of feeling, by awakening in himself the possibility of experiencing it' (UnC, p.340).

Freud here is confronting perhaps the major problem of his analysis: the issue of whether the experience of the uncanny is necessarily confined to individual psychological experience or whether there can be a general theory (psychoanalytic and/or aesthetic) of a general phenomenon designated as the uncanny. Such a question clearly represents in miniature a problem at the heart of psychoanalysis; a problem which, once again, brings us back to the question of authority and priority.

Mark Edmundson has described Freud's work in the following way: 'Freud's writing at its most formidable does two things simultaneously. It provides persuasive myths of normative development, and it records, as symbolic action, Freud's overcoming of all normative standards.'[24] What Edmundson means is that Freud's presentation of the 'myths of normative development' are themselves acts of rhetorical persuasion. Freud's strange extraction of himself from the experience of the uncanny represents his need to figure himself in his writing as an objective observer of psychological states of disorder. Freud requires his readers to view his analysis of the uncanny as canny, as an authoritative interpretation of aesthetic texts, an interpretation free from the distortions, repressions and blindnesses productive of the psychological experience of the uncanny. Such a self-positioning, as I have already remarked, is an unpersuasive account of Freud's reading of 'The Sandman' and the literature of the uncanny. Recognition of this central problem within Freud's text has led commentators to highlight various ways in which Freud, in order to make persuasive his supposedly canny (objective) interpretation, misreads Hoffmann's narrative. Kofman writes that '[Freud's] desire for unity which drives the investigation finds itself under attack at every turn from the need to introduce distinctions and divisions: even if, by several *tours de force*, Freud tries to erase these differences in favour of unity'.[25] Cixous makes a similar point at the beginning of her commentary: 'Everything takes place as if the *Unheimliche* went back to Freud himself in a vicious interchange between pursued and pursuer . . . the *Unheimliche* is at the root of Freud's analysis?'.[26]

What Kofman and Cixous bring out here is the way in which Freud treats Hoffmann's story as both an aesthetic production *and* as a text to be analysed; to be treated, that is, as the product of a case of (disordered) individual mental functioning. This brings us to another in the series of possible candidates for repression in Freud's analysis. Such an alternative candidate emerges as Freud attempts to relate the phenomenon of the uncanny to the theory of the castration complex. The misreadings highlighted by Freud's commentators appear to be produced by, among the other causes I have already referred to, Freud's desire to read the castration complex into Hoffmann's story. The castration complex is the 'unity' Freud desires to impose on the uncanny narrative of 'The Sandman'. This interpretative desire represses, as Freud's commentators have pointed out, key features of the narrative. The final candidate for repression, at this level, becomes the uncanniness for Freud of women, female identity and sexuality.

The first section of the paper is devoted to an examination of the concept of the uncanny from two distinct perspectives. Freud produces a long list of dictionary definitions of the words *heimlich* and *unheimlich* before going on to look at the phenomenon from the perspective of individual psychological examples. As Kofman remarks, the appearance of mutually informing investigative techniques is something of a rhetorical ploy, since Freud delivers his working definition of the concept prior to his etymological and psychological examples. Freud pre-empts these instances with the following remark: 'I will say at once that both causes lead to the same result: the uncanny is that class of the frightening which leads us back to what is known of old and long familiar' (UnC, p.340).

Freud backs up this working definition by treating the word 'canny' in terms of what he was elsewhere to call an 'antithetical primal word': a word which can contain contradictory or opposed meanings. The word canny has, among other things, to do with what is familiar, what is known and what is recognisable. The uncanny has to do with what is hidden and unfamiliar. However, as Freud points out, Schelling's comments assert that the uncanny (*unheimliche*) is that which 'ought to have remained secret and hidden but has come to light' (UnC, p.345). The uncanny thus comes to contain both what is hidden and what has come to light, what is revealed.

A certain resolution of these meanings begins to suggest itself when Freud looks at Grimm's dictionary, which stresses the canny as an idea of home. The home is canny, it is what is familiar and known, and yet it is a place which is separated from the 'eyes of strangers'. The home, a place of familiarity, depends, we might say, on the idea of its differentiation from an *other*, from the *not-home*, an idea which pulls it from the realm of what is revealed to the realm of what is concealed.

In essence, we are at the heart of Freud's new science of psychoanalysis here; a science which accounts for the existence at the very centre of the home of the unhomely, the *Other*. Having come this far, with a strong sense that this subject of the uncanny might provide some kind of substantiation for the principal tenets of psychoanalysis, Freud moves on to the next section, in which various examples are investigated.

This section begins with Freud engaging with the work of E. Jentsch, particularly his suggestion that a central technique for producing the effect of the uncanny is the use in fiction of automata or of states in which human beings seem to be reduced to mechanical entities or to be driven by mechanical forces. These figures, as Freud points out, are often related in literature to the theme of the 'double'. Freud also takes up Jentsch's suggestion that such effects are the stock-in-trade of the German Romantic writer, E. T. A. Hoffmann. Freud immediately departs from his precursor in analysis, however, when he asserts that the example of an automaton in the story 'The Sandman' is in no way the cause of that story's profound uncanniness. He writes: 'The main theme of the story is, on the contrary, something different, something which gives it its name, and which is always re-introduced at critical moments: it is the theme of the "Sand-Man" who tears out children's eyes' (UnC, p.348).

This disagreement with Jentsch over the function of the female automaton has, quite understandably, been the focal point of most recent commentaries on Freud's paper. Freud even goes so far as to suggest that, because there appears to be an element of satire revolving around the figure, this provides confirmation that it cannot be the main focus of the story or of its uncanny effects. Jentsch's assertion that the use of automata might be a major technique in producing the uncanny prompts Freud to focus on the writings of Hoffmann. When he gets down to looking at one of Hoffmann's stories in which an automaton is used, however, Freud denies that it has anything to do with the uncanny effect that story produces.

Weber writes that Freud's whole interpretation of 'The Sandman' is predicated on the assumption that there exists behind the narrative surface of the story 'an original Ur-text which itself is fully free of all distortion and repetition, and which antedates the fantasy-work of the writer'.[27] Such a belief in a stable, latent meaning behind the story, which as I have already said is for Freud determined by the castration complex (both as it is fictionalised in the story and as a determining element in the psychological constitution of that story's author, E. T. A. Hoffmann), leads Freud to direct his interpretative gaze exclusively towards the story of the male protagonist's (Nathaniel) movement towards death. Freud's interpretation of 'The Sandman' makes much of the figure of eyes in the story.[28] A fear revolving around the protagonist's eyes – losing his own or having them damaged, yet also a fear of other people's eyes – undoubtedly represents the structural motif of the narrative as a whole. Freud is able to make a direct connection between this theme and the castration complex since, as he points out, psychoanalysis has long known 'the substitutive relation between the eye and the male organ' (UnC, p.352). The castration complex is indeed founded on a fundamentally visual scene. As Freud describes it in his important paper 'Some psychical consequences of the anatomical distinction between the sexes',[29] little girls 'notice the penis of a brother or playmate, strikingly visible and of large proportions, at once recognize it as the superior counterpart of their own small and inconspicuous organ, and from that time forward fall a victim to envy for the penis.' Little boys, on the other hand, are horrified at the absence (of a penis) they see in their female counterparts: 'he sees nothing or disavows what he has seen, he softens it down or looks about for expedients for bringing it into line with his expectations.' This astonishing sight of the nothingness or lack in his female counterpart leads the little boy into 'horror of the mutilated creature or triumphant contempt for her', a feeling which often lasts into the adult life of the male.[30] Freud writes, offering one last example of the uncanny at the conclusion of section II: 'It often happens that neurotic men declare that they feel there is something uncanny about the female genital organs. This *unheimliche* place, however, is the entrance to the former *Heim* (home) of all human beings, to the place where each one of us lived once upon a time and in the beginning' (UnC, p.368).

Freud, however, as his commentators have pointed out, seems caught in his own form of blindness, his own scopic distortion. I have begun to refer to some of the elements which Freud leaves out of his reading. The whole issue of the tale's formal structure, its sporadic use of the epistolary mode, its playful shifting between narrative voices, the element of social satire involved in the episode of the female automaton, and various other details, are evaded or remain unseen by Freud. However, the most striking of all blindspots in Freud's interpretation occurs in his treatment of the tale's conclusion.

Freud's desire to read 'The Sandman' in terms of the castration complex requires him to draw an analogy between four figures: the two male antagonists in the narrative, Coppola and Coppelius; Nathaniel's father; the supposed 'bad' father imago of the Sandman himself. Such a requirement explains further why Freud should have rejected Jentsch's analysis of the female automaton. For Jentsch the effect of the uncanny attaches itself to such figures since it is an affective phenomenon which has to do with intellectual uncertainty. Freud's account of the uncanny depends not on the state of uncertainty but on the re-emergence of the repressed. Commenting on Nathaniel's fall to death from a tower after having apparently spied the figure of Coppelius–(Coppola)–Sandman walking towards him and his fiancée Clara from below, Freud writes:

> uncertainty disappears in the course of Hoffmann's story, and we perceive that he intends to make us, too, look through the demon optician's spectacles or spy-glass – perhaps, indeed, that the author in his very own person once peered through such an instrument. For the conclusion of the story makes it quite clear that Coppola the optician really *is* the lawyer Coppelius and also, therefore, the Sand-Man. (UnC, pp.351–2)

This is perhaps the most striking moment in Freud's reading of 'The Sandman': within it the extent of his misreading of the tale emerges dramatically. It is not only important to note, against Freud, that Hoffmann does in fact leave the relation between Coppelius (and thus Coppola) and the Sandman uncertain, it is even more important to recognise the complete redirection of sight involved in Freud's reading. As Kofman and Weber point out, Nathaniel's horror as he looks through the spy-glass does not ensue from sight of Coppelius (Sandman). Nathaniel is not looking down from the tower at all but towards his supposed beloved, Clara. As Weber puts it: 'Freud . . . has eyes only for the Sand-Man.' He goes on to assert that, unlike Freud, Nathaniel 'knows where danger lurks and there is no mistaking what he is compelled to see'. Clara, 'poison and antidote at once' is the person 'whom he . . . seeks to hurl from the tower, before he himself leaps'.[31]

Reiterating Weber's main points, Kofman adds that Nathaniel's use of the spy-glass functions as symbolic centre of the episode: 'Through the spy-glass, it is the face of Clara, the fiancée he thought that he would finally be able to marry, which appears terrifying to him, a veritable Medusa's head, as he imagined her in his poem'.[32] The spy-glass represents Nathaniel's major problem in the tale, which is, quite simply, his imprisonment in an imaginary structure within which women are whores and/or angels, 'poison' and/or 'antidote'.

It would appear that whatever light the theory of the castration complex has shed on Hoffmann's tale it has left Freud, its inventor, blind not only to important formal elements in the tale but to a whole area of meaning centred on the issue of the protagonist's relationship to and imaginative construction of women. The figure of the female automaton re-emerges in importance at this point as a further symbolisation of Nathaniel's difficulty with women, his imagining of them in the roles of passive beauties or demonically controlled, uncanny forces.

The theory of the castration complex, cornerstone of Freud's psychoanalytic explanation of the aetiology of sexual difference, appears to be the very thing which obstructs Freud's interpretative vision. A reader who has followed the line of argument I have been presenting this far will no doubt begin to recollect the next stage of Freud's paper, after he has concluded his reading of 'The Sandman'. In this section a discussion of the uncanny effect of repetition is illuminated by various personal asides, or autobiographical examples. As readers we begin to wonder how in control of the 'latent meaning' of these memories of uncanny repetition Freud actually is. Freud's repetitive returns to the red light district, in particular, are a rather disturbing attempt to elucidate the uncanny effect of the repetition of the same thing. The 'painted women' in the windows seem strangely reminiscent of the figure of the female automaton, although nothing Freud writes links them to that figure.

Why does Freud employ this example? It appears to establish a mode of intellectual uncertainty in precisely the same way as Hoffmann's story, so that instead of asking whether Coppelius equals Coppola equals the Sandman, we ask whether the painted women equal Olympia equal woman as the uncanny. Such equivalences begin to suggest a transference in which Freud is no longer the analyst of the patient Nathaniel but shares in Nathaniel's mode of blindness/ hysteria. Such transferences equally begin to transform Hoffmann from a position as analysand to the unrecognised analyst of Freud.

The issue of the compulsion to repeat leads Freud through comments on the animistic worldview and its residue in modern life, until he attains a kind of synopsis of his whole interpretation. The uncanny, Freud declares, is that which is frightening because it is something repressed which recurs. This insight explains the antithetical meaning of the word: 'for this uncanny is in reality nothing new or alien, but something which is familiar and old-established in the mind and which has become alienated from it only through the process of repression' (UnC, p.363–4). This is the definition which Bloom fixes on as Freud's original contribution to the aesthetics of the sublime. Indeed, having attained this definition, Freud proceeds to what might be called a moment of apotheosis:

> The Middle Ages quite consistently ascribed all such maladies [epilepsy and madness] to the influence of demons, and in this their psychology was almost correct. Indeed, I should not be surprised to hear that psychoanalysis, which is concerned with laying bare these hidden forces, has itself become uncanny to many people for that very reason. In one case, after I had succeeded – though none too rapidly – in effecting a cure in a girl who had been an invalid for many years, I myself heard the view expressed by the patient's mother long after her recovery. (UnC, p.366)

Freud's science of the mind becomes here the explainer of madness and disease. It becomes that mode of thought which has finally solved the great mysteries and which has explained the true import of earlier ages' insights. Psychoanalysis has made canny the areas of life which were previously uncanny and in doing so it has appeared to many people to be uncanny itself. Freud here is a kind of Christ figure; he cures people of their physical disorders and he exorcises demons. Yet is not such a parallel itself a return of the repressed, a desire for priority and authority which emerges from within Freud's apparently cool, rational discourse? Rather like the psychoanalyst, Sigmund Freud, riding on a night-train, suddenly being confronted by his double, that other, literary, uncanny Freud, who appears so repulsive to the public father of the scientific discipline of psychoanalysis.

If this is Freud's point of *daemonisation*, then the whole of the third section might be said to revolve around Freud's *kenosis*, a process of self-wounding in which he resubmits his decisive definitions of the uncanny to the problematic relationship (or non-relationship) between psychology and aesthetics. A reconsideration of this issue forces Freud back to a compromise with the theory of intellectual uncertainty, at least as regards the uncanny in literature. The section concludes with Freud distinguishing between a certainty concerning the causes of the uncanny in lived experience and an uncertainty concerning the uncanny in literature. Freud states that the storyteller's ability to play with our sense of reality provides him with far greater opportunities for generating the uncanny than are available in real life. 'We react to his inventions', Freud adds, 'as we would have reacted to real experiences; by the time we have seen through his trick it is already too late and the author has achieved his object' (UnC, p.374). The reader might well feel that Freud is not so much stating general aesthetic laws here as retrospectively rationalising the process of transference he has experienced in his engagement with literature in this very paper. An impression which might well be reinforced by his next statement: 'But it must be added that his success is not unalloyed. We retain a feeling of dissatisfaction, a kind of grudge against the attempted deceit.'

This reading of 'The uncanny' has been oriented towards explaining why Freud ends that paper expressing a grudge against literature. Bloom's interpretation of the paper as manifesting a drive for priority and authority seems accurate enough. What does not seem convincing is the assessment of Freud as a factitious writer who has anticipated all possible criticisms and all possible interpretations. The kind of critique I have been developing and extending here takes its cue from a much wider critique of Freud, which again centres on the construction of the female in Freud's work. If Freud's drive for priority and authority in 'The uncanny' is compromised by the very principle which is meant to establish its explanatory authority – the theory of the Oedipus complex and its accompanying phenomenon, the castration complex – then this only serves to mirror the manner in which Freud's writings have found their general claim to authority challenged through a radical questioning and problematisation of the psychoanalytic representation of women. The most important point about this general challenge to Freud's authority – a point which offers the possibility of marshalling the above material into a final revision of the theory of facticity – is that its most radical and far-reaching expressions have occurred not from positions *outside* the psychoanalytic movement, not by authors wishing to reject completely the discourse inaugurated in the writings of Freud, but from within that movement and that discourse.[33]

This is the characteristic form in which innovations and transformations in psychoanalysis tend to occur. Lacan's assertion that psychoanalysis needed to get back to the radical elements in Freud's writing, Kristeva's sense of the crucial role Freud plays in the revision of Marxist dialectics, are famous examples of the manner in which radical transformations in the psychoanalytic movement (involving an inevitable critique of certain elements in Freud's work) tend to go hand-in-hand with a reassertion of the original (authoring) position of Freud for that movement. It is this process, along with a similar process in the discourse of Marxism, which led Foucault to describe both Freud and Marx as 'authors of discourse'.[34] Foucault states that psychoanalysis and Marxism are special kinds of discourse because they are discursive practices in which their 'initiation . . . is heterogeneous to its subsequent transformations'. A 'return to the origin' is a function built into both psychoanalysis and Marxism as discourses, so that 're-examining Freud's texts modifies psychoanalysis itself just as a re-examination of Marx's would modify Marxism'.[35]

At the beginning of this section I suggested that on one level Bloom's description of Freud as a factitious author was convincing. By that I mean that Freud's function as the author of that discourse we call psychoanalysis remains unchallengeable so long as the discursive practice of psychoanalysis continues. Yet, of course, this is hardly the same thing as suggesting that Freud is beyond criticism and represents the particular kind of authority Bloom intends by his term facticity.

The manner in which feminist psychoanalytical writers have challenged Freud demonstrates what is at stake in this distinction. This questioning of Freud's construction of women, particularly his theory of the Oedipus and castration complexes in the female infant, dates back to the twenties and early thirties.[36] This tradition can be said to have enjoyed a brilliant and devastating re-emergence in the work of Luce Irigaray, particularly her long meditation on Freud's various writings on female sexuality, 'The blind spot of an old dream of symmetry'.[37]

Irigaray finds within Freud's writings on female sexuality similar breaks, diversions, distortions and absences to those I have been referring to in his paper 'The uncanny'. For Irigaray, Freud's writings represent a special moment in Western metaphysics in which the 'old dream of symmetry' is brought to a kind of culmination. What Irigaray means by the 'old dream of symmetry' is the patriarchal valorisation of unity and identity which, because it bases and centres these values in men and masculine desire, occludes feminine difference. Freud's discourse culminates and yet in that way manifests, lays open to view, discloses, a patriarchal logic to which the 'author' of that discourse remained blind.

On this reading, Freud remains an uncanny cultural figure; but hardly because he retains authority and priority of the sort Bloom's agonistic theory of meaning postulates. Freud is an uncanny figure because within his own work 'something which [ought] to have remained hidden . . . has come to light'.

Irigaray's work supports Bloom's claims for the cultural centrality of Freud. Her work can also be said to support Bloom's understanding of the continued influence of Freud over Western cultures as one necessarily bound up in processes of misreading, in an agon over authority and power. Yet her reading of Freud is also a graphic demonstration of the manner in which Bloom's own representation of Freud, and indeed his whole theory of meaning, tradition and influence, depends on a patriarchal ideology, which would have us believe that the Father is an unchallengeable figure (trope). I refer again here to the passage from Bloom quoted in my last chapter (see RST, p.120).

To challenge that repetition of the 'old dream of symmetry' in Bloom necessarily involves challenging Bloom's account of poetic meaning as the product solely of intratextual processes of revisionism. Which is to say that, for example, Freud's cultural power and authority is not reducible to his originating genius for rhetorical invention. Something else is involved in the meaning of Freud's writing than his undoubted agon with the literary and philosophical texts of tradition and our agon with the texts that agon produced. That 'something else' is Freud's and our own involvement with ideological structures, with sociocultural meanings which are by definition transcendent of all particular textual articulations and which make the intratextual agon over meaning observable in such a discursive formation as psychoanalysis mean something more than a psychopoetic drive for individual authority and power.

Jay Clayton and Eric Rothstein, in a survey of the distinct yet frequently competing histories of the terms influence and intertextuality, have recently argued that, for those modes of criticism which are concerned to trace the political and ideological features of literary texts, the term influence has often seemed more useful than the term intertextuality. The former term, they suggest, appears to allow for a mode of agency, of the human struggle within history, which the latter term would seem to diminish or even exclude.[38]

My revisions of Bloom's theory of influence (intratextuality) have not sought to replace the concept with a version of the currently more popular notion of intertextuality. Rather, I have been arguing that intratextuality and intertextuality, or what in chapter 4 was described in terms of the scene of instruction and the scene of writing, need to be understood as two sides of the same coin, or, to alter the figure, recto and verso. Another way of stating this is that my attempts to produce counter-readings of Stevens, Wordsworth, Shelley and Freud, which sought to revise the Bloomian reduction of meaning and revisionism to an intratextual dimension, have still, none the less, found a certain revised Bloomianism indispensable. What that intratextual level allows us to see is the manner in which, in literary texts, historical conflicts over sociocultural power and authority are often figured through conflicts over literary authority and power, and how what might initially look like specifically literary conflicts over the canon and over meaning invariably express and emerge from wider historical conflicts. Why do we always seem to be forced into positions of totalisation: to be *for* a concept like influence and thus *against* a concept like intertextuality, or vice versa? There are many possible answers, but one is, surely, that we tend to conflate (confuse) concepts with the personalities that invent, redefine or popularise them. This has been my point throughout this study, a point made against Bloom's psychopoetic theory of influence, yet which could not have been made in the manner it has been without that profoundly insightful, maddeningly blind, eminently challengeable work.

# Notes

## Historical and cultural contexts: movements beyond formalism

1. References to major works by Bloom will follow the key below:

(*Agon*) *Agon: Towards a theory of revisionism* (New York: Oxford University Press, 1982).
(AI) *The Anxiety of Influence: A theory of poetry* (New York: Oxford University Press, 1973).
(BF) 'The breaking of form', in *Deconstruction and Criticism*, ed. Bloom (New York: Seabury Press, 1979).
(BV) *The Breaking of the Vessels* (Chicago and London: Chicago University Press, 1982).
(FCI) *Figures of Capable Imagination* (New York: Seabury Press, 1976).
(KC) *Kabbalah and Criticism* (New York: Seabury Press, 1975).
(MM) *A Map of Misreading* (New York: Oxford University Press, 1975).
(PI) *Poetics of Influence: New and selected criticism* (New York: Henry R. Schwab, 1988).
(PR) *Poetry and Repression: Revisionism from Blake to Stevens* (New Haven and London: Yale University Press, 1976).
(RST) *Ruin the Sacred Truths: Poetry and belief from the Bible to the present* (Cambridge, Mass. and London: Harvard University Press, 1989).
(RT) *The Ringers in the Tower: Studies in Romantic tradition* (Chicago and London: Chicago University Press, 1971).
(SM) *Shelley's Mythmaking* (1959), 2nd edn (Ithaca, New York: Cornell University Press, 1969).
(VC) *The Visionary Company: A reading of English Romantic poetry*, revised and enlarged edn (Ithaca and London: Cornell University Press, 1971).
(WS) *Wallace Stevens: The poems of our climate* (Ithaca and London: Cornell University Press, 1977).
(*Yeats*) *Yeats* (New York: Oxford University Press, 1970).

2. Edward Said, *The World, the Text, and the Critic* (London: Faber and Faber, 1984), p.4.
3. J. Hillis Miller, 'Stevens' rock and criticism as cure, 2', in *The Georgia Review* 30, 2 (1976), p.341.
4. J. Hillis Miller, 'Tradition and difference', in *Diacritics* 2, 4 (1972), pp.6–13.
5. Edward Said, op. cit., pp.151–2.
6. Frank Lentricchia, 'Harold Bloom: The spirit of revenge', in *After the New Criticism* (1980), 2nd edn (London: Methuen, 1983), pp.318–46; Paul A. Bové, *Destructive Poetics: Heidegger and modern American poetry* (New York: Columbia University Press, 1980), pp.7–31; Daniel T. O'Hara, 'The genius of irony: Nietzsche in Bloom', in *The Yale Critics: Deconstruction in America*, Jonathan Arac, Wlad Godzich and Wallace Martin (eds) (Minneapolis: Minnesota University Press, 1983), pp.109–32, expanded version published in *The Romance of Interpretation: Visionary criticism from Pater to de Man* (New York: Columbia University Press, 1985), pp.55–92; Jonathan Arac, 'Harold Bloom: History and judgement', in *Critical Genealogies: Historical situations for postmodern literary studies* (New York: Columbia University Press, 1987), pp.11–23. For further discussions of the formalistic side of Bloom's criticism, see the following: Jerome J. McGann, 'Formalism, savagery and care: Or, the function of criticism once again', in *Critical Inquiry* 2, 3 (1976), pp.605–30; Peter de Bolla, *Harold Bloom: Towards historical rhetorics* (New York and London: Routledge, 1988), p.31; James R. Kincaid, 'Antithetical criticism: Harold Bloom and Victorian poetry', in *Victorian Poetry* 14, 4 (1976), p.370.
7. Paul de Man, 'Literary history and literary modernity', in *Blindness and Insight: Essays in the rhetoric of contemporary criticism* (1971), 2nd edn, revised and enlarged (London: Methuen, 1983), pp.142–65.
8. Ibid., pp.163–4.
9. Ibid., p. 163.
10. Ibid.
11. Ibid.
12. Ibid.
13. Ibid., p.150.
14. Jerome J. McGann, *Romantic Ideology: A critical investigation* (Chicago and London: University of Chicago Press, 1983), p.91.
15. Friedrich Nietzsche, 'On the uses and disadvantages of history for life' (1874), in *Untimely Meditations*, trans. by R. J. Hollingdale (Cambridge: Cambridge University Press, 1983), p.70–1.

## Chapter 1: Bloom and the re-evaluation of Romanticism

1. Harold Bloom, 'A new poetics', in *The Yale Review* 47, 1 (1957), p.133.
2. David Fite, *Harold Bloom: The rhetoric of Romantic vision* (Amherst: Massachusetts University Press, 1985), p.16.
3. Ibid., p.17.
4. Frank Lentricchia, *After the New Criticism* (1980), 2nd edn (London: Methuen, 1983), p.326.
5. Kelvin Everest, *English Romantic Poetry: An introduction to the historical context and the literary scene* (Milton Keynes and Philadelphia: Open University Press, 1990), p.22.
6. See M. H. Abrams, *Natural Supernaturalism: Tradition and revolution in Romantic literature* (New York and London: W. W. Norton, 1973). Hartman's essay 'Romanticism and anti-self-consciousness' has clear affiliations to Bloom's arguments here and was collected in *Romanticism and Consciousness: Essays in criticism*, ed. by Harold Bloom (New York: W. W. Norton, 1970), pp.46–56; reprinted in Geoffrey Hartman's *Beyond Formalism: Literary essays, 1958–1970* (New Haven and London: Yale University Press, 1970), pp.298–310.
7. This passage should be compared and contrasted to Frye's account of the final anagogic stage of his system in *Anatomy of Criticism: Four essays* (Princeton: Princeton University Press, 1957), pp.115–28. The particular essay by Frye that Bloom is attacking in his 'The internalization of quest romance' is 'The Romantic myth', in Frye's *A Study of English Romanticism* (1968), 2nd edn (Hemel Hempstead: Harvester Wheatsheaf, 1983), pp.3–49.

## Chapter 2: Anxieties of influence: deidealisation, reduction and Bloom's poetics of conflict

1. See Bloom's Foreword to Thomas Weiskel, *The Romantic Sublime: Studies in the structure and psychology of transcendence* (1976), 2nd edn (Baltimore and London: Johns Hopkins University Press, 1986), p.ix. This Foreword is incorporated as part of RST, pp.117–22.
2. Kenneth Connelly, review of *Yeats*, in *The Yale Review* 60, 3 (1971), p.397.
3. William V. Pritchard, 'Mr. Bloom in Yeatsville', in *The Partisan Review* 38, 1 (1971), p.109.

4. Sandra Seigal, 'Prolegomenon to Bloom: The opposing self', in *Diacritics* 1, 4 (1971), p.36.
5. Northrop Frye, 'The rising of the moon' (1965), republished in *Spiritus Mundi: Essays on literature, myth, and society* (Bloomington and London: Indiana University Press, 1976), pp.245–74.
6. Daniel T. O'Hara, *The Romance of Interpretation: Visionary criticism from Pater to de Man* (New York: Columbia University Press, 1985), p.84. See also O'Hara's 'The freedom of the master', in *Contemporary Literature* 21, 4 (1980), p.656.
7. Peter de Bolla has written one of the most complete accounts of the various misconceptions which have collected around Bloom's theory of influence: see Peter de Bolla, *Harold Bloom: Towards historical rhetorics* (New York and London: Routledge, 1988), pp.15–35. He has also discussed the figure of 'going beyond' in Bloom's work, linking it to the traditional rhetorical figure of hyperbaton (ibid., p.133) and thus to Bloom's theory of poetic crossings, while also showing how it works as a motif in Bloom's treatment of both traditional and deconstructive accounts of poetic rhetoric (ibid., p.81).
8. Ibid., p.16; Robin Jarvis, *Wordsworth, Milton and the Theory of Poetic Relations* (London: Macmillan, 1991), pp.77–83.
9. See Jarvis, ibid., p.80; and R. D. Havens, *The Influence of Milton on English Poetry* (1922), 2nd edn, (New York: Russell and Russell, 1961). For further comparisons between Havens and Bloom, see James Reiger, 'Wordsworth unalarmed', in *Milton and the Line of Vision*, ed. by J. A. Wittreich, Jr (London: Wisconsin University Press, 1975), pp.185–208 (p.186); and Stuart A. Ende, 'The melancholy of the descent of poets: Harold Bloom's *The Anxiety of Influence: A theory of poetry*', in *Boundary – 2*, 2, 3 (1974), p.609.
10. James Arrt Aune, 'Burke's late blooming: Trope, defence, and rhetoric', in *Quarterly Journal of Speech* 69, 3 (1983), p.331.
11. Elizabeth Bruss, *Beautiful Theories: The spectacle of discourse in contemporary criticism* (Baltimore and London: Johns Hopkins University Press, 1980), p.310.
12. See the interview with Bloom in Imre Salusinszky, *Criticism and Society* (New York and London: Methuen, 1987), p.51.
13. Geoffrey Hartman, 'War in heaven: A review of Harold Bloom's *Anxiety of Influence*', first published in *Diacritics* 3, 1 (1973), pp.26–32 and republished in Hartman's *The Fate of Reading and Other Essays* (Chicago and London: University of Chicago Press, 1975), pp.41–56.
14. Geoffrey Hartman, *The Fate of Reading*, ibid., pp.48–9.
15. Ibid., p.50.
16. Fredric Jameson, *The Political Unconscious: Narrative as a socially symbolic act* (London: Methuen, 1981), p.79. Pierre Macherey, *A Theory of Literary Production* (1966), trans. Geoffrey Wall (London and New York: Routledge, 1978).

17. Jay Clayton and Eric Rothstein, 'Figures in the corpus: Theories of influence and intertextuality', in *Influence and Intertextuality in Literary History*, Jay Clayton and Eric Rothstein (eds) (Wisconsin and London: Wisconsin University Press, 1992), pp.10–11.
18. Susan Stanford Freidman, 'Weavings: Intertextuality and the (re)birth of the author', in *Influence and Intertextuality*, Jay Clayton and Eric Rothstein (eds), p.154.
19. Ibid., p.166.
20. Sean Hand, 'Missing you: Intertextuality, transference, and the language of love', in *Intertextuality: Theories and practices*, Michael Worton and Judith Still (eds) (Manchester and New York: Manchester University Press, 1990), p.85.
21. Julia Kristeva, 'Word, dialogue and novel' (1966), in *The Kristeva Reader* (ed.) Toril Moi (Oxford: Basil Blackwell, 1986), p.36.
22. It is interesting to note that Walter Jackson Bate, in his *The Burden of the Past and the English Poet* (London: Chatto and Windus, 1971), frequently represents what Bloom was around the same time coming to describe as the anxiety of influence both as a burden related to the influence of one giant precursor, notably Milton, and also as a phenomenon to do with the sense of the sheer accumulation of influences upon the single would-be poet: (see p.4). Jean-Pierre Mileur's analysis of Bloom and the concept of revisionism can also be said to focus on a similar issue: see *Literary Revisionism and the Burden of Modernity* (Berkeley and Los Angeles: California University Press, 1985), pp.78–191.
23. Salusinszky, op. cit., p. 69.
24. See Frank Kermode, 'Institutional control of interpretation', in *Salmagundi* 43, 1 (1979), pp.72–86; 'Canon and period', in *History and Value* (Oxford: Clarendon Press, 1988), pp.108–27; also Kermode's 'The argument about canons', in *An Appetite for Poetry: Essays in literary interpretation* (Glasgow: William Collins, 1989), p.189–207.
25. One of the problems with Kermode's argument, and of course even more so with Bloom's, is that, as Alastair Fowler points out, there are many kinds of canons functioning at any one time in society: Fowler posits at least six different kinds of canon in his 'Genre and literary canon', in *New Literary History* 11, 1 (1979), pp.97–119.
26. Christine Froula, 'When Eve reads Milton: Undoing the canonical economy', in *Canons*, ed. Robert Von Hallberg (Chicago and London: Chicago University Press, 1984), p.154.

## Chapter 3: Maps of misreading

1. See M. H. Abrams, 'Structure and style in the greater Romantic lyric', in *The Correspondent Breeze: Essays on Romanticism* (New York and London: W. W. Norton, 1984), pp.76–108.

168  *Notes*

2. Robert Scholes, review of AI, in *The Journal of English and Germanic Philology* 73, 2 (1974), p.267.
3. Gerald Graff, 'Fear and trembling at Yale', in *The American Scholar* 46, 4 (1977), p.472.
4. Joseph N. Riddel, review of KC and PR, in *The Georgia Review* 30, 4 (1976), pp.992–3.
5. Joseph N. Riddel, 'Juda becomes New Haven', in *Diacritics* 10, 2 (1980), pp.17–34.
6. Paul de Man, 'Review of Harold Bloom's *Anxiety of Influence*', in *Blindness and Insight: Essays in the rhetoric of contemporary criticism* (1971), 2nd edn (London: Methuen, 1983), pp.267–76.
7. Ibid., p.267.
8. There are a number of discussions of de Man's review of *The Anxiety of Influence*. Of these a handful exhibit an awareness of the 'misreading' or strategic misunderstanding involved in de Man's critique. See the following: Wlad Godzich, 'Harold Bloom as rhetorician', in *Centrum* 6, 1 (1978), pp.43–9; Shuli Barzilai, 'A review of Paul de Man's "review of Harold Bloom's *Anxiety of Influence*" ', in *Yale French Studies*, vol. 69, *The Lesson of Paul de Man*, pp.134–41. Also see discussions in David Fite's *Harold Bloom: The rhetoric of Romantic vision* (Amherst: Massachusetts University Press, 1985), pp.163–7, and in Peter de Bolla's *Harold Bloom: Towards historical rhetorics*, (New York and London: Routledge, 1988), pp.70–4.
9. Paul de Man, op. cit., p.274.
10. Ibid., p.275.
11. Paul de Man, 'A new vitalism', in *The Massachusetts Review* 3, 3 (1962), pp.618–23.
12. Paul de Man, *Blindness and Insight*, p.272.
13. Paul de Man, 'Semiology and rhetoric', in *Allegories of Reading: Figural language in Rousseau, Nietzsche, Rilke, and Proust* (New Haven and London: Yale University Press, 1979), pp.3–19.
14. J. Hillis Miller, *The Linguistic Moment: From Wordsworth to Stevens* (Princeton: Princeton University Press, 1985), p.54.
15. Kenneth Burke, 'The four master tropes', in *A Grammar of Motives* (New York: Prentice Hall, 1945), pp.503–17.
16. Peter de Bolla, op. cit., pp.37–8.
17. In KC Bloom takes the complex system worked out by Moses Codervero and argues for its analogical appropriateness as a founding model for both the map of misprision and the scene of instruction. Centred on the concept of the sefirotic tree – with its ten *sefirot* or *behinot*, each an interpenetrating 'reading' or 'misprision' of the adjacent *behinot* – the Kabbalistic system, with its relational stages, becomes the perfect model for Bloom's already developed six-stage map. See 'Kabbalah and criticism', in KC, pp.49–92. For a usefully concise discussion of this appropriation of the Kabbalistic Sefirah, see Warwick Gould's 'A misreading

of Harold Bloom', in *English* 26, 1 (1977), pp.40–54. Bloom's appropriation of Kabbalah relies heavily on the work of Gershom Scholem. See his *Major Trends in Jewish Mysticism* (1941), 2nd edn (New York: Schocken, 1946) and *Kabbalah* (New York: Quadrangle, 1974).
18. Paul de Man, *Allegories of Reading*, pp.119–31.
19. Ibid., pp.124–5.
20. Ibid., p.125.
21. Ibid., p.131.
22. Peter de Bolla, op. cit., p.107.
23. Ann Wordsworth, 'An art that will not abandon the self to language: Bloom, Tennyson, and the blind world of the wish', in *Untying the Text: A post-structuralist reader*, ed. Robert Young (Boston: Routledge and Kegan Paul, 1981), p.212.
24. David Fite, op. cit., p.111.
25. See Frank Kermode, *Wallace Stevens* (Edinburgh and London: Oliver and Boyd, 1954), p.45; and Helen Vendler, *On Extended Wings: Wallace Stevens' longer poetry* (Cambridge, Mass. and London: Harvard University Press, 1969), p.52.
26. Robin Jarvis has recently produced a 'post-Bloomian' revision of the concept of mockery in poetic allusion in his *Wordsworth, Milton, and the Theory of Poetic Relations* (London: Macmillan, 1991), pp.106–35. Jarvis's point, that a certain kind of allusion or allusiveness can be produced which deliberately mocks the reader's own drive to interpretation as well as the poet's own will-to-identity and the precursor's own rhetoric of authority has close affinities to the reading I am advocating here. It should also be noted that the work of M. M. Bakhtin on parody constitutes a substantial theoretical support for the kind of reading I am developing. 'The comedian as the letter c' can be seen, on this basis, as making the sub-genre of quest-romance the 'object of representation'. M. M. Bakhtin, *The Dialogical Imagination: Four essays* (1975), ed. Michael Holquist, trans. Caryl Emerson and Michael Holquist (Austin: Texas University Press, 1981).
27. See Stevens's letter to Harriet Monroe, 21 December 1921, in *Letters of Wallace Stevens*, ed. Holly Stevens (London: Faber and Faber, 1966), p.224; Stevens's letters hereafter referred to as L.
28. See 'From the journal of Crispin', in *Wallace Stevens: A celebration*, Frank Doggett and Robert Buttel (eds) (Princeton: Princeton University Press, 1980), pp.30–45. Bloom omits all reference to the 'Journal', although it has been known about since 1974. The fact that this earlier version is now known to exist could be said to add another dimension to the problematic instability and excessiveness of the text[s] Bloom is mapping. Whether or not Bloom would feel the need to alter his six-part mapping of the 'Comedian', when dealing with the four-part 'Journal', again highlights the questionable authority of Bloom's map when applied to this text[s].

170  Notes

29. I am using *Wallace Stevens: The palm at the end of the mind*, ed. Holly Stevens (New York: Vintage Books, 1972), this being the edition Bloom cites in WS. References hereafter will be to PEM and to the appropriate page number, line numbers not being printed in this edition. This passage, p.60.
30. 'From the journal of Crispin', p.39. See Louis L. Martz's discussion of these lines, and the 'Journal' as a whole, in his ' "From the journal of Crispin": An early version of "The comedian as the letter c" ', in *Wallace Stevens: A celebration*, pp.3–29.
31. 'From the journal of Crispin', p.37.
32. Wallace Stevens, *The Necessary Angel: Essays on reality and the imagination* (1942) (London: Faber and Faber, 1984), p.18–19.

## Chapter 4: Scenes of instruction: The limits of Bloom's psychopoetics

1. See Bloom's review 'Poets' politics', in *The Virginia Quarterly Review* 47, 2 (1971), pp.314–17.
2. Bloom's theory of the poetic scene of instruction owes much to Hartman's treatment of Wordsworth's translation of 'the Puritan quest for evidences of election into the most ordinary emotional contexts'. See Geoffrey Hartman, *Wordsworth's Poetry, 1787–1814* (1964), 2nd edn (Cambridge, Mass. and London: Harvard University Press, 1971), p.5. See also Timothy Bahti, 'Wordsworth's rhetorical theft', in *Romanticism and Language*, ed. Arden Reed (London: Methuen, 1984), p.86.
3. Jonathan Culler, 'Presupposition and intertextuality', in *The Pursuit of Signs: Semiotics, literature, deconstruction* (London: Routledge and Kegan Paul, 1981), pp.107–11. Neil Hertz, *The End of the Line: Essays in psychoanalysis and the sublime* (New York: Columbia University Press, 1985), p.40–60.
4. Jacques Derrida, 'Freud and the scene of writing' (1966), in *Writing and Difference* (1967), trans. Alan Bass (London: Routledge and Kegan Paul, 1978).
5. Ibid., p.199.
6. Bloom's theory of a kind of primal narcissism in the poetic psyche, and his theory of the precursor's absorption into the poetic id, are indebted to the discussion of repression in Freud's 'Analysis terminable and interminable'. See Sigmund Freud, *Collected Papers*, vol. 5, ed. James Strachey (London: The Hogarth Press, 1950), pp.339–40. For Bloom's discussions of this passage, see *Agon*, p.114; also AI, p.88–9. Bloom's theory is also dependent, as I show below, on Freud's essay 'On narcissism: an introduction' (1914), in *Pelican*

*Freud Library*, vol. 11, *On Metapsychology: The theory of psychoanalysis*, ed. Angela Richards (Harmondsworth: Penguin, 1984), pp.61–97. See Bloom, RT, p.17; AI, p.88–9; *Agon*, p.105.
7. Elizabeth Bruss, *Beautiful Theories: The spectacle of discourse in contemporary criticism* (Baltimore and London: Johns Hopkins University Press, 1982), p.326.
8. Anika Lemaire, *Jacques Lacan*, trans. David Macey (London: Routledge and Kegan Paul, 1977), p.6.
9. Elizabeth Bruss, op. cit., pp.328–9.
10. Cathy Caruth, 'Speculative returns: Bloom's recent work', in *Modern Language Notes* 98, 5 (1983), p.1291.
11. Peter de Bolla, *Harold Bloom: Towards historical rhetorics* (New York and London: Routledge, 1988), pp.46–53.
12. *Wordsworth and Coleridge: Lyrical ballads, 1805*, 3rd edn, ed. Derek Roper (Plymouth: Northcote House, 1987), 'Tintern Abbey', ll.148–50. All further references to 'Tintern Abbey' will be marked 'TA' and will be from this edition.
13. Marjorie Levinson, 'Insight and oversight: Reading "Tintern Abbey" ', in *Wordsworth's Great Period Poems: Four essays* (Cambridge and New York: Cambridge University Press, 1986), pp.14–57.
14. Ibid., p.16.
15. For an extremely useful and informative account of these years and of why they should have produced a 'fear of writing' in Wordsworth, see Nicholas Roe, *Wordsworth and Coleridge: The radical years* (Oxford: Clarendon Press, 1988).
16. Marjorie Levinson, op. cit., pp.16–17.
17. Ibid., p.23.
18. Ibid., pp.29–30.
19. Ibid., p.33.
20. I am using MS 1 here, as published by Jonathan Wordsworth as 'Appendix 2. The Prospectus to *The Recluse*', in *The Borders of Vision* (Oxford: Clarendon Press, 1982), pp.387–90. This reference ll.7–9. All further references will be marked 'Pros'.
21. All references to *The Prelude*, unless otherwise stated, will be from the 1805 edition as published in *William Wordsworth: The prelude, 1799, 1805, 1850*, Jonathan Wordsworth, M. H. Abrams, and Stephen Gill (eds) (New York and London: W. W. Norton, 1979) and will be cited P. with book and line numbers following. This reference is from P.III. ll.286–95.
22. Peter de Bolla, op. cit., p.49.
23. 'William Wordsworth, 'Letter to the Bishop of Llandaff', in *The Prose Works of William Wordsworth*, 3 vols, W. J. B. Owen and Jane Worthington Smyser (eds) (Oxford: Clarendon Press, 1974), vol. 1, p.32.
24. 'Preface' to *Lyrical Ballads*, op. cit., p.25.

172  *Notes*

25. Hayden White, *Tropics of Discourse: Essays in cultural criticism* (Baltimore and London: Johns Hopkins University Press, 1978), p.94.
26. Raman Selden, *Practising Theory and Reading Literature: An introduction* (New York and London: Harvester Wheatsheaf, 1989), p.11.
27. Neil Hertz, op. cit., pp.40–60.
28. I am using the 1850 edition here, partly because it is the version employed by Neil Hertz, op. cit., pp.40–60; and partly because it is a more compact expression of the themes I am highlighting.
29. Neil Hertz, ibid., pp.58, 59.
30. See Timothy Bahti's discussion of the manner in which Hartman and Bloom interpret the trope of 'flood' in Book V of *The Prelude*, in 'Figures of interpretation, the interpretation of figures: A reading of Wordsworth's "dream of the Arab" ', in *Studies in Romanticism* 18, 4 (1979), p.624.
31. *Paradise Lost*, ed. Alastair Fowler (London: Longman, 1971), Book 1. ll.19–26.
32. Nicholas Roe, 'Wordsworth, Milton, and the politics of poetic influence', in *Yearbook of English Studies* 19, (1989), pp.112–26.
33. Ibid., p.115.
34. Ibid., p.118.
35. *Selected Prose of T. S. Eliot*, ed. Frank Kermode (London: Faber and Faber, 1975), p.177.

# *Chapter 5: Lies against time: Transumptive allusion, diachronic rhetoric and the question of history*

1. For John Hollander on the metaleptic troping upon the leaves, see *The Figure of Echo: A mode of allusion in Milton and after* (Berkeley, Los Angeles and London: California University Press, 1981), p.120–2; for Bloom's earlier work on this trope, see MM, pp.135–9.
2. Peter de Bolla, *Harold Bloom: Towards historical rhetorics* (New York and London: Routledge, 1988), p.121. I am indebted to de Bolla for my discussion of diachronic rhetoric and transumption in this chapter.
3. John Hollander, op. cit., p.99.
4. Ibid., pp.64–72.
5. Ibid., p.64.
6. Ibid., p.62.
7. Puttenham is quoted in Hollander, op. cit., p.142 and by Bloom in MM, p.103.
8. Harold Bloom, 'James Dickey: From "The other" through *The Early Motion*', in *The Southern Review* 21, 1 (1985), p.73.

Notes 173

9. For a useful analysis of Bloom's Judaic critique of the concept of *figura*, see Susan Handelman's *The Slayers of Moses: The emergence of rabbinic interpretation in modern literary theory* (Albany: State University of New York Press, 1982), pp.186–8. For an analysis of Bloom's distinction between transumption and *figura* in the context of modern theories of revisionism, see Jean-Pierre Mileur, *Literary Revisionism and the Burden of Modernity*, pp.100–19. For Erich Auerbach's work on *figura*, see his 'Figura', in *Scenes in the Drama of European Literature* (1959), 2nd edn (Manchester: Manchester University Press, 1984), pp.11–76: see also *Mimesis: The representation of reality in western literature* (1946), 3rd edn, trans. William R. Trask (Princeton: Princeton University Press, 1968), pp.73–6, 156–62, 194–202. For Bloom's criticisms of Auerbach, see PR, pp.87–92 and RST, pp.38–50.
10. Hans Jonas, *The Gnostic Religion: The message of the alien god and the beginnings of Christianity* (1958), 2nd edn, revised (London: Routledge, 1992). See the section on 'Gnostic allegory', pp.91–9.
11. Bloom has pursued his association between American poetics and the Gnostic tradition in various Chelsea House introductions: see, for example, *Nathaniel West's 'Miss Lonelyhearts'*, Modern Critical Interpretations (New York: Chelsea House, 1987), pp.1–9; *Herman Melville's 'Moby Dick'*, Modern Critical Interpretations (New York: Chelsea House, 1986), pp.1–11; *Thomas Pynchon's 'Gravity's Rainbow'*, Modern Critical Interpretations (New York: Chelsea House, 1986), pp.1–9.
12. John Hollander, op. cit., p.114.
13. Ibid., p.115.
14. See Peter de Bolla, 'Disfiguring history', in *Diacritics* 16, 4 (1986), pp.49–58.
15. Peter de Bolla, *Harold Bloom: Towards historical rhetorics*, pp.134–43.
16. Ibid., p.133.
17. Ibid., pp.135–43.
18. Ibid., p.136.
19. See PR, pp.83–111. The conclusion of this essay is republished in an extended form in Bloom's Preface to *Shelley's Prose or The Trumpet of a Prophecy* (1954), 3rd edn, ed. David Lee Clark (London: Fourth Estate, 1988).
20. Judith Chernaik, *The Lyrics of Shelley* (Cleveland and London: Case Western Reserve University Press, 1972), pp.8–31.
21. Ibid., p.30.
22. G. Kim Blank, *Wordsworth's Influence on Shelley: A study of poetic authority* (London: Macmillan, 1988), p.4.
23. Ibid., pp.5–6.
24. Timothy Clark's re-evaluation of the concept of 'sensibility' in Shelley also highlights the period between 1815–1817 as a crucial

phase. It was in 1815 that Shelley first began to formulate his 'science of mind' which, as Clark demonstrates, represents a rigorous analysis of the positionality of the poet conceived as a particularly receptive/sensitive being: see Timothy Clark, *Embodying Revolution: The figure of the poet in Shelley* (Oxford: Clarendon Press, 1989).
25. 'To Wordsworth' in *The Poems of Shelley*, vol. 1, 1804–17, Geoffrey Matthews and Kelvin Everest (eds) (London and New York: Longman, 1989). All further references to poems in the *Alastor* volume will be from this edition. All other references will be taken from *Shelley: Poetical works* (1905), ed. Thomas Hutchinson, new edn corrected by G. M. Matthews (Oxford: Oxford University Press, 1970) and will be cited as Poems with line numbers following.
26. G. Kim Blank, op. cit., p.6.
27. Ibid., p.69.
28. See 'London, 1802' in *William Wordsworth: The poems*, 2 vols, ed. John O. Hayden, vol. 1 (Harmondsworth: Penguin, 1977), pp.579–80.
29. William Hazlitt, *Complete Works*, Centenary Edition, 21 vols, *The Spirit of the Age* and *Conversation of James Northcliffe, Esq., R.A.*, vol. 11, ed. P. P. Howe (London and Toronto: J. M. Dent, 1932), pp.37–8.
30. P. M. S. Dawson, 'Shelley and class', in *The New Shelley: Later twentieth-century views*, ed. G. Kim Blank (London: Macmillan, 1990), pp.34–41. See also Dawson's *The Unacknowledged Legislator: Shelley and politics* (Oxford: Clarendon Press, 1980).
31. See 'Translated from the Greek of Moschus', 'Sonnet from the Italian of Dante Alighieri' and 'Guido Cavalcanti to Dante Alighieri' in Matthews and Everest. Blank, in *Wordsworth's Influence on Shelley*, argues for the close thematic relationship between the Cavalcanti translation and 'To Wordsworth' (p.48). Richard Holmes makes a similar point in *Shelley: The pursuit* (1974), 2nd edn (Harmondsworth: Penguin, 1987), p.308.
32. P. M. S. Dawson, *The Unacknowledged Legislator*, p.70.
33. A full analysis of the influence of Wordsworth on Shelley's use of this image-complex would, as I have already suggested, need to examine his revisionary reading of *The Excursion*. See *The Excursion* (1814) (Oxford and New York: Woodstock Books, 1991). The manner in which the various roles and positions I have been examining in Shelley's figure of the poet can be said to be separated out among the different characters in Wordsworth's poem is clearly an important issue, one with poetic and ideological implications.
34. Jerome J. McGann, *Romantic Ideology: A critical investigation* (Chicago and London: University of Chicago Press, 1983), p.111.
35. Ibid., p.118.
36. David Wyatt, 'Bloom, Freud and America', in *The Kenyon Review* 6, 3 (1984), pp.59–66.

37. It was in 1965 that Bloom published his first major essay on Emerson and the American tradition 'The central man: Emerson, Whitman, Wallace Stevens' (RT, pp.217–33) and there is a degree of reflexivity in Bloom's subsequent dating of the revival of Emerson's reputation in the American canon: see Bloom *Henry David Thoreau's 'Walden'*, Modern Critical Interpretations (New York: Chelsea House, 1987), pp.1–2. See also Bloom's 'Mr. America' in *New York Review of Books*, 22 November 1984, p.19; this essay is reprinted in revised form as 'Emerson: power at the crossing' in PI, pp.309–23 (see p.309).
38. *Henry James's 'The Portrait of a Lady'*, Modern Critical Interpretations (New York: Chelsea House, 1987), p.2.
39. 'Harold Bloom on poetry', in *The New Republic*, 29 November 1975, p.24.
40. *Henry David Thoreau's 'Walden'*, op. cit., pp.1–2.
41. Joseph N. Riddel, 'Juda becomes New Haven', in *Diacritics* 10, 2 (1980), pp.17–18.

# Chapter 6: Literary cultures: facticity and the return of originality

1. Harold Bloom, 'The analysis of character' in *Major Literary Characters*, 51 vols (New York: Chelsea House, 1990– ).
2. Marjorie Levinson, 'The New Historicism: Back to the future', in *Rethinking Historicism: Critical readings in romantic history*, M. Levinson, M. Butler, J. J. McGann, and P. Hamilton (eds) (Oxford: Basil Blackwell, 1989), p.18.
3. Jerome J. McGann, *Romantic Ideology: A critical investigation* (Chicago and London: University of Chicago Press, 1983), p.48.
4. Ibid.
5. Marjorie Levinson, op. cit., pp.49–50.
6. Louis Montrose, 'Professing the Renaissance: The poetics and politics of culture', in *The New Historicism*, ed. H. Aram Veseer (New York and London: Routledge, 1989), p.18.
7. Ibid., p.23.
8. Stephen Greenblatt, *Shakespearean Negotiations: The circulation of social energy in Renaissance England*, (Oxford: Clarendon Press, 1988), p.7.
9. Ibid., pp.1–20.
10. Ibid., p.6.
11. Ibid., p.7.
12. Ibid.
13. Ibid., p.12.
14. Bloom defends his version of character analysis in the General Intro-

duction to the new Chelsea House series *Major Literary Characters*, 'The analysis of character', op. cit.
15. Barry V. Qualls, 'Abishag's king', in *Raritan* 11, 3 (1992), p.105.
16. See Chapter 1, 'What is religious criticism?', in Bloom's *The American Religion: The emergence of the post-Christian nation* (New York: Simon and Schuster, 1992), pp.21–44. On the evidence of this book it might perhaps be more accurate to say that it is not Judaic tradition and culture but rather modern modes of Gnosticism which form the central focus of this new 'religious' approach to criticism: see also Bloom's 'Whoever discovers the interpretation of these sayings . . .', in *The Gospel of Thomas: The hidden sayings of Jesus*, ed. and trans. Marvin Meyer (San Francisco: Harper Collins, 1992), pp.111–21.
17. Michel Foucault, 'What is an author?', in *Textual Strategies: Perspectives in post-structuralist criticism*, ed. José V. Harari (Ithaca, New York: Cornell University Press, 1979), p.159. I am using the revised version of Foucault's paper rather than the version which can be found in Michel Foucault, *Language, Counter-Memory, Practice: Selected essays and interviews*, ed. Donald F. Bouchard, trans. Donald F. Bouchard and Sherry Simon (Oxford: Blackwell, 1977), pp.113–38, and which presents a translation of Foucault's original paper, first presented to the Société Française de Philosophie in 1969.
18. See Elizabeth Wright's useful survey of recent interpretations of 'The uncanny', in *Psychoanalytic Criticism: Theory in practice* (London and New York: Methuen, 1984), pp.137–50. Wright follows this with an account of Bloom's contribution to psychoanalytic literary criticism, focussing largely on the issue of the uncanny (see pp.150–6).
19. Ibid., p.143.
20. Sigmund Freud, 'The uncanny', in *Pelican Freud Library*, vol. 14, *Art and Literature*, ed. Albert Dickson (Harmondsworth: Penguin, 1985), pp.336–76 (p.339). Hereafter referred to as UnC. Bloom's reference occurs in *Agon*, p.101–2.
21. Neil Hertz, 'Freud and the Sandman', in *The End of the Line: Essays in psychoanalysis and the sublime* (New York: Columbia University Press, 1985), pp.97–121 (pp.118–19). Both Hertz and Bloom refer to a similar statement in *Beyond the Pleasure Principle*, in which Freud asserts that: 'Priority and originality are not among the aims that psychoanalytic work sets itself'. *Pelican Freud Library*, vol. 11, *On Metapsychology: The theory of psychoanalysis*, ed. Angela Richards (Harmondsworth: Penguin, 1984), p.275.
22. Of recent commentaries on 'The uncanny' I will be concentrating on the following: Neil Hertz, op. cit.; Samuel Weber, 'The sideshow or: Remarks on a canny moment', in *Modern Language Notes* 88, 6 (1973), pp.1102–33; Hélène Cixous, 'Fiction and its phantoms: A reading of Freud's *Das Unheimliche* ("The uncanny")', in *New Literary History* 7, 3 (1976), pp.525–48; Sarah Kofman, 'The double is/

and the Devil: The uncanniness of *The Sandman (Der Sandmann)*', in *Freud and Fiction* (1974), trans. Sarah Wykes (Cambridge: Polity Press, 1991), pp.119–62; Elizabeth Wright, op. cit.
23. Elizabeth Wright, op. cit., p.144.
24. Mark Edmundson, *Towards Reading Freud: Self-creation in Milton, Wordsworth, Emerson, and Sigmund Freud* (Princeton: Princeton University Press, 1990), p.xii.
25. Sarah Kofman, op. cit., pp.123–4.
26. Hélène Cixous, op. cit., p.526.
27. Samuel Weber, op. cit., 1119.
28. I do not intend to produce yet another paraphrase of Hoffmann's tale in this discussion. The question of paraphrase is of course a central issue in Freud's misreading of 'The Sandman'. As Hertz points out, there are two distinct paraphrases offered in Freud's account: the first representing its 'manifest surface', the second, 'offered in a long and stunningly condensed footnote' (see UnC., p.353–4) representing the latent meaning (see Hertz, pp.103–13). For the tale itself, see *Tales of Hoffmann*, selected, trans. and ed. R. J. Hollingdale (Harmondsworth: Penguin, 1982), pp.85–125.
29. Sigmund Freud, 'Some consequences of the anatomical distinction between the sexes', in *Pelican Freud Library*, vol. 7, *Sexuality*, ed. Angela Richards (Harmondsworth: Penguin, 1977), pp.325–57.
30. Ibid., pp.335–6.
31. Samuel Weber, op. cit., p.1121.
32. Sarah Kofman, op. cit., p.133.
33. Juliet Mitchell makes this point in her 'Introduction – 1', in *Feminine Sexuality: Jacques Lacan and the Ecole Freudienne*, Juliet Mitchell and Jacqueline Rose (eds), trans. Jacqueline Rose (London: Macmillan, 1982), pp.1–26.
34. Michel Foucault, op. cit., pp.153–7.
35. Ibid., pp.156–7.
36. For an illuminating discussion of what is traditionally known as the 'Jones–Freud' debate, but which in fact involved various female psychoanalysts, see Zenia Odes Fliegel, 'Feminine psychosexual development in Freudian theory', in *The Psychoanalytical Quarterly* 42, 3 (1973), pp.385–98. For a general survey of feminist critiques of Freud, see 'Introduction' in *The (M)other Tongue: Essays in feminist psychoanalytic interpretation*, Shirley Nelson Garner, Claire Kahane, and Madelon Sprengnether (eds) (Ithaca and London: Cornell University Press, 1985), pp.15–29.
37. Luce Irigaray, *Speculum of the Other Woman* (1974), trans. Gillian C. Gill (Ithaca, New York: Cornell University Press, 1985), pp.11–129.
38. Jay Clayton and Eric Rothstein, 'Figures in the corpus: Theories of influence and intertextuality', in *Influence and Intertextuality in Literary History*, Jay Clayton and Eric Rothstein (eds) (Wisconsin and London: Wisconsin University Press, 1992), pp.10–11.

# Glossary of terms

This is a short glossary of some of the more theoretically specific or obscure terms used in this book. My policy has been to concentrate mainly on those terms which, because of space, have not been submitted to a full analysis and description in the book itself. Some of Bloom's more challenging terms do not, therefore, appear in this glossary. I have also endeavoured to restrict the definitions to those most applicable to the manner in which these terms and concepts function in this study. For this reason, readers wishing to know more about the terms below should consult more substantial glossaries and reference works.

The following have all proved useful in compiling this glossary: M. H. Abrams, *A Glossary of Literary Terms*, 5th edn (Chicago: Holt, Rinehart and Winston, 1988); Chris Baldick, *The Concise Oxford Dictionary of Literary Terms* (Oxford: Oxford University Press, 1990); J. A. Cuddon, *A Dictionary of Literary Terms*, revised edn (Harmondsworth: Penguin, 1979); H. B. English and A. C. English, *A Comprehensive Dictionary of Psychological and Psychoanlytical Terms* (London: Longman, 1958); Jeremy Hawthorne, *A Concise Glossary of Contemporary Literary Theory* (New York: Edward Arnold, 1992); Alex Preminger, *The Princeton Encyclopedia of Poetry and Poetics*, enlarged edn (London: Macmillan, 1974); *The Oxford English Dictionary*, 2nd edn (Oxford: Clarendon Press, 1989).

**aetiology**: the location of a cause; hence, the psychoanalytic search for the *aetiology* of neurosis.
**anagogic**: from the tradition of allegorical writing and interpretation. The *anagogic* stage is the fourth stage in allegory: the other stages being the *literal*, the *typological* or historical, and the *tropological* or moral. The *anagogic* stage, in which a complete spiritual vision is achieved or communicated, is of particular importance in Northrop Frye's adaptation of allegorical interpretation: see **Archetypal Criticism**.
**analysand**: the person analysed in the psychoanalytic session.
**analysee**: the person doing the analysis in the psychoanalytic session.

**Antithetical:** from *antithetic*, direct opposites. Bloom uses the word in two distinct yet related ways. The first corresponds to Freud's concept of *antithetical primal words* and is defined by Bloom as 'the counter-placing of rival ideas in balanced or parallel structures [or] words . . .'. The second corresponds to Yeats's concept of the *anti-self* or *antithetical self*, and is based on the 'anti-natural, or the "imaginative" opposed to the natural' (MM, p.88).

**Apollonian:** Apollo, the Greek god of music, medicine, youth and light, is usually compared to Dionysus, the god of vegetation and wine. Nietzsche employs a distinction between the *Apollonian* and the *Dionysian* to mark a distinction between the rational, that faculty on which civilisation is built, and the instinctual, that faculty which is repressed in civilised life and yet which constantly reasserts itself.

**Aporia:** a logical contradiction beyond rational resolution. The *aporetic* nature of literary texts is a central preoccupation in *deconstruction* and the modes of criticism influenced by it.

**Apotropaic:** from the Greek, 'averting evil', 'to turn away'. The OED defunction is as follows: 'Having or reputed to have the power of averting evil influence or ill luck.' If we keep the word 'influence' but transpose 'poetic' or 'daemonic' for 'evil' in this definition, we begin to understand why this should be one of Bloom's favourite adjectives.

**Archetypal Criticism:** an *archetype* is an original model or pattern (prototype) from which copies are made. *Archetypal criticism* is a practice of interpretation promoted in the work of Northrop Frye. For Frye, literary texts exist within a 'literary universe' grounded in universal and timeless *archetypal* patterns.

**Auto-eroticism:** the arousal and/or gratification of a person's sexual feelings without the involvement of another person. Since sexuality in psychoanalysis has an extremely broad definition, this process can be said to take very different forms.

**Belated:** the state of being late, after the fact. The state of being *belated* corresponds to the experience of having been pre-empted by the past. This concept is, therefore, crucial for Bloom, who views all Western culture, since the Enlightenment, as *belated*. It should be noted, however, that in his recent work, Bloom has tended to backdate considerably the onset of a dominant sense of *belatedness* in Western culture.

**Caesura:** a break in the metrical pattern of a poetic line. In *poststructuralist* theory this word comes to signify a break in logic.

**Castration complex:** the fear in males of losing their genitals; in females, the fantasy of having once possessed a penis, now lost. In Freud, the *aetiology* of this complex takes us back to the *Oedipus complex* (q.v.).

**Catachresis:** often related to mixed or misused metaphor. A misapplication of a *figure*, making it difficult to relate it back to its literal usage. In deconstruction *catachresis* is important, since it represents the manner in

which rhetorical uses of language do not necessarily depend on a simple deviation from the literal.
**Chiasmus**: in rhetoric, a complex yet ordered (criss-crossed) arrangement of words or clauses which can be rearranged in a number of ways without altering the meaning of the whole to which each part belongs.
**Constative**: see **Performative**.
**Covering Cherub**: the angel posted at the gates of Eden after the expulsion of Adam and Eve. In Bloom, an image for the manner in which the *precursor* blocks the *ephebe* from originality and meaning.
**Crossings**: see **Topos**.
**Cultural materialism**: a mode of cultural interpretation, including literary interpretation, which, since the early 1980s, has emerged from the work of various influential thinkers, including Raymond Williams, Louis Althusser, Michel Foucault and M. M. Bakhtin. Critics of this school are interested in the manner in which cultural 'texts' are produced by and help to reproduce specific cultural discourses. *Cultural materialism* is often compared to *New Historicism* (q.v.).
**Davhar**: the Hebrew word for 'word'. Contrasted by Bloom to the Greek *logos*: see **Logocentricism**. In Bloom's comparison, *davhar* possesses the attributes of an action, *logos* possesses the attributes of rational description.
**Deconstruction**: a movement in philosophy and in literary theory, dating from the late 1960s, based on the work of the French philosopher Jacques Derrida. See **Aporia, Catachresis, Ecriture, Logocentrism, Metaphysics, Supplementarity**.
**Diachronic**: the study of something over time. *Diachrony* is contrasted to *synchrony*, which is the study of something, such as language, at a particular moment of time.
**Dionysian**: see **Apollonian**.
**Discourse**: an important but complex word in modern linguistics, philosophy and literary theory. A discourse, for Michel Foucault, is a group of statements, governed by rules of formation, objects of attention, linguistic and conceptual strategies, which determine the way in which the world can be understood and described at any specific historical moment. Given the notion that the manner in which we experience the world is determined by language, Foucault argues that various *discursive formations* combine to produce historically specific *epistemes*: worldviews, structures of knowledge, ideological constructions of the world. In Foucault and in the work of M. M. Bakhtin, a study of *discourse* or *discursive formations* necessarily involves a study of the modes of power, the ideological positions, which are supported by various discrete *discursive practices*: medical language, penal language, the language of criticism, philosophy, psychoanalysis, educational institutions, and so forth.
**Dualism**: in philosophy *dualism* represents the belief that mind and matter exist separately. *Dualism* is contrasted to idealism, materialism and also to *monism* (q.v.).

**Ecriture:** the French word for 'writing'. An important word/concept in *post-structuralist* theory. In Derrida's *deconstructive* philosophy, the traditional opposition which privileges speech over writing is reversed. *Ecriture*, for Derrida, represents the differential nature of all language.
**Ego:** see **Super-ego**.
**Energia:** the Latin word for 'energy'.
**Ephebe:** from the Greek word for a 'young citizen'. In Bloom the word denotes a young, *belated* 'citizen' of the realm of poetry. Bloom's use of the word foregrounds the quasi-Oedipal, agonistic nature of being a poet, since all *ephebes* have their *precursor*.
**Epistolary mode:** from the word epistle, a written message to an absent person: a letter.
**Essentialism:** an approach and/or belief that things have inherent qualities. Such a belief leads to the premiss that essences not only exist but can be located. *Essentialist humanism* is that view which posits an essential human nature beyond the influences of society, history and all other factors.
**Ethos:** Aristotle defines this as the 'character' of the orator as presented to an audience. *Ethos* is frequently contrasted to *pathos*, the Greek word for that element in an address or a text which creates the feelings of pity or sorrow in an audience.
**Extrinsic criticism:** the literary theorists Wellek and Warren group modes of literary criticism into either *extrinsic* or *intrinsic* modes. The former category covers all the approaches which look to contexts apparently 'outside' the literary text in order to establish its meaning. The latter approach reverses this procedure.
**Family romance:** in Freud's essay 'Family Romances' he describes the manner in which parents are fantasised by their children. Children construct fanstasies in order to explain their early, ambivalent feelings concerning their parents. Bloom adopts this term and applies it to the imaginary relations he sees at the heart of the poetic process.
**Figura:** Bloom, in his use of this word, follows the work of Erich Auerbach, who has traced the development of a particular approach to *figurative* language in the Christian tradition of Biblical interpretation. Auerbach relates *figura* to the Christian notion that *figures* (persons), events, objects and acts of speech prefigure events in the New Testament and in times still to come. Auerbach thus links *figura* to the idea of *type* and *anti-type* in the Christian tradition of allegorical interpretation of the Old and New Testaments: David is a *type* for Christ as *anti-type*. David is thus both a real, historical figure, but also a *figure* (*figura*), a sign for something else, i.e. Christ. This mode of reading the Bible can thus be called *figural criticism*, but should not be confused with the kind of *figural* or *figurative criticism* exemplified by Bloom and de Man: see **Figure**.
**Figure:** As Bloom states, in Quintillian, *tropes* and *figures* are compounded, although the former concept is ultimately subsumed under the latter. On

this view, 'A *trope* is a word or phrase used in some way that is not literal; a *figure* is any kind of discourse departing from common usage' (MM, p.93, my emphasis). Classical rhetoric also complicates things by attempting, often rather unsuccessfully, to make a distinction between 'figures of thought', which expand the semantic level of words, and 'figures of speech', which merely affect, through the process of *figuration*, a given audience. In modern, theoretical practice, including the work of Bloom, there is much overlap between *figure* and *trope*. A *figurative* mode of language is a variety of language which contains a high level or number of *tropes*. Both *figure* and *trope* designate words or phrases which deviate from literal or common usage. The kind of interpretative approach which concentrates on the *figurative* nature of literary language, and perhaps even on its own *figurative* status as text, as in the work of Bloom and de Man, can be described as *figural* or *figurative* criticism. This is not to be confused with the more traditional kind of *figural criticism* described above: see **Figura**. The former kind of criticism is sometimes described as *tropological criticism*, *tropology* being the study of the 'system' or the 'grammar' of *tropes* (metaphor, *metonymy*, *synecdoche*, etc.).

**Formalism:** in literary criticism and theory any approach that emphasises the form over the content of a text can be described as a mode of *formalism*. *Formalism* is, then, a way of reading literature which concentrates on the opaque nature of literary language, its construction in and through language, and thus its lack of direct referentiality, its inability to represent or speak directly about the world 'outside' it. This term, however, is too broad to be of much use in itself, and the kinds of approach which can be categorised under it exhibit fundamental differences from each other: see **New Criticism, Russian Formalism, Structuralism**.

**Genius loci:** 'spirit of place'. A term which is important in the study of Wordsworth's poetry but also relates to the idea, in rhetoric, of *topoi* or 'commonplaces': see **Topos**.

**Gnosticism:** an ancient, Judaeo-Christian heresy which asserts that the God of the Bible is in fact a secondary deity, a 'demiurge', and that the true God exists outside the material universe. Associating the creation of the universe with the Fall, the Gnostics argued that the true God remains hidden from all those within the universe. Proper knowledge (*gnosis*, enlightenment) of the alien, true God can only be achieved through a negation of all the forms of knowledge, including orthodox religious teaching, established in the fallen universe. The Gnostic practitioner is thus, for Bloom, a perfect example of the 'strong' 'poet', being a severe misreader of all prior texts and a supreme individualist.

**Hegelian negative:** the German philosopher Hegel argued for a theory of dialectics in which the fusion of a thesis and an antithesis produces a synthesis, a new thing or concept containing but not reducible to the two former terms. Bloom's description of the *deconstructive* practice of reading as producing a kind of *Hegelian negative* is meant to place *deconstruction* back in a Continental, rather than an American, intellectual tradition, and to highlight the fact that the result of such a mode of reading is not knowledge but a negation of the possibility of knowledge.

**Hermeneutic circle:** a concept, important in modern *hermeneutics*, which emphasises the problem that in order to understand a part of the text the reader must have a sense of the whole text, yet a sense of the whole text depends upon knowledge of its parts. The *hermeneutic circle* thus involves the problem of the 'foreknowledge' and/or the presuppositions we bring to an interpretation of a text.

**Hermeneutics:** the theory and practice of interpretation, originally of the Bible but now, in modern usage, of all texts.

**Hypostasisation:** to represent something as if it were a substance.

**Id:** that aspect of the unconscious which is not in contact with the world or with the rational mind and which manifests itself only though the experience in the individual of instinctual drives. See **Super-ego**.

**Impersonality thesis:** *New Criticism* follows T. S. Eliot in arguing that the function of great art is not to express but to escape from 'personality'. The work of art itself, rather than the authorial creator of that work, is emphasised by this principle.

**Infans:** a young child; precisely, a child prior to the acquisition of language. For the psychoanalytic theorist Jacques Lacan the notion of the *infans* is important, since it is only with the acquisition of language that identity occurs. Identity, for Lacan, therefore, is fundamentally social and linguistic.

**Intertext:** the text to which another text refers to or points towards *intertextually*. An important term in the work of critics such as Michael Riffaterre, for whom the function of interpretation is to locate in as precise a way as possible the texts on which other texts rely for their meaning.

**Intrinsic criticism:** see **Extrinsic criticism**.

**Introjection:** a complex term in psychoanalysis. Bloom focuses on its meaning as the absorption of the external world into the subjective 'self'; a response to the external world which views that world as if it were part of the 'self'. In psychoanalysis, however, various other definitions of *introjection* emphasise the process in which the 'self' projects its own identity into inanimate objects or into the position of other people. As a word, therefore, *introjection* tends to merge with its supposed opposite, *projection*. In psychoanalysis, *projection* is the mistaken attribution of one's own feelings, fears or characteristics to others. Both of these terms, as Bloom, after Freud, reminds us, tend towards an animistic vision of the world.

**J writer:** the first of the series of authors credited with composing the first part of the Hebrew Bible. Also referred to as the *Yahwist*, because of the author's specific nomination of God.

184  *Notes*

**Kabbalah:** sometimes spelt *Cabbala* and meaning 'tradition'. The *Kabbalah* is the tradition of oral instruction which was inherited by the Rabbinic scribes and formed the basis for their interpretations of the *Torah* (the 'Law' or Pentateuch, first five books of the Hebrew Bible) in both the Mishnah and the Talmud. More specifically, *Kabbalism* is the tradition of mystical interpretation of the Hebrew Bible which fed into Christian sects and became mixed, in the medieval and Renaissance periods, with the art and theory of alchemy.

**Logocentricism:** a crucial concept in *deconstruction*. From *logos*, a word which combines 'reason' and 'the Word' (in the New Testament Christ is described as 'the Word'/*logos*). Derrida denotes as *logocentric* all systems of thought which rely on the idea of presence and identity. Such *logocentric* concepts, he argues, form the 'centre' of the various structures or systems erected within *Western metaphysics* and do not account for the differential nature of language: see **Ecriture, Metaphysics, Supplementarity.**

**Lurianic:** from Isaac Luria, of sixteenth-century Kabbalist.

**Merkabah:** the vision of God in a chariot presented, notably, in Ezekiel and again in Revelations. This image is, according to some, the one exception to the Hebraic rejection of icons or images of divinity.

**Metalepsis:** Bloom sometimes describes this trope as the *metonymy* (q.v.) of a *metonymy*. Quintillian describes it as a *metonymy* in which that which is substituted is itself figurative. This *trope* is closely related to *catachresis*.

**Metaphysics:** the mode of philosophical thought which deals with first principles, such as being, substance, cause, time, space. Modern *poststructuralist*, and particularly *deconstructive*, theory seeks to challenge and ultimately unravel the claims of *Western metaphysics*.

**Metonymy:** a rhetorical figure in which the name of an aspect or a part of a thing is applied to (substitutes for) another thing.

**Misprision:** in Bloom, another word for misreading. This word functions particularly to signify the consequences of an act of misreading.

**Modernism:** see **Post-modern.**

**Monism:** the belief that there is only one being, or one supreme Being, in existence; also those theories which deny the fundamental distinction (duality) between mind and body: see **Dualism.**

**Mythopoeic:** that kind of poetry which has close affinities to myth. Thus *mythopoeia* would be the study of the mythic qualities of poetry or of its relation to myth.

**New Criticism:** a *formalist* mode of literary criticism and theory dominant in the Anglo-American academic arena between the 1930s and the 1950s: see **Impersonality thesis.**

**New Historicism:** a mode of criticism, dating from the early 1980s to the present, which combines an attention to the historical and ideological nature of texts with a *post-structuralist* approach to language and representation: see **Cultural materialism.**

**Oedipus complex:** Freud's theory that in early stages of psychological development little boys develop a desire to join sexually with their mothers and, as a consequence, develop a resentment against their fathers. For Freud, female infants have their own version of this complex: see **Castration complex, Family romance.**

**Optative mood:** in grammar, the *optative mood* of a verb is that mood in which the expression of desire or wish is predominant. Bloom applies this phrase as a general description to one aspect of Emerson's writings.

**Paradigmatic:** the associative element in any piece of language; opposed to the combinatory element in any piece of language, the *syntagmatic* level. Every word in any given sentence will be chosen from a possible list of associated words. Language works on a *syntagmatic* or linear plane in which meaning is produced by the total combination of words, each chosen from a *paradigmatic*, associative series or register.

**Pathos:** see **Ethos.**

**Performative:** from modern theories of speech acts. A *performative* is an utterance which does something (i.e. 'I promise to pay my bill') rather than says something about the world. The latter kind of utterance is often called a *constative*.

**Phenomenology:** a movement in philosophy, beginning with the work of Edmund Husserl, which attempts to investigate the world as a product of consciousness rather than as a field of objects independent of consciousness. This movement has influenced a number of philosophical and critical schools, including existentialism, the 'Geneva School' of literary criticism and various modes of literary theory which concentrate on the response (consciousness) of the reader in the act of interpretation.

**Post-Enlightenment:** the phase of history, or of literary or philosophical history, beginning in the latter part of the eighteenth century at the close of the Enlightenment period. For Bloom, the *Post-Enlightenment* phase begins slightly earlier and is identical to the phase of cultural history he would call, alternatively, Romantic or Modern.

**Post-modern:** the current period in Western culture, coming after the *Modernist* stage, during the first few decades of this century. *Post-modernism* is seen as continuing the radical break with traditional forms of thought and expression initiated by *Modernism*, but it extends such a project beyond any level countenanced by *Modernism*. If both *Modernism* and *Post-modernism* rely on the appearance of discontinuity, formlessness and modes of indeterminacy, the former can be said to contain these appearances within an overall structure, while the latter attempts to resist such a move.

**Post-structuralism:** the movement in theory which succeeded *Structuralism*. Like *Post-modernism, Post-structuralism* is a mode of thought and practice which denies the possibility of explaining the world by recourse to universal or absolute or totalising systems or structures.

**Pragmatism**: a mode of philosphical thought, primarily American, which argues that the basis of any understanding of a concept or phenomenon lies in their practical consequences in the world.
**Precursor**: Bloom employs this term to designate that specific past poet against whom the *ephebe* poet attempts to defend him- or herself.
**Primal repression**: Bloom makes much of this concept from Freud's latter period. In his latter work, Freud posited the possibility of an initial act of repression prior to object-consciousness. A *primal repression* would, in a sense, be an initial act of repression made before there was anything specific for the psyche to repress.
**Primal scene**: in psychoanalysis the *primal scene* is an event in which some initial form of sexual experience occurs. In the *primal scene fantasy*, the older child fantasises that it remembers witnessing its parents engaged in the sexual act.
**Projection**: see **Introjection**.
**Repetition-compulsion**: a mechanism of psychological defence in which an irrational compulsion to repeat, often a rather simple action, represses and yet negatively manifests or exposes an anxiety.
**Revisionism**: this term has a general currency in historical and political thought, often of a pejorative variety. On this level *revisionism* is the rewriting of history for ideological purposes: there are *revisionistic* accounts of Marxist thought and of recent German history, for example. In Bloom, *revisionism* is a key concept, representing the basic nature of all *belated* writing. If all writing, but particularly all literary writing, in the modern world, is *belated*, then all writing is necessarily parasitical on original vision, and is thus *revisionary*.
**Scopic**: from the Latin and Greek 'to look at' and 'to examine'.
**Signified**: from Saussure's theory of the sign. The *signified* is the concept designated by a particular sound or image, a *signifier*.
**Signifier**: see **Signified**.
**Signifying practice**: an important concept in the work of Roland Barthes and Julia Kristeva. A *signifying practice* can be described as a particular mode of discourse in which the struggle for meanings between individual *subjects* and dominant social systems is played out.
**Structuralism**: the theoretical movement which, at various times and in various places, during the twentieth century, has argued for the possibility of understanding culture and cultural productions on the basis of the 'science' of linguistics. Thus in *Structuralism* any definable aspect of cultural life can be seen as a system or code functioning in a manner analogous to language.
**Subject**: in modern theory the *subject* designates the idea that consciousness is not a natural and/or individual phenomenon, but, rather, something constructed ideologically. In most theoretical uses of the term, therefore, there is a conscious pun which combines consciousness (the orthodox notion of 'subjectivity') with subjection (the construction and

positioning, frequently repressive, of the 'self' or sense of 'self' through ideology).
**Sublime:** as an aesthetic term the classical notion of the *sublime* contains the sense of what is beyond normal perception with that which is lofty, elevated, and also that which is obscure or mysterious. Due to the renewed interest in this subject in the eighteenth century, the *sublime* constituted an important element in Romanticism. The German Enlightenment philosopher Kant differentiated between the *dynamical sublime*, which involves a sense of a natural phenomenon too large for normal perceptual categories, and the *mathematical sublime*, involving the sense of an uncontainable excess or series of repeated things.
**Super-ego:** in Freud, the part of the psyche in which is located the internalised voice(s) of authority, initially parental, and which attempts to influence the *ego*, that part of the psyche which has direct contact with the external world, against the influence of the *id*.
**Supplementarity:** a key term in *deconstruction*. Derrida's *deconstruction* of *Western metaphysics* involves a disruption of established oppositions. Derrida argues that traditional *metaphysics* relies on the privileging of one of the two terms in the oppositions which form the foundation of thought and belief: e.g. male over female, the rational over the irrational, the literal over the figurative. *Supplementarity*, as a concept, represents deconstruction's characteristic move, in which a *demonstration* of the conceptual priority of a traditionally subordinated term in an important opposition helps to disrupt the entire system established upon the basis of that opposition. Derrida argues, in other words, that those terms which are traditionally seen as *supplementary* are, in fact, from a conceptual point of view, *primary*.
**Synchronic:** see **Diachronic**.
**Synecdoche:** a rhetorical *figure* in which a part substitutes for the whole or the whole substitutes for a part.
**Syntagmatic:** see **Paradigmatic**.
**Taxonomy:** the classification of a system or field in terms of its essential parts, or laws, or principles.
**Tetralogy:** a series of four related works, traditionally literary works.
**Topos:** in rhetoric *topoi* are 'commonplaces' or 'places of invention'; specific parts or places of an address or text traditionally associated with specific *tropes*. *Topos*, as an idea, thus suggests that, in an address or text, the speaker should move through pre-established stages, involving conventional rhetorical stances, in order for the address or text to be understood and thus to be effective. Bloom relates *topos* to the notion of the *genius loci*; he also develops a theory of *poetic crossings* from an analysis of *topoi*. For Bloom, poems move through three *crossings* or moments of crisis, in which whatever meaning those texts appear to possess is collected. Bloom's theory of *poetic crossings* presents an additional level in his theory that *post-Enlightenment* poems depend on a pre-established map of

images, *tropes* and defences. In short, Bloom's theory of *crossings* allows him to argue that reading poetic texts involves a location and interpretation of various places in a text, *topoi*, in which specific *tropes* and defences are replaced by others. The *poetic crossings* are: the *Crossing of Election*, the *Crossing of Solipsism* and the *Crossing of Identification* (see WS, pp.402–4).

**Torah**: the Hebrew word for the law or instruction, thus the first five books of the Hebrew Bible, the Mosaic Law or Pentateuch.

**Transference**: an essential aspect of the psychoanalytic session, in which the *analysand* displaces disordered feelings for another person or persons (often the parents) onto the *analysee*.

**Trope**: see **Figure**.

**Typology**: from the allegorical practice of interpretation: see **Anagogic**, **Figura**.

**Vichian**: pertaining to Giambattista Vico (1668–1744), Italian philosopher and author of *The New Science*.

**Writing**: see **Ecriture**.

# Bibliography

## Works by Bloom

A complete bibliography of Bloom's work is currently being prepared by Roy Sellars for Gale Press.

'A new poetics', in *The Yale Review* 47, 1 (1957), pp.130–3.
*Shelley's Mythmaking* (1959), 2nd edn (Ithaca, New York: Cornell University Press, 1969).
*The Visionary Company: A reading of English Romantic poetry* (1961), rev. edn (Ithaca and London: Cornell University Press, 1971).
*Blake's Apocalypse: A study in poetic argument* (1963), 2nd edn (Ithaca, New York: Cornell University Press, 1970).
*From Sensibility to Romanticism: Essays presented to Fredrick A. Pottle*, Harold Bloom and Fredrick W. Hilles (eds) (New York: Oxford University Press, 1965).
Commentary, in *The Complete Poetry and Prose of William Blake* (1965), newly rev. edn, ed. David V. Erdman (New York: Anchor Press/ Doubleday, 1982), pp.894–970.
*Yeats* (New York: Oxford University Press, 1970).
*Romanticism and Consciousness: Essays in criticism*, ed. Harold Bloom (New York: W. W. Norton, 1970).
*The Ringers in the Tower: Studies in Romantic tradition* (Chicago and London: University of Chicago Press, 1971).
'Poets' politics', in *The Virginia Quarterly Review* 47, 2 (1971), pp.314–17.
*The Anxiety of Influence: A theory of poetry* (New York: Oxford University Press, 1973).
*Romantic Poetry and Prose*, The Oxford Anthology of English Literature, Harold Bloom and Lionel Trilling (eds) (New York: Oxford University Press, 1973).
*Victorian Poetry and Prose*, The Oxford Anthology of English Literature, Harold Bloom and Lionel Trilling (eds) (New York: Oxford University Press, 1973).

## Bibliography

*A Map of Misreading* (New York: Oxford University Press, 1975).
*Kabbalah and Criticism* (New York: Seabury Press, 1975).
'Harold Bloom on poetry', in *The New Republic*, 29 November 1975, pp.24–6.
*Poetry and Repression: Revisionism from Blake to Stevens* (New Haven and London: Yale University Press, 1976).
*Figures of Capable Imagination* (New York: Seabury Press, 1976).
*Wallace Stevens: The poems of our climate* (Ithaca and London: Cornell University Press, 1977).
*Deconstruction and Criticism*, ed. Harold Bloom (New York: Seabury Press, 1979).
*The Flight to Lucifer: A Gnostic fantasy* (New York: Vintage Books, 1980).
*Agon: Towards a theory of revisionism* (New York: Oxford University Press, 1982).
*The Breaking of the Vessels* (Chicago and London: University of Chicago Press, 1982).
'Mr. America', in *New York Review of Books*, 22 November 1984, pp.19–24.
'James Dickey: From "The other" through *The Early Motion*', in *The Southern Review* 21, 1 (1985), pp.63–78.
*Modern Critical Interpretations*, 132 vols (New York: Chelsea House, 1985– ).
*Modern Critical Views*, Series 1, 115 vols (New York: Chelsea House, 1985– ).
Foreword, in Thomas Weiskel, *The Romantic Sublime: Studies in the structure and psychology of transcendence* (1976), 2nd edn (Baltimore and London: Johns Hopkins University Press, 1986), pp.vii–x.
Interview, in *Criticism and Society*, ed. Imre Salusinszky (New York and London: Methuen, 1987), pp.45–73.
*Poetics of Influence: New and selected criticism* (New Haven: Henry R. Schwab, 1988).
Preface, in *Shelley's Prose or The Trumpet of a Prophecy* (1954), 3rd. edn, corrected, ed. David Lee Clark (London: Fourth Estate, 1988).
*Ruin the Sacred Truths: Poetry and belief from the Bible to the present* (Cambridge, Mass. and London: Harvard University Press, 1989).
*Major Literary Characters*, 51 vols (New York: Chelsea House, 1990– ).
*The Book of J*, trans. David Rosenberg, interpreted Harold Bloom (London: Faber and Faber, 1991).
*The American Religion: The emergence of the post-Christian nation* (New York: Simon and Schuster, 1992).
'Whoever discovers the interpretation of these sayings . . .', in *The Gospel of Thomas: The hidden sayings of Jesus*, trans. and ed. Marvin Meyer (San Francisco: Harper Collins, 1992), pp.111–21.

## Secondary works

Abrams, M. H., *Natural Supernaturalism: Tradition and revolution in Romantic literature* (New York and London: W. W. Norton, 1973).
Abrams, M. H., *The Correspondent Breeze: Essays on Romanticism* (New York and London: W. W. Norton, 1984).
Arac, Jonathan, Wlad Godzich and Wallace Martin (eds) *The Yale Critics: Deconstruction in America* (Minneapolis: Minnesota University Press, 1983).
Arac, Jonathan, *Critical Genealogies: Historical situations for post-modern literary studies* (New York: Columbia University Press, 1987).
Auerbach, Erich, *Mimesis: The representation of reality in western literature* (1946), 3rd edn, trans. William R. Trask (Princeton: Princeton University Press, 1968).
Auerbach, Eric, *Scenes in the Drama of European Literature* (1959), 2nd edn (Manchester: Manchester University Press, 1984).
Aune, James Arrt, 'Burke's late blooming: Trope, defence, and rhetoric', in *The Quarterly Journal of Speech* 69, 3 (1983), pp.328–40.
Bahti, Timothy, 'Figures of interpretation, the interpretation of figures: A reading of Wordsworth's "dream of the Arab" ', in *Studies in Romanticism* 18, 4 (1979), pp.601–27.
Bahti, Timothy, 'Wordsworth's rhetorical theft', in *Romanticism and Language*, ed. Arden Reed (London: Methuen, 1984), pp.86–124.
Bakhtin, M. M., *The Dialogical Imagination: Four essays*, ed. Michael Holquist, trans. Caryl Emerson and Michael Holquist (Austin: Texas University Press, 1981).
Barzilai, Shuli, 'A review of Paul de Man's "review of Harold Bloom's *The Anxiety of Influence*" ', in *Yale French Studies*, vol. 69, *The Lesson of Paul de Man*, pp.134–41.
Bate, Walter Jackson, *The Burden of the Past and the English Poet* (London: Chatto and Windus, 1971).
Blank, G. Kim, *Wordsworth's Influence on Shelley: A study of poetic authority* (London: Macmillan, 1988).
Bolla, Peter de, 'Disfiguring history', in *Diacritics* 16, 4 (1986), pp.49–58.
Bolla, Peter de, *Harold Bloom: Towards historical rhetorics* (New York and London: Routledge, 1988).
Bové, Paul A., *Destructive Poetics: Heidegger and modern American poetry* (New York: Columbia University Press, 1980).
Bruss, Elizabeth, *Beautiful Theories: The spectacle of discourse in contemporary criticism* (Baltimore and London: Johns Hopkins University Press, 1982).
Burke, Kenneth, *A Grammar of Motives* (New York: Prentice Hall, 1945).
Caruth, Cathy, 'Speculative returns: Bloom's recent work', in *Modern Language Notes* 98, 5 (1983), pp.1286–96.

## 192  Bibliography

Chernaik, Judith, *The Lyrics of Shelley* (Cleveland and London: Case Western Reserve University Press, 1972).
Cixous, Hélène, 'Fiction and its phantoms: A reading of Freud's *Das Unheimliche* ("The uncanny")', in *New Literary History* 7, 3 (1976), pp.525–48.
Clark, Timothy, *Embodying Revolution: The figure of the poet in Shelley* (Oxford: Clarendon Press, 1989).
Clayton, Jay and Eric Rothstein (eds), *Influence and Intertextuality in Literary History* (Wisconsin and London: Wisconsin University Press, 1992).
Connelly, Kenneth, review of *Yeats*, in *The Yale Review* 60, 3 (1971), pp.394–403.
Culler, Jonathan, *The Pursuit of Signs: Semiotics, literature, deconstruction* (London: Routledge and Kegan Paul, 1981).
Dawson, P. M. S., *The Unacknowledged Legislator: Shelley and politics* (Oxford: Clarendon Press, 1980).
Dawson, P. M. S., 'Shelley and class', in *The New Shelley: Later twentieth-century views*, ed. G. Kim Blank (London: Macmillan, 1990), pp.34–41.
Derrida, Jacques, *Writing and Difference* (1967), trans. Alan Bass (London: Routledge and Kegan Paul, 1978).
Doggett, Frank and Robert Buttel (eds), *Wallace Stevens: A celebration* (Princeton: Princeton University Press, 1980).
Edmundson, Mark, *Towards Reading Freud: Self-creation in Milton, Wordsworth, Emerson, and Sigmund Freud* (Princeton: Princeton University Press, 1990).
Eliot, T. S., *Selected Prose of T. S. Eliot*, ed. Frank Kermode (London: Faber and Faber, 1975).
Ende, Stuart A., 'The melancholy of the descent of poets: Harold Bloom's *The Anxiety of Influence: A theory of poetry*', in *Boundary – 2* 2, 3 (1974), pp.608–15.
Everest, Kelvin, *English Romantic Poetry: An introduction to the historical context and the literary scene* (Milton Keynes and Philadelphia: Open University Press, 1990).
Fite, David, *Harold Bloom: The rhetoric of Romantic vision* (Amherst: Massachusetts University Press, 1985).
Fliegel, Zenia Odes, 'Feminine psychosexual development in Freudian theory', in *The Psychoanlytical Quarterly* 42, 3 (1973), pp.385–98.
Foucault, Michel, 'What is an author?', in *Textual Strategies: Perspectives in post-structuralist criticism*, ed. José V. Harari (Ithaca, New York: Cornell University Press, 1979), pp.141–60.
Foucault, Michel, *Language, Counter-Memory, Practice: Selected essays and interviews*, ed. Donald F. Bouchard, trans Donald F. Bouchard and Sherry Simon (Oxford: Blackwell, 1977).
Fowler, Alastair, 'Genre and literary canon', in *New Literary History* 11, 1 (1979), pp.97–119.

Freud, Sigmund, *Collected Papers*, vol. 5, ed. James Strachey (London: The Hogarth Press, 1950).
Freud, Sigmund, *Pelican Freud Library*, vol. 7, *Sexuality*, ed. Angela Richards (Harmondsworth: Penguin, 1977).
Freud, Sigmund, *Pelican Freud Library*, vol. 11, *On Metapsychology: The theory of psychoanalysis*, ed. Angela Richards (Harmondsworth: Penguin, 1984).
Freud, Sigmund, *Pelican Freud Library*, vol. 14, *Art and Literature*, ed. Albert Dickson (Harmondsworth: Penguin, 1985).
Froula, Christine, 'When Eve reads Milton: Undoing the canonical economy', in *Canons*, ed. Robert Von Hallberg (Chicago and London: University of Chicago Press, 1984), pp.149–75.
Frye, Northrop, *Anatomy of Criticism: Four essays* (Princeton: Princeton University Press, 1957).
Frye, Northrop, *A Study of English Romanticism* (1968), 2nd edn (Hemel Hempstead: Harvester Wheatsheaf, 1983).
Frye, Northrop, *Spiritus Mundi: Essays on literature, myth, and society* (Bloomington and London: Indiana University Press, 1976).
Garner, Shirley Nelson, Claire Kahane and Madelon Spregnether (eds), *The (M)other Tongue: Essays in feminist psychoanalytic interpretation* (Ithaca and London: Cornell University Press, 1985).
Godzich, Wlad, 'Harold Bloom as rhetorician', in *Centrum* 6, 1 (1978), pp.43–9.
Gould, Warwick, 'A misreading of Harold Bloom', in *English* 26, 1 (1977), pp.40–54.
Graff, Gerald, 'Fear and trembling at Yale', in *The American Scholar* 46, 4 (1977), pp.467–78.
Greenblatt, Stephen, *Shakespearean Negotiations: The circulation of social energy in Renaissance England* (Oxford: Clarendon Press, 1988).
Handelman, Susan A., *The Slayers of Moses: The emergence of rabbinic interpretation in modern literary theory* (Albany: State University of New York Press, 1982).
Hartman, Geoffrey, *Wordsworth's Poetry, 1787–1814* (1964), 2nd edn (Cambridge, Mass. and London: Harvard University Press, 1971).
Hartman, Geoffrey, *Beyond Formalism: Literary essays, 1958–1970* (New Haven and London: Yale University Press, 1970).
Hartman, Geoffrey, *The Fate of Reading and Other Essays* (Chicago and London: University of Chicago Press, 1975).
Havens, R. D., *The Influence of Milton on English Poetry* (1922), 2nd edn (New York: Russell and Russell, 1961).
Hazlitt, William, *Complete Works*, Centenary Edition, 21 vols, ed. P. P. Howe (London and Toronto: J. M. Dent, 1930–4).
Hertz, Neil, *The End of the Line: Essays in psychoanalysis and the sublime* (New York: Columbia University Press).
Hoffmann, E. T. A., *Tales of Hoffmann*, selected, trans. and ed. R. J. Hollingdale (Harmondsworth: Penguin, 1982).

Hollander, John, *The Figure of Echo: A mode of allusion in Milton and after* (Berkeley, Los Angeles and London: California University Press, 1981).
Holmes, Richard, *Shelley: The pursuit* (1974), 2nd edn (Harmondsworth: Penguin, 1987).
Irigaray, Luce, *Speculum of the Other Woman* (1974), trans. Gillian C. Gill (Ithaca, New York: Cornell University Press, 1985).
Jameson, Fredric, *The Political Unconscious: Narrative as a socially symbolic act* (London: Methuen, 1981).
Jarvis, Robin, *Wordsworth, Milton, and the Theory of Poetic Relations* (London: Macmillan, 1991).
Jonas, Hans, *The Gnostic Religion: The message of the alien god and the beginnings of Christianity* (1958), 2nd edn, revised (London: Routledge, 1992).
Kermode, Frank, *Wallace Stevens* (Edinburgh and London: Oliver and Boyd, 1954).
Kermode, Frank, 'Institutional control of interpretation', in *Salmagundi* 43, 1 (1979), pp.72–86.
Kermode, Frank, *History and Value* (Oxford: Clarendon Press, 1988).
Kermode, Frank, *An Appetite for Poetry: Essays in literary interpretation* (Glasgow: William Collins, 1989).
Kincaid, James R., 'Antithetical Criticism: Harold Bloom, and Victorian poetry', in *Victorian Poetry* 14, 4 (1976), pp.365–82.
Kofman, Sarah, *Freud and Fiction* (1974), trans. Sarah Wykes (Cambridge: Polity Press, 1991).
Kristeva, Julia, *The Kristeva Reader*, ed. Toril Moi (Oxford: Basil Blackwell, 1986).
Lemaire, Anika, *Jacques Lacan*, trans. David Macey (London: Routledge and Kegan Paul, 1977).
Lentricchia, Frank, *After the New Criticism* (1980), 2nd edn (London: Methuen, 1983).
Levinson, Marjorie, *Wordsworth's Great Period Poems: Four essays* (Cambridge and New York: Cambridge University Press, 1986).
Levinson, Marjorie, 'The New Historicism: Back to the future', in *Rethinking Historicism: Critical readings in Romantic history*, M. Levinson, M. Butler, J. J. McGann and P. Hamilton (eds) (Oxford: Basil Blackwell, 1989), pp.18–63.
Macherey, Pierre, *A Theory of Literary Production* (1966), trans. Geoffrey Wall (London and New York: Routledge, 1978).
Man, Paul de, 'A new vitalism', in *The Massachusetts Review* 3, 3 (1962), pp.618–23.
Man, Paul de, *Blindness and Insight: Essays in the rhetoric of contemporary criticism* (1971), 2nd edn (London: Methuen, 1983).
Man, Paul de, *Allegories of Reading: Figural language in Rousseau, Nietzsche, Rilke, and Proust* (New Haven and London: Yale University Press, 1979).

McGann, Jerome J., 'Formalism, savagery, and care: Or, the function of criticism once again', in *Critical Inquiry* 2, 3 (1976), pp.605–30.
McGann, Jerome J., *Romantic Ideology: A critical investigation* (Chicago and London: University of Chicago Press, 1983).
Mileur, Jean Pierre, *Literary Revisionism and the Burden of Modernity* (Berkeley and Los Angeles: California University Press, 1985).
Miller, J. Hillis, 'Tradition and difference', in *Diacritics* 2, 4 (1972), pp.6–13.
Miller, J. Hillis, 'Stevens' rock and criticism as cure, 2', in *The Georgia Review* 30, 2 (1976), pp.330–48.
Miller, J. Hillis, *The Linguistic Moment: From Wordsworth to Stevens* (Princeton: Princeton University Press, 1985).
Milton, John, *Paradise Lost*, ed. Alastair Fowler (London: Longman, 1971).
Mitchell, Juliet and Jacqueline Rose (eds), trans. Jacqueline Rose, *Feminine Sexuality: Jacques Lacan and the Ecole Freudienne* (London: Macmillan, 1982).
Montrose, Louis, 'Professing the Renaissance: The poetics and politics of culture', in *The New Historicism*, ed. H. Aram Veseer (New York and London: Routledge, 1989), pp.15–36.
Nietzsche, Friedrich, *Untimely Meditations*, trans. R. J. Hollingdale (Cambridge: Cambridge University Press, 1983).
O'Hara, Daniel T., 'The freedom of the master', in *Contemporary Literature* 21, 4 (1980), pp.649–61.
O'Hara, Daniel T., *The Romance of Interpretation: Visionary criticism from Pater to de Man* (New York: Columbia University Press, 1985).
Pritchard, William H., 'Mr. Bloom in Yeatsville', in *The Partisan Review* 38, 1 (1971), pp.107–112.
Qualls, Barry V., 'Abishag's king', in *Raritan* 11, 3 (1992), pp.105–16.
Reiger, James, 'Wordsworth unalarmed', in *Milton and the Line of Vision*, ed. J. A. Wittreich, Jr (London: Wisconsin University Press, 1975), pp.185–208.
Riddel, Joseph N., review of *Kabbalah and Criticism* and *Poetry and Repression*, in *The Georgia Review* 30, 4 (1976), pp.989–1006.
Riddel, Joseph N., 'Juda becomes New Haven', in *Diacritics* 10, 2 (1980), pp.17–34.
Roe, Nicholas, *Wordsworth and Coleridge: The radical years* (Oxford: Clarendon Press, 1988).
Roe, Nicholas, 'Wordsworth, Milton, and the politics of poetic influence', in *Yearbook of English Studies* 19 (1989), pp.112–26.
Said, Edward, *The World, the Text, and the Critic* (London: Faber and Faber, 1984).
Scholem, Gershom, *Major Trends in Jewish Mysticism* (1941), 2nd edn (New York: Schoken, 1946).
Scholem, Gershom, *Kabbalah* (New York: Quadrangle, 1974).

Scholes, Robert, review of *The Anxiety of Influence*, in *The Journal of English and Germanic Philology* 73, 2 (1974), pp.266–8.
Selden, Raman, *Practising Theory and Reading Literature: An introduction* (New York and London: Harvester Wheatsheaf, 1989).
Shelley, P. B., *Shelley: Poetical Works* (1905), ed. Thomas Hutchinson, new edn corrected by G. M. Matthews (Oxford: Oxford University Press, 1970).
Shelley, P. B., *The Poems of Shelley*, vol. 1, 1804–17, Geoffrey Matthews and Kelvin Everest (eds) (London and New York: Longman, 1989).
Seigal, Sandra, 'Prolegomenon to Bloom: The opposing self', in *Diacritics* 1, 4 (1971), pp.35–8.
Stevens, Wallace, *The Necessary Angel: Essays on reality and the imagination* (1942) (London: Faber and Faber, 1984).
Stevens, Wallace, *Letters of Wallace Stevens*, ed. Holly Stevens (London: Faber and Faber, 1966).
Stevens, Wallace, *Wallace Stevens: The palm at the end of the mind*, ed. Holly Stevens (New York: Vintage Books, 1972).
Vendler, Helen, *On Extended Wings: Wallace Stevens' longer poetry* (Cambridge, Mass. and London: Harvard University Press, 1969).
Weber, Samuel, 'The sideshow or: Remarks on a canny moment', in *Modern Language Notes* 88, 6 (1973), pp.1102–33.
White, Hayden, *Tropics of Discourse: Essays in cultural criticism* (Baltimore and London: Johns Hopkins University Press, 1978).
Wordsworth, Ann, 'An art that will not abandon the self to language: Bloom, Tennyson and the blind world of the wish', in *Untying the Text: A post-structuralist reader*, ed. Robert Young (London and New York: Routledge and Kegan Paul, 1981), pp.207–22.
Wordsworth, Jonathan, *The Borders of Vision* (Oxford: Clarendon Press, 1982).
Wordsworth, William, *The Prose Works of William Wordsworth*, 3 vols, ed. W. J. B. Owen and Jane Worthington Smyser (Oxford: Clarendon Press, 1974).
Wordsworth, William, *William Wordsworth: The Poems*, 2 vols, ed. John O. Hayden (Harmondsworth: Penguin, 1977).
Wordsworth, William, *William Wordsworth: The prelude, 1799, 1805, 1850*, Jonathan Wordsworth, M. H. Abrams and Stephen Gill (eds) (New York and London: W. W. Norton, 1979).
Wordsworth, William, *Wordsworth and Coleridge: Lyrical ballads, 1805*, 3rd edn, ed. Derek Roper (Plymouth: Northcote House, 1987).
Wordsworth, William, *The Excursion* (1814) (Oxford and New York: Woodstock Books, 1991).
Worton, Michael and Judith Still (eds), *Intertextuality: Theories and practices* (Manchester and New York: Manchester University Press, 1991).
Wright, Elizabeth, *Psychoanalytic Criticism: Theory in practice* (London and New York: Methuen, 1984).
Wyatt, David, 'Bloom, Freud, and America', in *The Kenyon Review* 6, 3 (1984), pp.59–66.

# Index

Abrams, M. H., xix, 1, 5, 7, 41, 147
American tradition (Bloom on), 26, 38, 62, 63–4, 65, 128–33, 136
Ammons, A. R., 130
Aristotle, 58
Arnold, Matthew, 104
Ashbery, John, 28, 42, 130, 131, 132
Auerbach, Eric, 111, 173 n.9, 181
Aune, James Arrt, 26

Bakhtin, M. M., 36, 169 n.26, 180
Barthes, Roland, 36, 186
Bate, Walter Jackson, xix, 167 n.22
Bishop, Elizabeth, 130, 131
Blake, William, 3, 4, 5, 8, 12, 13–14, 44, 81, 141, 145
Blank, G. Kim, 118, 119, 174 n.33
Bolla, Peter de, 17, 18, 49–50, 51, 57, 87, 96, 106–7, 113, 114, 115, 166 n.7
Browning, Robert, 20–1
Bruss, Elizabeth, 28, 83, 84
Buber, Martin, 3, 14
Burke, Kenneth, 28, 49

canon (canon-formation), 2, 39–40, 53, 69–71, 98, 104, 145, 146, 149
Caruth, Cathy, 85
Chernaik, Judith, 117
Cixous, Hélène, 152, 153
Clark, Timothy, 173–4 n.24
Clayton, Jay, 35, 162
Codervero, Moses, 168 n.17
Coleridge, S. T., 88, 92, 106–7, 121
'Covering Cherub', 9, 142
Crane, Hart, 131
criticism *see* interpretation
crossings, poetic, 80, 187–8
Culler, Jonathan, 72
Cultural Materialism, 138, 180

Dante Alighieri, 4, 116, 122, 141
Dawson, P. M. S., 121–2, 123
deconstruction, xi, xix, xx, xxii, xxiii, 21, 34, 35, 45, 46, 48, 56, 57, 58, 59, 60, 77–8, 89, 106, 108, 109, 131, 179, 180, 181, 182–3, 184, 187
Derrida, Jacques, 73, 74–5, 76, 77, 78, 80, 83, 84, 86, 87, 111, 134, 180, 181, 184, 187
Descartes, René, 4–5, 6
Dickinson, Emily, 131
Dodds, E. R., 37
Donne, John, 115

Edmundson, Mark, 152
Eliot, T. S., xx, xxi, 3, 21, 70, 104, 183
Emerson, R. W., 27, 33, 38, 54, 57, 61, 64, 115, 128–33, 137, 175 n.37, 185
Everest, Kelvin, 5–6

facticity, 132, 137–8, 143–8
figura, 111, 116, 182
Fite, David, 4, 12, 58
Fletcher, Angus, xvii
Fliegel, Zenia Odes, 177 n.36
formalism, xvii, xviii–xxiv, 5, 18, 29, 125, 182, 184
Foucault, Michel, xix, 36, 84, 149, 160, 176 n.17, 180
Fowler, Alistair, 167 n.25
Freidman, Susan Stanford, 36
Freud, Anna, 25
Freud, Sigmund, 6, 7, 8–9, 10, 17, 21, 22–5, 26, 33, 34, 35, 58, 73–4, 75, 76, 77, 78, 79, 80, 82, 83, 84, 85, 86, 87, 136, 137, 138, 142, 144, 145, 146, 147, 148, 149, 150–62, 170–1 n.6, 176 n.21, 177 n.28, 179, 181, 183, 185, 186, 187

## Index

Frost, Robert, 131
Froula, Christine, 39
Frye, Northrop, xx-i, 1, 2, 3, 4, 7–8, 9, 14, 42, 70, 135, 147, 165 n.7, 178, 179

Galileo, 110
Gennette, Gerard, 60
Gnosticism, 14, 39, 58, 79, 111–12, 130, 148, 182
Godwin, William, 125
Goethe, John Wolfgang von, 84
Graff, Gerald, 42–3
Greenblatt, Stephen, 134, 140–1

Handelman, Susan, 173 n.9
Hardy, Thomas, 20
Hartman, Geoffrey H., xvii, xviii, xix, 1, 7, 30–1, 32, 88, 89, 97, 170 n.6
Havens, R. D., 18
Hazlitt, William, 121
Hegel, Georg Wilhelm Freidrich, 6, 57, 58, 139, 148
Heine, Heinrich, 139
Hertz, Neil, 72–3, 98, 99, 151, 152, 172 n.28, 176 n.21, 177 n.28
Hoffmann, E. T. A., 151, 153–9
Hollander, John, 29, 108, 109, 112, 172 n.1
Homer, 69, 84, 130, 143
Husserl, Edmund, 185
Huxley, T. H., 37

Irigaray, Luce, 161
influence, xiv, 14, 15–16, 17–18, 20, 23, 26, 28, 48–9, 52, 55, 64, 72, 73, 75–6, 77, 79, 116, 121, 125, 126, 127, 132, 162
  anxiety of, xviii, xxiii, xxxiv, 9, 10, 11, 16, 25, 37–8, 40, 46, 48, 49, 67, 68, 88, 128
  source-study, compared to, 17, 18–21, 51
interpretation, xviii, xix, xx, xxi, xxiii, 2, 4, 13, 15, 16, 17, 18, 19, 20, 21, 29, 30, 32–4, 35, 39, 41–3, 45, 46–5, 54, 56, 60–1, 64, 71, 73, 81, 84, 89, 106, 107, 108–9, 111–12, 113–14, 115, 136, 138, 139, 140, 142
intertextuality, 19–20, 35–7, 55, 72, 73, 86, 88, 90, 104, 108, 115, 121, 132, 141, 149, 162, 183

Jakobson, Roman, 97
Jameson, Fredric, 34–5

Jarvis, Robin, 18, 169 n.26
Jentsch, E., 154, 155, 156
Johnson, Dr, 110
Jonas, Hans, 111–12
Judaic tradition, 76, 147, 148–9
  Greek tradition, compared to, 73, 76, 80, 147, 148–9
J-writer (Yahwist), 85, 132, 137, 138, 143, 144, 145, 146, 147, 149, 183

Kabbalism, 33, 49, 51, 58–9, 60, 76, 77, 79, 80, 130, 168–9 n.17, 184
Kant, Immanuel, 72, 187
Keats, John, 11, 35
Kermode, Frank, 39, 62, 167 n.25
Kierkegaard, Soren, 31, 78–9
Kofman, Sarah, 152, 153, 157
Kristeva, Julia, 36–7, 81, 160, 186

Lacan, Jacques, 83–4, 160, 183
language, poetic, 47, 72
  trope and defence in, 45, 46, 47, 49
Leavis, F. R., 104
Lemaire, Anika, 83
Lentricchia, Frank, 5, 6, 29, 41
Levinson, Marjorie, 92–3, 94, 138
Locke, John, 6
Luria, Isaac, 49, 184

Macherey, Pierre, 34–5
Man, Paul de, xvii, xviii, xix, xxi-iv, 1, 43–6, 47–8, 51, 56–7, 58, 59, 60, 78, 89, 134, 168 n.8, 181, 182
map of misreading, 21, 41–3, 44, 45, 48, 49–54, 59, 60, 61, 63, 71–2, 119, 187–8
Marvell, Andrew, 141
Marx, Karl, 6, 160
Marxist literary criticism, xviii, 34–5
McGann, Jerome J., xxiii, 34, 101, 125, 139, 140
meaning (Bloom's theory of), xi, 16, 19, 29, 30, 31, 32, 37, 38–9, 46, 49, 50, 52, 55, 57, 58, 59–60, 77–8, 112–13, 131, 137, 140, 142, 148–9, 162
Mileur, Jean-Pierre, 173 n.9
Miller, J. Hillis, xix, 1, 43, 48, 134
Milton, John, 5, 18, 26, 28, 39, 81, 87, 88, 89, 90, 91, 94–5, 96, 97, 101–2, 103–4, 108, 110, 111, 112, 113, 114, 116, 117, 120–1, 127, 130, 134, 141

Moschus, 122
Monroe, Harriet, 62
Montrose, Louis, 134, 140
monumentalism, xxiii-iv

New Criticism, xviii, xix, xx, 1, 2–3, 12, 18, 21, 134, 183, 184
New Historicism, xviii, 2, 134, 135, 138–40, 184
Newton, Isaac, 6, 98
Nietzsche, Friedrich, xxiii-iv, 33, 47, 56, 73, 74, 76, 128, 179

O'Hara, Daniel T., 14, 64

Pater, Walter, 33
Piaget, Jean, 82, 83
Plato, 58
poetry *see* text, poetic
Pope, Alexander, 38
post-modernism, 136, 185
post-structuralism, xviii, xix, xxi, 45, 72, 108, 134, 138, 140, 141, 142, 144, 146, 184, 185
Proust, Marcel, 136
Puttenham, George, 110
psychopoetics (Bloom's theory of), xi, xiv, xx, 7, 8–9, 21–4, 25, 44, 72–3, 77, 81–4, 85–6, 142

reading *see* interpretation
revisionary ratios, 20, 25–8, 44, 50, 52, 65, 66, 67, 90, 119, 159
revisionism, xviii, 2, 28, 72, 77, 83, 131, 186
rhetoric, xxi, 24, 44, 45–6, 47, 49, 50, 56–7, 58–60, 62, 75, 78, 89, 105–9, 110, 113, 114, 115, 116, 128, 129, 130, 131, 136
Richards, I. A., 67
Riddel, Joseph N., 43, 131, 132
Riffaterre, Michael, 35–6, 183
Roe, Nicholas, 103–4, 171 n.15
Romanticism, xi, xxiii, 1–10, 11, 12, 14, 15, 22, 24, 27, 37, 42, 44, 45, 49, 58, 67, 70, 104, 113, 114, 125, 128, 130, 138, 139–40, 187
  quest romance in, 4, 5, 7, 8, 9, 42, 62, 63, 64
Rorty, Richard, 136
Rothstein, Eric, 35, 162
Rousseau, Jean-Jacques, 47

Said, Edward, xviii, xix-xx, 29

scene of instruction, primal, 52, 69, 71, 72, 73–4, 75, 76, 78–86, 88, 90, 92, 93, 94, 96, 97–8, 101, 102, 103, 107
Schelling, Friedrich Wilhelm, 154
Scholem, Gershom, 169 n.17
Scholes, Robert, 42, 43
Schopenhauer, Artur, 147
Seigal, Sandra, 13
Selden, Raman, 97
Shakespeare, William, 97, 98, 135, 137, 138, 143–4, 146, 149
Shelley, P. B., 3, 7, 8, 12, 13–14, 20–1, 27, 108, 116–28, 162
Simons, Hi, 67
Spenser, Edmund, 5, 42
Stein, Gertrude, 131
Stevens, Wallace, 26, 28, 35, 61–8, 106, 107, 108, 109, 119, 131, 132, 162
structuralism, 15, 186
sublime, 27, 66, 72, 73, 75, 80, 81, 87, 88, 98, 102, 104, 118, 119, 129, 150, 151, 187
Swinburne, Algernon Charles, 20

text, poetic xx, xxii, 3, 18, 19, 20, 22, 29, 34, 42, 46, 48, 51, 52, 53, 55, 57, 71, 78, 105–6, 162
  dyad, xviii, 19
  lie against time, 30, 109
  monad, xviii, 2
  triad, 19, 106
tradition, literary, 15–16, 28, 29, 31, 35, 53, 54, 55, 70–1, 72, 76, 102, 104, 106, 110, 114, 135–7, 145, 149
transumption, 28, 75, 80, 85, 91, 108, 109, 110–13, 114, 116, 117, 125, 126, 127, 128, 129, 130, 131, 132
Trilling, Lionel, xvi, 22

uncanny, 132, 145, 150, 151–9, 161

Vendler, Helen, 62, 63
Vico, Giambattista, 78, 79–80, 178

Weber, Samuel, 152, 155, 157
Weiskel, Thomas, 12
White, Hayden, 97
Whitman, Walt, 26, 27, 57, 61, 64, 108, 131, 132
Williams, Raymond, 139, 180
Wittgenstein, Ludwig, 85, 147
Wordsworth, Ann, 57
Wordsworth, Dorothy, 91, 92

Wordsworth, William, 5, 15, 27, 63, 65, 81, 82, 86, 87–104, 115, 117, 118–21, 122, 123, 124, 125, 126, 127, 130, 162

Wright, Elizabeth, 151, 152
Wyatt, David, 128

Yeats, W. B., 2, 12–16, 20, 23, 179